THE SPECTACLE OF DISINTEGRATION

THE SPECTACLE OF DISINTEGRATION

◆

MᶜKENZIE WARK

VERSO

London • New York

First published by Verso 2013
© McKenzie Wark 2013

1 3 5 7 9 10 8 6 4 2

Verso
UK: 6 Meard Street, London W1F 0EG
US: 20 Jay Street, Suite 1010, Brooklyn, NY 11201
www.versobooks.com

Verso is the imprint of New Left Books

ISBN-13: 978-1-84467-957-7

British Library Cataloguing in Publication Data
A catalogue record for this book is available from the British Library

Library of Congress Cataloging-in-Publication Data
A catalog record for this book is available from the Library of Congress

Typeset in Cochin by MJ & N Gavan, Truro, Cornwall
Printed in the US by Maple Vail

Contents

In memory of:

Mark Poster
The mode of information
Bernard Smith
Place, taste and tradition
Adam Cullen
The otherness when it comes

It may not be what it looks to lack totality.

Anna Mendelssohn

I sense the River Neckinger beneath the paving slabs, the queasy toxicity shifting to St. Saviours dock.

Laura Oldfield Ford

I Widening Gyres

A person of sharp observation and sound judgment governs objects rather than being governed by them.

Baltasar Gracián

When the storm hit the Hansa Carrier, twenty-one shipping containers fell from its decks into the Pacific Ocean, taking some 80,000 Nike sneakers with them. Seattle-based oceanographer Curtis Ebbesmeyer used the serial numbers from the sneakers that washed up on the rain coast of North America to plot the widening gyre of ocean-going garbage that usually lies between California and Hawaii. Bigger than the state of Texas, it is called the North Pacific Subtropical Gyre, and sailors have known for a long time to steer clear of this area from the equator to fifty degrees north.

It's an often windless desert where not much lives. Flotsam gathers and circles, biodegrading into the sea. Unless it is plastic, which merely photo-degrades in the sun, disintegrating into smaller and smaller bits of sameness. Now the sea here has more particles of plastic than plankton. The Gyre is a disowned country of furniture, fridges, cigarette lighters, televisions, bobbing in the sea and slowly falling apart, but refusing to go away.[1]

New Hawaii is the name some humorists prefer for the North Pacific Subtropical Gyre now that it has the convenience of contemporary consumer goods. Or one might call it a spectacle of disintegration. It is as good an emblem as any of the passing show of contemporary life, with its jetsam of jostling plastic artifacts, all twisting higgledy-piggledy on and below the surface of the ocean. Plastic and ocean remain separate, even as the plastic breaks up and permeates the water, insinuating itself into it but always alien to it.

The poet Lautréamont once wrote: "Old Ocean, you are the symbol of identity: always equal to yourself ... and if somewhere your waves are enraged, further off in some other zone they are in the most complete calm."[2] But this no longer describes the ocean, which now appears as far from equilibrium. It describes instead the spectacle, the Sargasso Sea of images, a perpetual calm surrounded by turbulence, at the center always the same.

When Guy Debord published *The Society of the Spectacle* (1967), he thought there were two kinds: the concentrated and the diffuse spectacle. The concentrated spectacle was limited to fascist and Stalinist states, where the spectacle cohered around a cult of personality. These are rare now, if not entirely extinct. The diffuse spectacle emerged as the dominant form. It did not require a Stalin or Mao as its central image. Big Brother is no longer watching you. In His place is little sister and her friends: endless pictures of models and other pretty things. The diffuse spectacle murmured to its sleeping peoples: "what appears is good; what is good appears."[3]

The victory of the diffuse spectacle over its concentrated cousin did not lead to the diffusion of the victor over the surface of the world. In *Comments on the Society of the Spectacle* (1988), Debord thought instead that an integrated spectacle had subsumed elements of both into a new spectacular universe. While on the surface it looked like the diffuse spectacle, which molds desire in the form of the commodity, it bore within it aspects of concentration, notably an *occulted state*, where power tends to become less and less transparent.

That the state is a mystery to its subjects is to be expected; that it could become occult even to its rulers is something else. The integrated spectacle not only extended the spectacle outwards, but also inwards; the falsification of the world had reached by this point even those in charge of it. Debord wrote in 1978 that "it has become ungovernable, this wasteland, where new sufferings are disguised with the names of former pleasures; and where the people are so afraid ... Rumor has it that those who were expropriating it have, to crown it all, mislaid it. Here is a civilization which is on fire, capsizing and sinking completely. Ah! Fine torpedoeing!"[4]

Since he died in 1994, Debord did not live to see the most fecund and feculent form of this marvel, this spectacular power that integrates both diffusion and concentration. In memory of Debord, let's call the endpoint reached by the integrated spectacle the *disintegrating spectacle*, in which the spectator gets to watch the withering away of the old order, ground down to near nothingness by its own steady divergence from any apprehension of itself. Debord: "that state can no longer be led strategically."[5]

And yet the spectacle remains, circling itself, bewildering itself. Everything is impregnated with tiny bits of its issue, yet the new world remains stillborn. The spectacle atomizes and diffuses itself throughout not only the social body but its sustaining landscape as well. As Debord's former comrade T. J. Clark writes, this world is "not 'capital accumulated to the point where it becomes image,' to quote the famous phrase from Guy Debord, but images dispersed and accelerated until they become the true and sufficient commodities."[6]

The spectacle speaks the language of command. The command of the concentrated spectacle was: OBEY! The command of the diffuse spectacle was: BUY! In the integrated spectacle the commands to OBEY! and BUY! became interchangeable. Now the command of the disintegrating spectacle is: RECYCLE! Like oceanic amoeba choking on granulated shopping bags, the spectacle can now only go forward by evolving the ability to eat its own shit.

The disintegrating spectacle can countenance the end of everything except the end of itself. It can contemplate with equanimity melting ice sheets, seas of junk, peak oil, but the spectacle itself lives on. It is immune to particular criticisms. Mustapha Khayati: "Fourier long ago exposed the *methodological myopia* of treating fundamental questions without relating them to modern society as a whole. The fetishism of facts masks the essential category, the mass of details obscures the totality."[7]

Even when it speaks of disintegration, the spectacle is all about particulars. The plastic Pacific, even if it is as big as Texas, is presented as a particular event. Particular criticisms hold the spectacle to account for falsifying this image or that story, but in the process thereby merely add legitimacy to the spectacle's claim that it can in general be a vehicle for the true. A genuinely critical approach to the spectacle starts from the opposite premise: that it may present from time to time a true fragment, but it is necessarily false *as a whole*. Debord: "In a world that really has been turned on its head, the true is a moment of falsehood."[8]

This then is our task: a critique of the spectacle as a whole, a task that critical thought has for the most part abandoned. Stupefied by its own powerlessness, critical thought turned into that drunk who, having lost the car keys, searches for them under the street lamp. The drunk knows that the keys disappeared in that murky puddle, where it is dark, but finds it is easier to search for them under the lamp, where there is light — if not enlightenment.

And then critical theory gave up even that search and fell asleep at the side of the road. Just as well. It was in no condition to drive. In its stupor, critical thought makes a fetish of particular aspects of the spectacular organization of life. The critique of content became a contented critique.[9] It wants to talk only of the political, or of culture, or of subjectivity, as if these things still existed, as if they had not been colonized by the spectacle and rendered mere excrescences of its general movement. Critical thought contented itself with arriving late on the scene and picking through the fragments. Or, critical thought retreated into the totality of philosophy. It had a bone to pick with *metaphysics*. It shrank from the spectacle, which is philosophy made concrete. In short: critical thought has itself become spectacular. Critical theory becomes *hypocritical theory*. It needs to be renewed not only in content but in form.

When the US Food and Drug Administration announced that certain widely prescribed sleeping pills would come with strong warnings about strange behavior, they were not only responding to reports of groggy people driving their cars or making phone calls, but also purchasing items over the internet.[10] The declension of the spectacle into every last droplet of everyday life means that the life it prescribes can be lived even in one's sleep. This creates a certain difficulty for prizing open some other possibility for life, even in thought.

Debord's sometime comrade Raoul Vaneigem famously wrote that those who speak of class conflict without referring to everyday life, "without understanding what is subversive about love and what is positive in the refusal of constraints, such people have a corpse in their mouth."[11] Today this formula surely needs to be inverted. To talk the talk of critical thought, of *biopolitics* and *biopower*, of the *state of exception, bare life, precarity,* of *whatever being,* or *object oriented ontology* without reference to class conflict is to speak, if not with a corpse in one's mouth, then at least a sleeper.

Must we speak the hideous language of our century? The spectacle appears at first as just a maelstrom of images swirling about the suck hole of their own nothingness. Here is a political leader. Here is one with better hair. Here is an earthquake in China. Here is a new kind of phone. Here are the crowds for the new movie. Here are the crowds for the food riot. Here is a cute cat. Here is a cheeseburger. If that were all there was to it, one could just load one's screen with better fare. But the spectacle is not just images. It is not just another name for the media. Debord: "The spectacle is a social relationship between people mediated by images."[12] The trick is not to be distracted by the images, but to inquire into the nature of this social relationship.

Emmalee Bauer of Elkhart worked for the Sheraton Hotel company in Des Moines until she was fired for using her employer's computer to keep a journal which recorded all of her efforts to avoid work. "This typing thing seems to be doing the trick," she wrote. "It just looks like I am hard at work on something very important."[13] And indeed she was. Her book-length *work* hits on something fundamental about wage labor and the spectacle, namely the separation of labor from desire. One works not because one particularly wants to, but for the wages, with which to then purchase commodities to fulfill desires.

In the separation between labor and desire lies the origins of the spectacle, which appears as the world of all that can be desired, or rather, of all the appropriate modes of desiring. "Thus the spectacle, though it turns reality on its head, is itself a product of real activity."[14] The activity of making commodities makes in turn the need for the spectacle as the image of those commodities turned into objects of desire. The spectacle turns the goods into The Good.

The ruling images of any age service the ruling power. The spectacle is no different, although the ruling power is not so much a ruling monarch or even a power elite anymore, but the rule of the commodity itself. The celebrities that populate the spectacle are not its sovereigns, but rather model a range of acceptable modes of desire from the noble to the risqué. The true celebrities of the spectacle are not its subjects but its objects.

Billionaire Brit retailer Sir Philip Green spent six million pounds flying some two hundred of his closest friends to a luxury spa resort in the Maldives. The resort offers water sports and a private beach for each guest. Much of the décor is made from recycled products, and there is an organic vegetable garden where residents can pick ingredients for their own meals.[15] "Sustainability" is the Viagra of old world speculative investment. Sir Philip is no fool, and neither is his publicist. This retailer of dreams has the good sense to appear in public by giving away to a lucky few what the unlucky many should hence forth consider good fortune. And yet while this story highlights the fantastic agency of the billionaire, the moral of the story is something else: even billionaires obey the logic of the spectacle if they want to appear in it.

The spectacle has always been an uninterrupted monologue of self-praise. But things have changed a bit. The integrated spectacle still relied on centralized means of organizing and distributing the spectacle, run by a culture industry in command of the means of producing its images. The disintegrating spectacle chips away at centralized means of producing images and distributes this responsibility among the spectators themselves. While the production of goods is out-sourced to various cheap labor countries, the production of images is *in-sourced* to unpaid labor, offered up in what was once leisure time. The culture industries are now the *vulture industries*, which act less as producers of images for consumption than as algorithms that manage databases of images that consumers swap between each other—while still paying for the privilege. Where once the spectacle entertained us, now we must entertain each other, while the vulture industries collect the rent. The disintegrating spectacle replaces the monologue of appearances with the appearance of dialogue. Spectators are now obliged to make images and stories for each other that do not unite those spectators in anything other than their separateness.

The proliferation of means of communication, with their tiny keyboards and tiny screens, merely breaks the spectacle down into bits and distributes it in suspension throughout everyday life. Debord: "The spectacle has spread itself to the point where it now permeates all reality. It was easy to predict in theory what has been quickly and universally demonstrated by practical experience of economic reason's relentless accomplishments: that the globalization of the false was also the falsification of the globe."[16] Ever finer fragments of the time of everyday life become moments into which the spectacle insinuates its logic, demanding the incessant production and consumption of images and stories which, even though they take place in the sweaty pores of the everyday, are powerless to affect it.

It is comforting to imagine that it is always someone else who is duped by the spectacle. Former movie star turned tabloid sensation Lindsay Lohan allegedly spent over one million dollars on clothes in a single year, and $100,000 in a single day, before consulting a hypnotist to try to end her *shopping addiction*. Lohan's publicist denied the story: "There is no hypnotist, and Lindsay loves clothes, but the idea that she spent that much last year is completely stupid."[17] The alleged excess of an other makes the reader's own relation to the spectacle of commodities seem *just right*. It's all about having the right distance. For Debord, "no one really believes the spectacle."[18] Belief, like much else these days, is optional. The spectacle is what it is: irrefutable images, eternal present, the endless yes. The spectacle does not require gestures of belief, only of deference. No particular image need detain us any longer than this season's shoes.

They call themselves the Bus Buddies. The women who travel the Adirondack Trailways Red Line spend five and even six hours commuting to high-paid jobs in Manhattan, earning much more money than they could locally in upstate New York. They are outlier examples of what are now called extreme commuters, who rarely see their homes in daylight and spend around a month per year of their lives in transit. It is not an easy life. "Studies show that commuters are much less satisfied with their lives than non-commuters." Symptoms may include "raised blood pressure, musculoskeletal disorders, increased hostility, lateness, absenteeism, and adverse effects on cognitive performance."[19] Even with a blow-up neck pillow and a blankie, commuting has few charms.

For many workers the commute results from a simple equation between their income in the city and the real estate they can afford in the suburbs, an equation known well by the real estate development companies. "Poring over elaborate market research, these corporations divine what young families want, addressing things like carpet texture and kitchen placement and determining how many streetlights and cul-de-sacs will evoke a soothing sense of safety. They know almost to the dollar how much buyers are willing to pay to exchange a longer commute for more space, a sense of higher status and the feeling of security."[20] By moving away from the city, the commuter gets the space for which to no longer have the time. Time, or space? This is the tension envelope of *middle-class* desire. Home buyers are to property developers what soldiers are to generals. Their actions are calculable, so long as they don't panic.

There are ways to beat the commute. Rush hour in São Paulo, Brazil features the same gridlocked streets as many big cities, but the skies afford a brilliant display of winking lights from the helicopters ferrying the city's *upper* class home for the evening. Helipads dot the tops of high-rise buildings and are standard features of São Paulo's guarded residential compounds. The helicopter speeds the commute, bypasses car-jackings, kidnappings—and it ornaments the sky. "My favorite time to fly is at night, because the sensation is equaled only in movies or in dreams," says Moacir da Silva, the president of the São Paulo Helicopter Pilots Association. "The lights are everywhere, as if I were flying within a Christmas tree."[21]

Many Paulistanos lack not only a helicopter, but shelter and clean water. But even when it comes with abundance, everyday life can seem strangely impoverished. Debord: "the reality that must be taken as a point of departure is dissatisfaction."[22] Even on a good day, when the sun is shining and one doesn't have to board that bus, everyday life seems oddly lacking.

Sure, there is still an under-developed world that lacks modern conveniences such as extreme commuting and the gated community. Pointing to this lack too easily becomes an alibi for not examining what it is the developing world is developing toward. And rather than a developed world, perhaps the result is more like what the Situationists called an *over-developed* world, which somehow overshot the mark.[23] This world kept accumulating riches of the same steroidal kind, pumping up past the point where a qualitative change might have transformed it and set it on a different path. This is the world, then, which lacks for nothing except its own critique.

The critique of everyday life—or something like it—happens all the time in the disintegrating spectacle, but this critique falls short of any project of transforming it. The spectacle points constantly to the more extreme examples of the ills of this world—its longest commutes, its most absurd disparities of wealth between slum dwellers and the helicopter class, as if these curios legitimated what remains as some kind of norm. How can the critique of everyday life be expressed in acts? Acts which might take a step beyond Emmalee Bauer's *magnum opus* and become collaborations in new forms of life? Forms of life which are at once both aesthetic and political and yet reducible to the given forms of neither art nor action? These are questions that will draw us back over several centuries of critical practice.

Once upon a time, there was a small band of ingrates—the Situationist International—who aspired to something more than this. Their project was to advance beyond the fulfillment of needs to the creation of new desires. But in these chastened times the project is different. Having failed our desires, this world merely renames the necessities it imposes as if they were desires. Debord: "It should be known that servitude henceforth truly wants to be loved for itself, and no longer because it would bring any extrinsic advantage."[24] Here we have an example of what the radical sociologist Henri Lefebvre called *historical drift*, where "the results of history differ from the goals pursued."[25]

The difficulty in the era of the disintegrating spectacle is to imagine even what the goal of history might be. Take the Tunisian revolution for instance. Mehdi Belhaj Kacem: "January 2011 is a May '68 carried through all the way to the end. It is a revolution that has more in common with the Situationists ... that is, a revolution carried out directly by the people, than with the Leninist or Maoist 'Revolution', in which an armed avant-garde takes over power and replaces one dictatorship with another..." Moreover, "for the first time in history it was the media—television, radio or newspapers—that played catch up to a new kind of democratic information ... That is one of the major 'situationist' lessons of this revolution: an absolute victory over one 'society of the spectacle.' Which means that, tomorrow, others, and not only Arab dictatorships, might fall."[26]

Let's concede to Mehdi his optimism, speaking so soon after the events. Let's concede also that he is probably correct in his assessment of the success in Tunisia of what are essentially Situationist organizational and communications tactics. One still has to wonder which way histories can drift once Big Brothers are deposed and exiled. Is to be freed from dictators the limit to the twenty-first century's desires? As the Situationists wrote in the wake of the success and failure of the Algerian revolution some forty-odd years previously: "Everywhere there are social confrontations, but nowhere is the old order destroyed, not even within the very social forces that contest it."[27] As we shall see, revolutions are not exceptions, they are constants—but so too are *restorations*.

The critique of everyday life is the critique of existing needs and the creation of new desires. The everyday is the site of tension between desires and needs. It is where the productive tension between them either halts or advances. Today we may safely say it has come to a halt. Everyday life has been so colonized by the spectacle of the commodity form that it is unable to formulate a new relation between need and desire. It takes its desire for the commodity as if it were a need.

The attempt to revolutionize everyday life, to forge a new relation between need and desire, was decisively defeated. The emblem of that defeat is the signal year 1968. Even if the transformation that seemed so imminent at the time was impossible, now it hardly appears at all. And yet the everyday may still function as a fulcrum of critique, even if the work upon which such a critique might now build is not to be found in the optimism that effloresces in 1968, but the grim determination of those who lived through and beyond the moment of failure, and yet did their best to keep the critical edge sharp.

Taking the everyday as a site for critical thought has several advantages. For one thing, you're soaking in it. It is not the special property of initiates of a particular kind of art or literature. It remains beyond the reach of even the most tactile and ductile of philosophies. Nor is it a domain walled off and subjected to the specialized tools of this or that kind of social science. Hence a critique of the everyday avoids a pre-emptive fashioning of a comfortable zone for thought detached from what is generally taken to matter to most people.

Lastly, the everyday has the peculiar property of being made up of slight and singular moments, little one-off events—situations— that seem to happen in between more important things, but which unlike those important things tend to flow into each other and connect up, flowing, finally, into some apprehension of a totality— a connection of sorts between things of all kinds. The trick is to follow the line that links the experience of concrete situations in everyday life to the spectacular falsification of totality.

These days extreme commuters may be working while they travel. The cellphone and the laptop make it possible to roll calls while driving or to work the spreadsheets while on the bus or train. They allow the working day to extend into travel time, making all of time productive rather than interstitial. Isn't technology wonderful? Where once, when you left the office, you could be on your own, now the cellphone tethers you to the demands of others almost anywhere at any time. Those shiny phones and handy tablets appear as if in a dream or a movie to make the world available at your command. The ads discreetly fail to mention that they rather put you at the world's command. The working day expands to fill up what were formerly workless hours and spills over into sleepless nights.

The thread that runs from the everyday moment of answering a cellphone or pecking away at a laptop on a bus to the larger total- ity plays out a lot further. Where do old laptops go to die? Many of them end up in the city of Guiyu in China's Pearl River Delta, which is something like the electronic-waste capital of the planet. Some sixty thousand people work there at so-called *recycling*, which is the new name for the old job of mining minerals, not from nature, but from this second nature of consumer waste.

It is work that, like the mining of old, imperils the health of the miners, this time with the runoff of toxic metals and acids. In Guiyu, "computer carcasses line the streets, awaiting dismemberment. Circuit boards and hard drives lie in huge mounds. At thousands of workshops, laborers shred and grind plastic casings into parti- cles, snip cables and pry chips from circuit boards. Workers pass the boards through red-hot kilns or acid baths to dissolve lead, silver and other metals from the digital detritus. The acrid smell of burning solder and melting plastic fills the air."[28] The critique of everyday life can seek out otherwise obscure connections between

one experience of life and another, looking for the way the commuter on a laptop and the e-waste worker melting chip boards are
connected. It considers the everyday from the point of view of how
to transform it, and takes nothing for granted about what is needed
or what is desired.

2 The Critique of Everyday Life

What good is knowledge if it isn't practiced? These days real knowledge lies in knowing how to live.

Baltasar Gracián

Henri Lefebvre started this line of thought with his 1947 book *The Critique of Everyday Life Volume 1* and raised it to a fine pitch with that book's second volume in 1961. But the group who really pushed it to its limit was the Situationist International, a movement which lasted from 1957 until 1972, and which its leading light Guy Debord would later describe as "this obscure conspiracy of limitless demands."[1]

While their project was one of "leaving the twentieth century," in the twenty-first century they have become something of an intellectual curio.[2] They stand in for all that up-to-date intellectual types think they have outgrown, and yet somehow the Situationists refuse to be left behind. They keep coming back as the bad conscience of the worlds of writing, art, cinema and architecture that claim the glamour of critical friction yet lack the nerve to actually rub it in. Now that critical theory has become hypocritical theory, the Situationist International keeps washing up on these shores like shipwrecked luggage. Are the Situationists derided so much because they were wrong or because they are right?

Consider how their legacy is isolated and managed. The early phase of the Situationist project, roughly from 1957 to 1961, is safety consigned to the world of art and architecture. Its leading lights, such as Pinot Gallizio, Asger Jorn, Michèle Bernstein and Constant Nieuwenhuys, all have books and articles dedicated to managing their memory.[3] The period from 1961 to 1972 is considered the political phase, and its memory is kept by various leftist sects who reprint the writings of Raoul Vaneigem, Guy Debord and René Viénet, and are mostly concerned with the critique of each other.[4] Of more interest to us now perhaps is Post-Situationist literature, in which former members or associates, including T. J. Clark, Gianfranco Sanguinetti and Alice Becker-Ho, restate or revise the theses of the movement, which runs more or less from 1972 to Debord's death in 1994.

The life and work of Guy Debord, the one consistent presence in the movement, is fodder for all kinds of recuperations. For biographers he is a grand grotesque, or a revolutionary idol, the hipster's Che Guevara. Certain enterprising critics have turned him into a master of French prose.[5] By recuperating fragments of the Situationist project within the intellectual division of labor, its bracing critique of everyday life as a totality, not to mention the project of constructing an alternative, tends to disappear into the footnotes.

In 2009 the French Minister of Culture, Christine Albanel, declared the archive of Guy Debord a *national treasure*. The archive, in the possession of Debord's widow, Alice Becker-Ho, contains a holograph of *Society of the Spectacle*, reading notes, notebooks in which Debord recorded his dreams, his entire correspondence, and the manuscript of a last, unfinished book, previously believed to have been destroyed. Yale University had already expressed interest in acquiring the archive, prompting the Bibliothèque Nationale, or French National Library, to make securing the Debord archive a priority.

The fund-raising arm of the Library holds an annual gala dinner to hit up its big benefactors for cash, and its 2009 event displayed Debord notebooks to tempt donors. Present were several board members, including Pierre Bergé (co-founder of Yves Saint Laurent) and Nahed Ojjeh (widow of the arms dealer Akram Ojjeh). Only €180,000 was raised, a fraction of what the Library had to find for Becker-Ho. "This evening depends upon the spectacular society," fund-raising chief Jean-Claude Meyer admitted in his speech. "It's ironic and, at the same time, a great homage." But if the Library could make an archive out of the Marquis de Sade, then anything is possible. The gala dinner took place in the Library's Hall of Globes, a monument to the presidency of François Mitterrand, who Debord particularly detested.[6]

The gulf that separates the present times from the time of the Situationist International passes through that troubled legacy of the failed revolution of 1968 and 1969 in France and Italy, in which Situationists were direct participants. There was no beach beneath the street. Whether such a revolution was possible or even desirable at that moment is a question best left aside. The installation of necessity as desire in the disintegrating spectacle is a consequence of a revolution that either could not or would not take place.

Even if a revolution could not take place in the late twentieth century, in the early twenty-first century it seems simply unimaginable.[7] It is hard not to suspect that the over-developed world has simply become untenable, and yet it is incapable of proposing any alternative to itself but more of the same. These are times in which the famous slogan from '68 — "be realistic, demand the impossible" — does indeed seem more realist than surrealist.

And yet these are times with a very uneasy relation to the legacy of such intellectual realists. Debord in particular is at once slighted and envied, as he was even in his own time. He was, by his own admission, "a remarkable example of what this era did not want."[8] He seemed to live a rather charmed life while doing nothing to deserve it. Debord: "I do not know why I am called 'a third rate Mephistopheles' by people who are incapable of figuring out that they have been serving a third rate society and have received in return third rate rewards … Or is it perhaps precisely because of that they say such things?"[9]

Not the least problem with Debord is that of all the adjutants of 1968 he was the one who compromised least on the ambitions of that moment in his later life. "So I have had the pleasures of exile as others have had the pains of submission."[10] Unlike Daniel "Danny the Red" Cohn-Bendit, he did not become a member of the European Parliament. As Debord wrote in 1985, looking back on the life and times of the Situationists: "It is beautiful to contribute to the ruination of this world. What other success did we have?" The key to the Situationist project of transforming everyday life is the injunction "to be at war with the whole world lightheartedly."[11] This unlikely conjuncture of levity with lucidity, of élan with totality, has rarely been matched.

It's not as if there aren't enough studies of the Situationist International and its epigones. While written in another context, these lines from Becker-Ho seem to apply: "Time and again in all the works dealing with the same subjects and sharing the same sources, one finds the same bits of information paraphrased more or less successfully, often with the same words endlessly repeated. Other people's findings, acknowledged in underhand fashion, re-emerge as so many new discoveries, stripped of quotation marks and references, and more often than not adding nothing to what is already known on the subject. But what this does is allow the whole field of information going unchallenged to be enlarged quantitatively, and on the cheap…"[12]

Culture is nothing if not what the Situationists called *détournement*: the plagiarizing, hijacking, seducing, detouring, of past texts, images, forms, practices, into others. The trick is to realize in the process the undermining of the whole idea of the author as owner, of culture as property, that détournement always implies.[13] Thus this study makes no claims to originality. Rather, in its act of inflating the whole field of information on the cheap, it seeks only to encourage others in this far from fine art of cultural inflation. The Situationist archive is there to be plundered. Unlike Becker-Ho, *The Spectacle of Disintegration* makes no proprietary claims, but it does set out to be a version of these materials of use to us *now*.[14] It's the past we need for the critique of this present.

Situationist thought is often imagined as a species of Marxism, particularly of the Hegelian variety. Sometimes it is regarded as the inheritor of the fringe romantic poetry of Arthur Rimbaud and the Comte de Lautréamont. Sometimes its project is imagined to be that of superseding the avant-garde movements of Dada and Surrealism, and presenting a spirited rival to contemporary movements as diverse as Fluxus, Oulipo or the Beats. Sometimes it is recalled as a precursor to punk rebellion, anarchist dumpster-diving or postmodern fabulousness.[15] That the Situationists took on the whole world does seem to align it with the more obstreperous of all these currents. What the Situationists fought against, much more vigorously than any of these movements, was their own success. The aim was to preserve something that could escape recuperation as mere art or theory. As Debord writes, "nothing has ever interested me beyond a certain practice of life. (It is precisely this that has kept me back from being an artist, in the current sense of the word and, I hope, a theoretician of aesthetics.)"[16]

The Situationists could be insolent, recalcitrant, insubordinate, but at their best their project of transforming everyday life had a playful quality. Everything is at stake, but the world is still a game. This attunement to life connects the Situationists to a quite different legacy. Michèle Bernstein, Gianfranco Sanguinetti and in particular Guy Debord were fond of quoting quite different sources which point toward different ancestors: Niccolò Machiavelli, Baltasar Gracián, Carl von Clausewitz and the Cardinal de Retz were, in their different ways, writers who tried to put into words the lessons of their own actions or the actions of others upon their time. Situationist writing thus belongs to that tradition of inquiries upon everyday life that ask: how is one to live? And that posit answers that are more than a critical theory, but form the tenets of a *critical practice*.

Debord was particularly fond of the *Mémoires* of the Cardinal de Retz (1613–79). A leader of the Fronde, that last aristocratic resistance to the imposition of absolutist monarchy in France, Retz contributes a quite particular orientation to everyday life that Situationist thought and action observes in its finest hours and neglects in its lesser moments. Writing a hundred years before Rousseau, Retz was not concerned with an armchair analysis of his inner life. He was crafting a public self, styling himself as a being in action. His *Mémoires* are an account of his successes and failures, but an account further perfected. A key quality with which Retz imbues his life is disinterestedness. His conduct of his affairs is something like a work of art or a well-played game. The chief aesthetic quality is being worthy of the events that befall him. He is versatile rather than a specialist. Often he acts from behind the scenes, an unseen power. The prevailing style is a certain appropriateness and consistency.

There is a certain aggrandizement to Retz, as there is to the Situationists, particularly Debord. Events are presented as if he was at the center of them. But what undercuts this seeming self-importance is a sense of the ridiculous quality of power in this world. Neither Retz nor Debord suffers fools gladly. Above all, this appreciation for human comedy relieves the writing of the bitterness of defeat. As Debord writes, in a style that is a modernized Retz: "I have succeeded in universally displeasing, and in a way that was always new."[17] To take this world seriously would be comic; to see the comedy of it is perfectly serious. What the Situationists share with Retz is a comic approach to life as a game which commits one to the cause of the world. Or to quote Debord, quoting Retz: "In bad times, I did not abandon the city; in good times, I had no private interests; in desperate times, I feared nothing."[18]

Like everything else, the Situationists got caught up in the spectacle. They became a mere image of themselves. Critical reception of them finds itself led by the nose into accepting a spectacular version, in which the whole project is reduced to Debord's personality, which is in turn reduced to a certain fanaticism.[19] Alain Badiou reduces Debord to psychoanalytic terms, as posing an image of the real against the symbolic and imaginary. Simon Critchley sees him as a religious rather than an ethical thinker. Jacques Rancière sees only aesthetic project.[20] Such readings take certain tactics at face value. Debord is not a modern Pascal, but a modern Retz; it is not faith but the game that is at stake.

"Of all modern writers," Debord said, quoting the eighteenth-century writer François-René Chateaubriand, "I am the only one whose life is true to his works."[21] Perhaps the most enviable thing about his life is that he managed to avoid wage labor. He did not work for the university or the media. And yet he produced several films, edited a journal, ran an international organization, and wrote a few slim books. Debord: "I have written much less than most people who write, but I have drunk much more than most people who drink."[22]

The drinking did him in. Peripheral neuritis is one of the more painful conditions from which a hard drinker can suffer. As a good Stoic, Debord put his affairs in order. He collaborated on a television documentary with Brigitte Cornand. He prepared his correspondence for publication with Alice Becker-Ho. He may (or may not) have burned certain documents. Then he shot himself in the heart. In the words of Louis-Ferdinand Céline, one of Debord's favorite writers: "When the grave lies open before us, let's not try to be witty, but on the other hand, let's not forget, but make it our business to record the worst of human viciousness we've seen without changing one word. When that's done, we can curl up our toes and sink into the pit. That's work enough for a lifetime."[23]

Debord was not by any means the only member of the Situationist International to leave her or his mark, and if other members did not exactly dazzle their century, they may yet have their chance to inform ours. The wager of this book is that critical practice needs to take three steps backwards in order to take four steps forward. First step back: the early, so-called *artistic* phase of the Situationists is richer than is usually imagined, and not so easily recuperated as mere art or architecture as is often supposed. Second step back: the political thought in action of the Situationists in the sixties is not well understood, and much of what transpired in this period still speaks to us today, if it is seen more broadly than May '68. An early book, *The Beach Beneath the Street*, set itself the challenge of retracing these two steps.

The Spectacle of Disintegration concerns itself with a third step back: that the defeat of May '68 did not mark the end of the Situationist project, even if the organization dissolved itself shortly afterwards. This book begins again with the story in the seventies, via the work not only of Debord but also his collaborations with his last comrade in the Situationist International, Giancarlo Sanguinetti, with Debord's second wife, Alice Becker-Ho, with his patron and film producer Gérard Lebovici, with professional filmmaker Martine Barraqué, with video documentarian Brigitte Cornand, and in the independent work of three former members of the Situationist International: T. J. Clark, Raoul Vaneigem and René Viénet. It is a disparate body of work through which we can read the last quarter of the twentieth century. They still dare us to outwit them, outmatch them. They dare us to stake something. There is more honor in failing that challenge than in refusing it.

This book is not a biography of Guy Debord. It is not a history of the Situationists. It is not literary criticism or art appreciation. Out of what is living and what is dead in the Situationist legacy it concerns itself mostly with what is living. If the Situationist slogan LIVE WITHOUT DEAD TIME is to be understood at all, it can only be in writing which treats its own archive as something other than dead time. The project is to connect Situationist theory and practice with everyday life today, rather than with contemporary art or theory. Hence the presence of certain anecdotes, cut from their journalistic context and taken on a journey, a detour, relieved of their fragmentary context and connected to a theoretical itinerary which treats them as moments of a lost totality. As the Situationists said: "One need only begin to decode the news such as it appears at any moment in the mainstream media in order to obtain an every-day x-ray of Situationist reality."[24]

Debord, like Retz and so many others, failed to transform the world of his own time, but this failure is the basis of a certain kind of knowledge. Right thinking in this tradition depends on the confrontation of thought with the world. History's winners are confirmed in their illusions; the defeated know *otherwise*. Debord: "But theories are made only to die in the war of time."[25] At least the Situationists found strategies for confronting their own time, to challenge it, negate it, and push it, however slightly, toward its end, toward leaving the twentieth century.

As impossible as that task was, leaving the twenty-first century may not be so easy. It is hard to know how to even imagine it. Perhaps a place to start, then, is by returning to some situations where it seemed possible to leave previous centuries. One of the virtues of writing in a Situationist vein is that it opened up the question of an activist reading of past revolutions. In our opening two chapters, we look back over the seventies writings of Clark and Vaneigem, but through their eyes look back again over the whole series of French revolutions and restorations. Then, we turn our attention to the rather critical accounts Sanguinetti and Viénet offered, from firsthand experience, of the Italian Autonomists and the Chinese Cultural Revolution, moments which, strangely, are back again, in a rather spectacular fashion, as touchstones for twenty-first-century political thought. After that, we pursue the tactics of Debord and Becker-Ho for keeping alive the spirit of contesting the totality as the era of the disintegrating spectacle was dawning.

3   Liberty Guiding the People

> To follow the times is to lead them.
>
> Baltasar Gracián

Suppose a team of archaeologists from an alien civilization came upon the ruins of the disintegrating spectacle, but all they had with which to understand it, besides some blasted fragments, was one or two books by T. J. Clark. What sort of sense would they make of it? Of course, we are already ourselves those very aliens. Much of what we now think of as what was once modern comes down to us in bits and pieces, as inscrutable as ancient Egyptian funeral art. But Clark's books might be singularly useful for this unearthed modern, since certain of his books quite consciously read the art of the nineteenth century as intimations for the twentieth century. As Clark reflects in *The Sight of Death*: "The advantage of the historical allegories in my previous books was that, if I was lucky, a point occurred at which the politics of the present was discovered in the histories — the distant histories — generated out of the object in hand."[1] These allegories might have further resonance in our own times.

One way to grasp the genesis of the disintegrating spectacle might be to rewind it, back before it sped up, before it flung apart. What Situationist writing might have going for it in this task is that, as Clark puts it: "It was the 'art' dimension, to put it crudely — the continual pressure put on the question of representational forms in politics and everyday life, and the refusal to foreclose on the issue of representation versus agency — that made their politics the deadly weapon it was for a while."[2] Clark can help us to formulate the problem of thinking aesthetics and politics together, within the vicissitudes of historical time.

Clark was, however briefly, a member of the Situationist International, and while his books are by no means a mere pendant to that fact, they respond to it; and respond, more particularly, to the stresses of a certain kind of political time through which Clark has lived. His writing was for him "a place to shelter from the storm. Doing art history — being an academic — was a compromise. It was as much as I had the nerve to do."[3] (An aside: And who am I, and who are you, dear reader, to ask of anyone anything more? Only those who throw stones can begrudge us our glass houses.)

Clark recalls standing on the edge of a demonstration in the late sixties, on the steps of the National Gallery in London, "discussing the (sad) necessity of iconoclasm in a revolutionary situation with my friend John Barrell, and agreeing that if ever we found ourselves part of a mob storming through the portico we ought to have a clear idea of which picture had to go the way of all flesh; and obviously it had to be the picture we would most miss."[4] Which picture would Clark choose? We shall find out later. Suffice now to say that it did not come to that, and perhaps just as well.

It is sometimes lost on readers familiar only with the opening overture of Debord's infamous book that the spectacle is not just some vast and totalizing shell that secretes itself out of the commodity form and envelopes all around it. While it may be the dominant form of social life, it is not the only one. Clark: "The spectacle is never an image mounted securely and firmly in place; it is always an account of the world competing with others, and meeting the resistance of different, sometimes tenacious forms of social practice."[5] Clark enlarges and refines the sense of the struggle over social form, and the role within the struggle played by the making of images. For while society may have become in part disciplinary, it has never ceased to be spectacular in its totality.[6]

If there is a limit to Clark — evident particularly in the later texts — it is in the way the auras of certain images start to become stand-ins for a contest of forces, struggling not just over what images can mean but also over what they can do. Clark: "If I cannot have the proletariat as my chosen people any longer, at least capitalism remains my Satan."[7] A Satan which art alone is not up to the task of confronting.

There are times when aesthetics and politics appear as discrete and free-standing categories. At other moments they can't help but fall over each other, which in the French context at least might be telegraphed by the following dates, and from the events that spill forth from them and evaporate into history: 1789, 1830, 1848, 1871, 1945, 1968; from the first *successful* French revolution, via the Paris Commune and the Liberation, to the last failed one. While Clark will have quite a bit to say about epochs of restoration, where art and politics interact only tangentially, of particular interest is the kind of time where they fuse. "Such an age needs explaining, perhaps even defending."[8]

Modernity is all about beginnings, and it might as well be said to begin with *The Death of Marat* (1793) by Jacques-Louis David (1748–1825). David shows Marat dead in his bath, clutching the letter written to him by his murderer. It's an image of a secular martyr, but not exactly a secular image. It was first shown at a ritual occasion, contrived by David. Quite a struggle went on over the meaning and ownership of the cult of Marat. While Marat was close to the Jacobin faction, the Enragés—the most radical expression of the most radical class, the sans-culottes—claimed him as one of their own. The image of Marat hovered for a moment, caught between the role of martyr to the state on the one hand, and friend to the sans-culottes and their demand for a thoroughly social revolution on the other.

"Surely never before had the powers-that-be in a state been obliged to improvise a sign language whose very effectiveness depended on its seeming to the People a language they had made up, and that therefore represented their interests."[9] The Jacobins had a tenuous grasp on state power. They relied on the sans-culottes for direct action against their enemies to the right, but having moved against the right, the Jacobins turned instead against their erstwhile allies to their left. The sans-culotte passion for direct democracy was a hindrance to the Jacobin claim to the state at a time of war.

The Death of Marat is a remnant of a historical event: the people's entry into history. For Clark, this is the cause of modernism itself, even if it doesn't usually know it. Robespierre and the Jacobins claimed to represent a pure and united people, forever to be purged of traitors, but this double act of representation, at once political and aesthetic, required vigilance. As for the people, as Clark put it with a chilling phrase: "It had to be killed in order to be represented, or represented in order to be killed."[10] Marat dead stood for the people, but the body was not up to the task. Representation as a whole isn't up to the task, but doesn't see it. The obsession with the false during the revolution did not lead to a questioning of representation in general.

Not the least extraordinary thing about David's version of Marat is that the whole top half of the portrait is a vast, blank space, a tissue of empty brushwork. It signals, in part, Marat's self-sacrificing austerity. For Clark, it is something more. Marat could hardly embody a revolution when nobody could confidently claim possession of its spirit. David's portrait could not quite work the old magic of the religious image, but nobody was quite ready to let the spiritual charm of images die. "Art had come out (been dragged out) of the Palais de Fontainebleau. That did not mean it was ready to understand its place in the disenchantment of the world. The whole history of modernism could be written in terms of its coming, painfully, to such an understanding."[11]

The blank wall behind Marat is "the endless, meaningless objectivity produced by paint not quite finding its objects, symbolic or otherwise, and therefore making do with its own procedures."[12] The revolution put in place a regime of the image in which for the first time the state was the representative of the people, but the people themselves could hardly be represented. The Jacobin notion of the people was empty, pure opposition to the parasites of the aristocracy. It was a problem that would take a century to resolve, and the name of that solution is the spectacle, but in solving the problem, the spectacle dissolves the people into itself—then itself dissolves.

The people appear on the historical stage in *Liberty Guiding the People* (1831), by Eugène Delacroix (1798–1863). It is an image of the myth of a revolution in which the bourgeoisie believed, if only for a little while. In 1830 the bourgeoisie has defeated tyranny and gained a constitution, all in three glorious days at the barricades. Delacroix's painting both restates and rephrases this myth. It repeats the forms of the popular lithographers, in that the barricade has become a stage, with characters propped on it rather than cowering behind it. Delacroix's Liberty is a woman, but not quite the conventional symbol. What unadorned Liberty reveals a little too much is the naked power of popular revolt. Delacroix's contemporary Honoré de Balzac saw in her eyes only "the flames of insurrection."[13] This is not exactly the liberty the bourgeois revolutionary bargained for.

Who exactly is Liberty guiding? The bourgeois in his top hat is surrounded by the rabble. If revolution is the door through which the people enter history, then it makes a troubling figure for bourgeois thought. Outnumbered, it might only be a matter of time before the rabble turns against their allies of the moment. And they did: By the time Delacroix's picture was hanging in the Salon of 1831, a new class war was on in earnest. The people didn't particularly want a constitution; they wanted bread and work and wages. They wanted a social revolution. The picture was an anachronism. It was quickly spirited out of sight, not to be seen again until the next revolution. What the bourgeoisie wants to remember henceforth is not revolution, but restoration. The revolution through which the people enter history is the revolving door that also spirits them back out if it again.

Delacroix's picture resurfaced in 1848, but he was not the painter of that revolution. Clark assigns that honor to Gustave Courbet (1817–77). By the 1840s, when Courbet came into his own as an artist, bourgeois power was an established fact. An insecure one, to be sure, but established, and artists could not but wonder "whether bourgeois existence was heroic, or degraded, or somehow conveniently both."[14] What would come to be known as the artistic and literary *avant-garde* was already an established part of cultural life, the antechamber of success. Also already in play was the avant-garde gambit of attacking the *forms* of the dominant order, whilst offering that order, knowingly or not, new forms.

The avant-garde rubs shoulders with, but is not the same as, *bohemia*. In mid-nineteenth-century Paris, bohemia was not yet a fantasy spun out of the *Scenes from Bohemian Life* of Henri Murger as *La Bohème* of Giacomo Puccini, let alone *Rent* by Jonathan Larson.[15] It was a genuine social class, outside of the ruling order, closer to the dangerous classes than the intellectuals. Clark calls them "the first debris of industrialism."[16] What bohemia lacked in aesthetic sophistication it made up for in recalcitrance. It was the genuine unassimilated force: "the real history of the *avant-garde* is the history of those who bypassed, ignored, or rejected it; a history of secrecy and isolation; a history of escape from the *avant-garde* and even from Paris itself."[17] Or in short, the only avant-garde worthy of mention is that which was unacceptable even to the avant-garde. Bohemia contains at least some element of the inassimilable waste product of spectacular society, what it pushes on ahead of itself, rather than what it leaves behind.

Clark identifies the bohemian's game as what Slavoj Žižek would later call over-identification. Clark: "the Bohemian caricatured the claims of bourgeois society. He took the slogans at face-value; if the city was a playground he would play; if individual freedom was sacrosanct then he would celebrate the cult twenty-four hours a day; laissez-faire meant what it said. The Bohemian was the dandy stood on his head."[18] Such a strategy had its limits. By the 1840s it offered little more than a shopworn romanticism, turned more toward nostalgia for the past that to present exigencies.

For Henri Lefebvre, romanticism is a viable strategy for advancing onto the symbolic terrain within what he calls the total semantic field.[19] It digs into the past to find the figures that still trouble the present. For Clark this is a temptation to be resisted. The promise of transforming everyday life has to be rooted in the materiality of everyday life itself. For Courbet, bohemia nevertheless offered a space within which to make a break with the expectations of the art world. His break from bohemia and its tired romanticism, in turn, would come via a return to his provincial roots.

From the bourgeois point of view, February 1848 was the beautiful revolution, but soon the bloom faded. Karl Marx: "The June revolution is the ugly revolution, the repulsive revolution, because realities have taken the place of words, because the republic has uncovered the head of the monster itself by striking aside the protective, concealing crown."[20] February was a bourgeois struggle to make again a constitution and secure its own power, with some few concessions made to popular power to secure its support. June was the uprising against bourgeois power when concessions proved not to concede enough. The avant-garde was for the revolution in February but against it in June; bohemia was not so biddable.

With the suppression of the popular forces, Courbet retreated to Ornan, and discovered, in the countryside, the missing element, something bohemian life couldn't supply—everyday life: "Courbet saw that the commonplace was not the life of other people, but his own life."[21] For Clark, the *Burial at Ornans* (1851) is one of Courbet's greatest achievements. It is an image of a religious ceremony, but it is not a religious image. It dissociates ritual from belief. It is not explicitly anti-clerical, which makes it all the more effective. Courbet pictures a kind of collective distraction, at once religious and secular, comic and tragic, sentimental and grotesque.

More challenging still is that it pictures the rural bourgeois. It confounds the myth of the unitary character of rural life, and at a time when the bourgeois replaced the aristocrat as the locus of peasant hatred. Courbet pictures the countryside at a time when power within it shifts toward the rural towns, and the countryside as a whole is absorbed within capital. Courbet at his best limns the relation between forces that animate the scene. His is a realism that thwarts art's supposed mission to imagine the *ideal*. The working of the canvas doesn't purify appearances, revealing an essence, but neither is it a fidelity to them.

With the defeat of the Parisian proletariat in June 1848, the role of Paris as center of political contest was for the moment eclipsed. What emerged in the shadow of Red Paris was Red France. The French peasantry had its own issues: land hunger, debts, rights to the commons. In 1848 the French peasantry arrives on the political stage as an actor in its own right. In 2010 the Thai peasantry did the same. After a populist prime minister was deposed in a judicial coup, the so-called Red Shirt movement came down from the countryside to Bangkok to try to force the end to a quasi-feudal political regime in which the monarchy presided over a state and army that represented only shifting compromises among business interests.

Early in March 2010 the Thai army reported the theft of six thousand assault rifles, but who stole them? Was it what the government called *terrorist elements* in the Red Shirt movement? Or did the army steal them from itself, so it could blame any violence in a coming confrontation on the opposition? When the Red Shirt demonstrations came later that same month, they were the biggest in Thai history, and largely peaceful, apart from a few grenade explosions in which nobody was killed. The Red Shirts poured what they claimed was their own blood on Parliament and called for elections to end the undemocratic rule—of the Democrat Party. Not getting what they wanted, they expanded their occupation from the Phan Fah Bridge to the Rajprasong intersection in the heart of Bangkok's tourist and commercial zone, and then into the nearby shopping district.

As part of a crackdown on Red Shirt–aligned media, including websites and radio stations, the army tried to shut down a TV station sympathetic to them. The Red Shirts stormed the station and occupied it, restoring broadcasts, at least temporarily. The army tried to retake Phan Fah bridge without success, killing two dozen people. The Red Shirts built bamboo barricades in the Rajprasong district, and held up a train coming from the Northeast carrying military vehicles.

A Red Shirt leader declared at this point that "we do not condone but we cannot control. There is no more control among the followers." Attempts at a ceasefire negotiation failed. Red Shirts forced their way into Chulanongkorn hospital near their Rajprasong barricades searching for troops, but they did not find any. The government added US$8 million to the Bangkok police budget. Khattiya Sawasdipol, a former army officer advising the Red Shirts, was shot in the head by a sniper while being interviewed by the *New York Times*.

In May, helicopters dropped leaflets on the demonstrators urging them to decamp, while they fired back with homemade rockets. Their encampment was surrounded, and the army launched an assault with armored cars. There were occasions of mutiny among the government forces, shooting at the army instead of the Red Shirts, but the government prevailed. Red Shirt leaders surrendered in an attempt to prevent further violence, only to be jeered at by an unrepentant rank and file. The stock exchange, banks and shopping centers went up in flames.[22] Whether or not one takes 1848 to be the moment when the peasantry enters history, in its own right, with its own demands, let's not pretend it ever left it.

The French peasantry in 1848 did not have websites or broadcast stations, but it did have its own forms of expression: songs, pictures, almanacs, secret societies meeting in the woods. The urban left would take some time grasping how to ally itself with all this. The party of order was quicker off the mark, casting the ethereal chains of religious devotion over the populace, while enacting laws to suppress traffic in popular almanacs.

This folk art was not as dangerous as it seemed. Far from being a pure expression of autonomous peasant consciousness, popular art had for a long time imitated that of the ruling classes. By the middle of the nineteenth century, it was a strange amalgam. Popular images included Napoleon and the Wandering Jew, Charles Fourier and the saints. Popular art carries new information but is full of reversals, distortions, exaggerations. Courbet appropriated this system of changes and inversions to make images for a dual public and with doubled meanings. "He exploits the area in which men still think and make images with materials long since falsified by history."[23]

Courbet's method, Clark claims, is what the Situationists call *détournement*: "Instead of reverence, a brutal manipulation of one's sources. Instead of pastiche, confidence in dealing with the past: seizing the essentials ... discarding the details, combining very different styles within a single image, knowing what to imitate, what to paraphrase, what to invent."[24] That there is a traffic between high and low art in Courbet is not all that original or notable. What matters is the direction: "Instead of exploiting popular art to revive official culture and titillate its special, isolated audience, Courbet did the exact opposite. He exploited high art—its techniques, its size, and something of its sophistication—in order to revive popular art."[25] Here is the key Situationist tactic *avant la lettre*.

Courbet confounded the expectations of both left and right: the left wanted a glorification of simple rural life; the right wanted the preservation of the myth of rural harmony. He addressed the possibility of a public that knew itself to be in a state of displacement. "Courbet's public was exactly this labyrinth, this confusion, this lack of firm outlines and allegiances. It was industrial society in the making, still composed of raw and explosive human materials."[26] His achievement was to appropriate from both high and low culture the means to give expression to the possibility not just of a popular art, but of a popular power with one foot in peasant rebellion and the other in the radical traditions of the urban tradesmen, bohemia and the dispossessed.

Courbet is the artist who both grappled with the most pressing problems of representation in his time and got the furthest with them: "In the middle of the nineteenth century both bourgeois and popular culture were in dissolution: the one shaken and fearful, trying to grapple with the fact of revolution; the other swollen with new themes and threatened by mass production. What might have happened—what Courbet for a while tried to make happen—was a fusion of the two."[27] But it was not to be. The vicissitudes of the art market made themselves felt soon enough, but far from being a failure of Courbet alone, this was a general failure.

The failure of a public, political art sets the stage for the more agreeable avant-garde of Impressionism, which discovers what can be achieved in the restricted space that remains. Impressionism is the art of the moment in which "the circumstances of modernism were not modern, and only became so by being given the form called 'spectacle.'"[28] In short, Impressionism was the art that traced the consequences for representation of the colonization of everyday life by the commodity form, even if it did not quite know it.

Impressionism knew itself to be the art of a Paris transformed by the urban planning of Baron Haussmann, and the moral panics that ensued from it. It was a vague but widespread feeling: "Something had gone from the streets; a set of differences, some density of life, a presence, a use."[29] Part of this feeling mapped a real transformation. Haussmann tried to evict the working class from its old quarters, leaving a Paris divided geographically by class. Bourgeois Paris would be in the west and working class in the north and east. The whole space of the city would be opened up to traffic. The political city, the city of the barricade, gives way to the city of circulation. The city as horizon of collective action has to be erased, but so too the city of distinct quarters, each a microcosm of trade and manufacture. Industry became a city-wide affair, with bigger markets, bigger players, tighter margins. In place of the small shop, the big department store, and with it the deskilling of retail. The shop assistant became a whole social category. One kind of capitalism supersedes another.

It was capital that changed things, but popular discourse blamed the city. In the 1860s people believed Paris was disappearing and being replaced by something unreal. Everyday life is becoming a matter of consumption rather than industry. "Paris was in some sense being put to death, and the ground prepared for the *consumer society.*"[30] The unitary world of the quarter, where everyone knows everyone and everyone can measure their social distance from each other directly, was disappearing.

What was so troubling was the anomie of everyday life, the interactions with so many anonymous strangers, who were not always what they seemed. Everyone seemed to be passing as what they were not. To navigate such a city takes maps, catalogues, field guides. The citizens of such a city can only interact with each other via representations that make its strange and fluctuating appearances legible. The city becomes spectacle, a city made to be looked at—for those on the make.

Not that this was to everybody's liking. In 1871, the Paris Commune would attempt to divert history onto another path. For the first time, the proletariat had its own revolution. While the representatives of the state retreated to Versailles, the communards became authors of their own history, if not at the level of government, then in everyday life. That the Commune had no real leaders might not be a weakness, and at least it had the wit to arm the people. It may not have understood power, but it understood the city, and intervened in its space. As Marx said, it suffered from too many trying to refight the old revolutions to grasp the originality of its situation. Or as the Situationists put it: "The Paris Commune succumbed less to the force of arms than the force of habit."[31]

"In our opinion, the Parisian insurrection of 1871 was the grand and highest attempt of the city to stand as the measure and norm of human reality," writes Henri Lefebvre.[32] Product of unique circumstances, and doomed from the start, when the ruling *Versaillese* return, the Commune closes a whole era of revolutionary politics, and perhaps not just politics. Clark: "After Courbet, is there any more 'revolutionary art'? After the Commune, and what Courbet did in that particular revolution, is there the possibility of any such thing?"[33] Charged with instigating the destruction of the Vendôme column during the Commune, Courbet faced imprisonment and exile, and became an enduring hero to the left.

The new city becomes the site for the painter who stays with the truth of appearances. But this imagining of the city is a kind of fetishism, an inability to see capital at work. Those workings are too spectral. Clark: "Capitalism was assuredly visible from time to time, in a street of new factories or the theatricals of the bourse; but it was only in the form of the city that it appeared as what it was, a shaping spirit, a force remaking things with ineluctable logic—the argument of freight statistics and double entry book keeping. The city was the sign of capital: it was there one saw the commodity take on flesh—and take up and eviscerate the varieties of social practice, and give them back with ventriloqual precision."[34] The city becomes the figure that both reveals and mystifies capital at work. Modern art becomes the art of this city, and, unknowingly, the keeper of at least a few capital secrets.

4 The Spectacle of Modern Life

Things have their seasons, and even certain kinds of eminence go out of style.

Baltasar Gracián

Modern art is good at symptoms. It is good at recording the perceptual effects of a certain kind of transformation of sensation, but not always so good at the diagram of forces that animates those appearances. Modern art invents a whole city of images of the city as images. Clark: "This, I should say, is the essential myth of modern life: that the city has become a free field of signs and exhibits, a marketable mass of images, an area in which the old separations have broken down for good. The modern, to repeat the myth once more, is the marginal; it is ambiguity, it is mixture of classes and classifications, it is anomie and improvisation, it is the reign of generalized illusion."[1] The separation of public and private life, and the invasion of both by the commodity form, is coming but is not yet perfected. The artist who worked this seam most assiduously was close to the Impressionists, but borrowed much from Courbet: Édouard Manet (1832–83).

The late nineteenth century is the time of the construction of the *middle class* as an entity separate from the proletariat. Manet shows with extraordinary clarity the sites in which it was produced: pop culture, the leisure industry, and suburbia. Three pictures, and three women's bodies, encapsulate this emerging spectacular regime, starting with Manet's *Olympia* (1863). By the 1860s, the bourgeoisie was used to the idea of an avant-garde. It had decided to be ironical about it. Manet still managed to find the weak point in bourgeois indifference.

The problem was not that *Olympia* was an image of a prostitute. It was not unusual for Salon pictures to be of prostitutes, but the acceptable image of the prostitute was the courtesan. The courtesan was what could be represented of prostitution. Money and sex could meet in private, in the brothel, or in the spectacle, in the representation of the courtesan. But the prostitute could not be made public. The courtesan is the acceptable image of modern desire. She was supposed to play at not being a prostitute. She was supposed to be the false coin in the realm of sexual purity. She was supposed to almost but not quite *pass* for respectable. She was what in twenty-first-century parlance offered something more than a mere hooker's hand-job. She is the ancestress of the *girlfriend experience*.[2]

The girlfriend experience was the invention of a pimp by the name of Jason Itzler. Other escort services offered the porn-star experience, where the client was supposed to receive something like the most perfectly commodified sex for his money. Itzler spotted a gap in the market for something else: "I told my girls ... we have to provide the clients with the greatest single experience ever, a Kodak moment to treasure for the rest of their lives. Spreading happiness, positive energy, and love, that's what being the best means to me. Call me a dreamer, but that's the NY Confidential credo." The women who worked for his NY Confidential were supposed to repeat a mantra to themselves before meeting their client, to the effect that he was actually her boyfriend of six months standing, whom she had not seen for three weeks.

Itzler found the perfect vehicle for such a service in 2004: Natalia McLennan, a former Canadian tap-dance champion. "I'm a little money making machine, that's what I am," recalls McLennan. "Yes, he sold the shit out of me, but he sold me as myself, someone anyone can be comfortable with, someone who really likes sex. Because the truth is, I do. I loved my job, totally." But, says Itzler, "If she ever did it with anyone for free, it would have broken my heart."

Both Itzler and McLennan seem conflicted about the nature of their business. McLennan: "Maybe it sounds crazy, but I never felt I was in it for the money." Itzler: "I thought I could save the world if I could bring together the truly elite people." Itzler even tried to turn NY Confidential into a reality TV show.[3] While hardly worthy of comparison to a Manet—and these days what is?—like *Olympia* the *NY Confidential* TV pilot blurred the boundaries of public and private, sex and love, money and gift. Itzler went to prison as much for a category mistake as a crime.

The name, for a start, is a joke: Olympia was a popular trade name for prostitutes. The brothel, like the Salon, put desire under the rubric of a classical goddess. *Olympia* undoes the category of the courtesan, or tries to. She is not a courtesan passing as a lady, but a hooker passing as a courtesan. Or rather, "she" is an artist, and artist's model — Victorine Meurent — passing as a hooker, passing as a courtesan.[4] This *Olympia* challenges the playful relation of money and desire. On its long road to disenchantment, the bourgeois lost faith in God, but it still believes in desire.

If even the image of prostitution escaped from the spectacle it would be an embarrassment. It implies that money has cuckolded even desire. "The fear of invasion amounted to this: that money was somehow remaking the world completely ... Such an image of capital could still not quite be stomached."[5] At least not in 1860; by 1960, things would be different, the frontier of what could not be stomached would be elsewhere, but was likely still being played out across women's bodies.

The official nude was supposed to be about something other than the naked body of desire. *Olympia* pictures also the disintegration of a genre. "If there was a specifically bourgeois unhappiness, it centered on how to represent sexuality, not how to organize or suppress it."[6] The nude became embarrassing. *Olympia* gave female sexuality a particular body, rather than an idealized and abstract one. It gave female sexuality not just a body to look at, but one that returned the viewer's gaze, and in returning it, created a space for a self reserved from the purchaser's look. The look it confounded was the look of both the art lover and the john.[7]

Argenteuil is about twelve kilometers from the heart of Paris, and by the early twenty-first century was one of its most populous suburbs, easily reached via the Transilien railway line. In the late nineteenth century it was still partly farmland, given over to grapes and the white asparagus named after it. The railway came in 1851. The market gardens gave way to factories, which were extensively bombed during the war, leading to a vast urban development plan in the postwar years, then suburban sprawl, and even a little gentrification in the prettier parts with a view of the city.

That this was Argenteuil's fate was not entirely clear in the late nineteenth century. It was a liminal space, to which the railway brought both factories and tourists, work and leisure, and sooner or later one had to yield to the other. For a while, it seemed destined to be a playground, a spectacular version of nature, made of parks and leisure zones. It framed the city with a more or less woody border. For the artists of the avant-garde, the suburb is a special zone, where the modern mix might be detected. "A landscape which assumed only as much form as the juxtaposition of production and distraction (factories and regattas)."[8]

Manet's *Argenteuil, les canotiers* (1874) is a big picture, made for the Salon. A couple sit by the riverside, boats behind them, and in the background, the factories on the other shore of the river. (The river, a vivid blue, is not quite as nature painted it. The color came from indigo dumped by a chemical factory upstream.) He looks at her; she stares into nothingness. Bored, perhaps, or indifferent, or blandly masking feelings for which there is no longer any public form or language. She is fashionably dressed, but the dress does not become her. She is uneasy.

Clark makes much of the disjointed quality of the picture. "Manet found flatness rather than invented it."[9] Her straw hat really is flat, a disc pinned at the back into a cone. "It is a simple surface; and onto that surface is spread that wild twist of tulle, piped onto the oval like cream on a cake, smeared on like a great flourishing brush mark, blown up to impossible size. It is a great metaphor, that tulle, and it is, yes, a metaphor of painting."[10] It is the brushy top half of *The Death of Marat* — domesticated.

Leisure can be a key site where the abstract workings of capital present themselves to the realm of sensation. "The subcultures of leisure and their representation are part ... of a process of spectacular reorganization of the city which was in turn a reworking of the whole field of commodity production."[11] The landscape of leisure emerges as the symbolic field for the conflicts of a spectacular identity. At stake are the forms of freedom, of accomplishment, naturalness, individuality.

These were traditionally bourgeois attributes, but the new

middle class claimed them as their own. *Canotiers* is an image of leisure that doesn't quite prove leisurely. The woman in her boating outfit and hat does not quite seem at ease. Leisure is not quite the free time it is supposed to be. Capital is already producing its own specific disappointments. In 2006 Anousheh Ansari, a successful telecommunications entrepreneur, spent A$20 million on a tourist trip — into space. But all she could think to do when she got there was look at the view and eat chocolate.[12]

Leisure becomes a site of tension, just like work. It is work. Manet's last painting, *A Bar at the Folies-Bergère* (1882), stocks all the ambiguities of the new, spectacular version of the popular. It's a scene from a café-concert, or what now might be called a nightclub. But in the late nineteenth century it was still something of a novelty, with its fake marble under electric light, its singers in ostentatious gowns, singing simple pop songs that are poor in melody but rich in inflection. Clark's claim for it is that the "café-concert produced the popular."[13] The café-concert generalized the instability of class. It made class contingent, a matter of passing, and called forth an art of mixture, transgression, ambiguity, in which the new middle class are the heroes, always angling for a way to exploit its edges.

This new middle class was creating a new class consciousness, which stressed what separated it from the proletariat, even if that claim struck the bourgeoisie, and its cultural functionaries, as ridiculous: "their probity was awful, their gentility insufferable, their snobbery outright comic."[14] And yet the avant-garde painters loved them, in their way. Their very ambiguity made them the perfect figure for the times. Modernist art tried to take its distance from the middle class and its entertainments, but artists are paradoxically fascinated by them. This usually served bourgeois interests. A characteristic of Situationist aesthetics and politics, with a nod back to Courbet, is to borrow modernism's contempt for the middle class, but for proletarian purposes.

Clark: "The middle class of the later nineteenth century, and even in the early years of the twentieth, had not yet invented an imagery of its own fate, though in due course it would do so with deadly effectiveness: the world would be filled with soap operas, situation comedies, and other small dramas involving the magic power of commodities…," not to mention the pilot for the *NY Confidential* reality TV show. "But for the time being it was obliged to feed on the values and idioms of those classes it wished to dominate; and doing so involved it in making the idioms part of a further system in which the popular was expropriated from those who produced it — made over into a separate realm of images which were given back, duly refurbished, to the *people* thus safely defined."[15] This inchoate spectacle learns to feed on, and transform, popular expression, extracting and selecting images. Hence the utility of modernism as a counter-project based on contempt for the result. But it is not as if there is a pure popular art that pre-exists its spectacular fate. The Situationist move is not to discard inauthentic pop in favor of an authentic popular, rather it is to appropriate the modernist critique of the popular as the basis for a new aesthetic and political project.

Clark: "It is above all collectivity that the popular exists to prevent, and doing so means treading a dangerous line."[16] It's the same line that threads through *The Death of Marat* and *Liberty Guiding the People*. The representation has to engage the real desires, frustrations, boredoms of its public. Yet it has to arrest these affects and make of them nothing more than spectacle. "Those who possess the means of symbolic production in our societies have become expert in outflanking any strategy which seeks to obtain such effects consistently; but they cannot control the detail of performance, and cannot afford to exorcise the ghost of totality once and for all from the popular machine."[17]

Armed with the techniques of the avant-garde, one can follow in Courbet's footsteps and re-appropriate the appropriators. The middle class are specialists of the image. "Popular culture provided the petit bourgeois aficionado with two forms of illusory 'class': an identity with those below him, or at least with certain images of their life; and a difference from them which hinged on his skill — his privileged place — as consumer of those same images."[18] This is the power of the middle class over the proletariat, its marking itself off both by its distance from the popular, and its possession of the power to mark that very distance. Hence the popularity in the early twenty-first century of reality shows in which workaday proles compete to become designers or chefs.[19] Becoming middle class means command of the surfaces of what now constitutes the popular, from a well-plated dish to kitchen renovations.

The middle class may be exempt from the rigors of manual labor, but it nonetheless encounters new kinds of labor, affective labor, cultural labor, for which it is hard to sustain much enthusiasm. Manet's *A Bar at the Folies-Bergère* shows a woman working behind a bar, fashionably made up. "The face she wears is the face of the popular ... but also of a fierce, imperfect resistance to any such ascription."[20] It might also be the face of someone whose feet ache. The other's leisure is her labor. It can't but provoke a certain boredom. Behind her is a mirror, which famously does not quite reflect the scene we see in front of it. The effect is cinematic. The mirror shows a moment before or after the one we see in front of it. There are two alternating moments, the act of serving, and waiting to serve. Which comes first? It doesn't matter. The picture is an alternation of these two moments, of working and waiting, and neither with any pleasure. She is, in a word, a *waitress*.

Once upon a time New York nightclubs catered to the aristocracy of the fabulous, to those with the looks, the style, or the connections to gain admittance to the world of the night.[21] That all changed with the invention of bottle service. Buy a table for some astronomical sum, and mere money will admit you to this world which once excluded the bridge-and-tunnel crowd, with their real jobs and neat suits. Sucking the credit cards out of their wallets became the main game, and the nightclubs became big business. Nightclubs ceased producing their own special kind of celebrity, and became dependent on attracting the sports and entertainment stars of their day. The nightclub became, in other words, just an enterprise dependent upon the spectacular, rather than one of its prime engines of efflorescence.

The game became one of attracting celebrities, who might in turn attract the bankers and hedge fund men for the VIP rooms. The general admission crowd down on the dance floor would be largely for decoration. The kinds of mixing of the classes that both troubled and thrilled Manet's contemporaries will now be carefully vetted. Managing such intercourse calls into being new kinds of labor. Rachel Uchitel was a VIP concierge director. She was an ambassador of client desire, making sure the big names and big spenders came to her club and kept on coming. "People say 'Oh Rachel, she's such a star fucker,' that I only hang out with celebs. No. I hang out with successful people. I hang out with people who matter, and I'm honored to." Uchitel became famous in her own right for fifteen seconds in connection with a famous sporting identity. The attention was not exactly welcome. Uchitel: "I have big breasts, yes. But I'm really offended by the notion that I used my sexuality."

Or anybody else's. For one of the roles of a VIP concierge director is to introduce people who matter to women they may find attractive. "It's not our job to get anybody laid," Uchitel insists.[22] But it was her job to populate the VIP rooms with women as attractive as they are discreet. Models, perhaps. Or almost-models. And it is the job of club promoters to bring these almost-models in. The contemporary nightclub, in other words, is a sophisticated machine for the highly selective mingling of money and sex. Or perhaps just the promise of sex, and sometimes just the promise of money. Whether the girls put out or the boys shell out is none of the club's concern.

The nightclub is now a long way from the café-concert, with its only partially organized traffic between money's desires and desire's money. Manet glimpses the beginnings of a spectacular industry that has since been perfected. Now that the threat of the dangerous classes seems half a world away, at least from a New York nightclub, the danger to guard against is not that the rabble might reject the desires on offer, but that it might rather embrace them with too much gusto. Leisure, sex and suburbia are no longer marginal sites within which new kinds of spectacular economy grow. They are the very center and essence of that spectacular economy.

5 Anarchies of Perception

There are occupations that enjoy universal acclaim, and others that matter more but are barely visible.

Baltasar Gracián

Camille Pissarro (1830–1903) offers a different kind of leisure in *Two Young Peasant Women* (1892). It is a painting of the end of the French peasantry, the fixing of something passing. Not that being a peasant was all that pleasant. It was hard work, but still, shot through with utopian promise.

Valuing peasant life was a way of resisting the disenchantment of the world, but Pissarro's painting is not an idealization of the image of the peasant as a remnant of the past. It is something more specific. Pissarro paints *idleness* as a moment within the field of work, as the peasant's ability to choose the moment to be idle. He found a way of looking at the people without being disciplinary or sentimental. There are certain things Pissarro's peasant women are not asked to be: figures of sympathy, for one. Clark rightly stresses the rarity of this as an achievement. Unlike Manet's women, they are indifferent to the gaze.

Pissarro's way of seeing is, in effect, *anarchist*. Not in the sense of painting a doctrine, but rather in working, through the act of making art, to a certain understanding of the social world. Anarchism is the theory of a freedom compatible with order. "It is the anarchist temper—vengeful, self-doubting, and serene—out of which *Two Young Peasant Women* comes."[1] Pissarro arrived at it through the materiality of painting itself. In this canvas, the singular and universal are no longer in opposition. It's something Pissarro wrestled with in trying to absorb the influence of Georges

Seurat, in whose distinctive paintings all dots are equal, but not the same.

For Pissarro, paintings are a way of thinking, of investigating vision and rendering it thinkable. The danger, as in Seurat, is that "Every act of submission to one's experience could turn into a system." But one could struggle against it, by immersion in a practice, of painting or something else, to get at the singular structure of sensation as one experiences it. Art is not an Idea cast into a few signs. It is more a matter of a singular sensation calling objects into being in its own way, with its own "folding of parts into wholes."[2] The anarchist critic Félix Fénéon, on Pissarro: "Finally a master of forms, he bathes them forever in a translucent atmosphere, and immortalizes, by means of the benign and flexible hieraticism he has just invented, their exalted interweave."[3]

Pissarro matters for Clark because of a need to recover a version of the history of socialism independent of either the social democracy of the Second International (1889–1916) or the Leninism of the Third International (1919–43). The First International (1864–76), for all its squabbles, was one in which anarchism was alive and well. Socialists pay a high price for suppressing their anarchist side, first with the capitulation to militarism of the Second International, and then by the authoritarianism of the Third.[4] In Pissarro's time, the anarchists at least resisted militarism, and stood apart from the nascent bureaucratic tendencies of the organized labor movement. For Clark what matters is always the internal difference within revolutionary movements, between a people and its representatives. This was already the case with the sans-culottes and David, the proletarians and Delacroix.

Socialist culture and politics, of which anarchism was then a component, were at the height of their power at the end of the nineteenth century. But socialism "had still to devise a set of forms in which the developing nature of bourgeois society—the cultural order of capitalism as well as the economic and political ones—could be described and resisted. Anarchism possessed some of the elements needed. In closing against anarchism, socialism deprived itself of far more than fire. It deprived itself of an imagination adequate to the horror confronting it, and the worse to come."[5]

The anarchists were geographers of the peasant condition. Pissarro certainly responded to the anti-urban strand in anarchism, its refusal to be seduced by labor and the machine. It was possible to read *The Conquest of Bread* by Peter Kropotkin together with Marx, to imagine agriculture as another route to praxis. "But at least anarchists knew already in the 1890s that fighting the state meant thinking geographically and biologically."[6] They counted among their number Elisée Reclus, veteran of the Paris Commune, acute critic of what was becoming of Marxisant socialism, and the founder of social geography. This is the space toward which Clark's viewing of *Two Young Peasant Women* opens.

David's *The Death of Marat* is a canvas that contains in embryo the two tendencies in modern representation. The top half points toward art's recognition of the disenchantment of the sign. In place of its magic, art will turn inward, and succeed by representing its own failure to represent anything else. The bottom half is something else. Here art struggles, and fails, to make a claim to enact a truth that is at once political and aesthetic: Marat's blood on the traitor's letter. But is the failure of the bottom half aesthetic or political? Perhaps it is not art that fails in this instance, or not art alone. Perhaps the failure is in calling on art to represent a people *in absentia*.

One could see Delacroix, Courbet, Manet and Pissarro as attempts to make some kind of painting work in the place of the dead Marat. Delacroix tries to affirm the presence of the people, and fails. What Courbet bequeaths to Manet is the possibility of a realism that finds the gap between appearances and the ruling ideas of their time. What Pissarro offers is the possibility of picturing an actual site in which some other life could be sensed. In their successes and failures is a legacy from which to thieve in the unending struggle of peoples to present themselves to history rather than be represented by the state or the commodity. In short, from the détournement of these formative moments of the nascent spectacle can come resources for a counter-practice to the spectacle in its current form.

Or so, perhaps, was Clark's proposition in his earlier books, up until *The Painting of Modern Life* (1985). In his later writing, particularly in *Farewell to an Idea* (1999), it's the works that descend from the top half of *The Death of Marat* that interest him, by Paul Cezanne, Pablo Picasso and Jackson Pollock. This is where modern art becomes the site of a certain kind of melancholia, the place where the impossibility of the projects launched by the bare half of *The Death of Marat* is registered. This is an art that becomes enclosed within the spectacle, gesturing crazily to what it can't picture, what it can't sense, what it can't know. Modernism is the spectacle in negative.[7] But it is still spectacle.

Debord dates the modern spectacle from the 1920s: "the society of the spectacle continues to advance. It moves quickly, for in 1967 it had barely 40 years behind it; though it had used them to the full."[8] This periodization is no mystery. The key incidents are the Bolsheviks' suppression of the Kronstadt rebellion against the Soviet state (1921) and German Social Democrats' acquiescence to the suppression of the German revolution by the far right (1919). Debord: "The same historical moment, when Bolshevism triumphed for itself in Russia and social democracy fought victoriously for the old world, also marks the definitive inauguration of an order of things that lies at the core of the modern spectacle's rule: this was the moment when an image of the working class arose in radical opposition to the working class itself."[9]

What Debord calls the concentrated spectacle has its roots in David and Delacroix; the diffuse spectacle arises out of the contradictory materials Manet and Pissarro explore. The concentrated spectacle merged elements of both. But what separates the spectacle proper from its nascent state is the incorporation, not of an amorphous people, but of the working class, and not as individuals but via the representation of class power. The disintegrating spectacle resembles the nascent state. Organized labor gradually ceases even to be its own image.

Clark's excavation of the nascent spectacle may well provide resources for thinking about its disintegrating remnants, and what he describes as "a terrible, interminable contest over how best to debauch and eviscerate the last memory—the last trace—of political aspiration."[10] For Clark, as for Debord, there's not much to mourn about the collapse of the Soviet Union and its client states, of what Debord called the concentrated spectacle. Debord rather presciently anticipates that its eclipse casts its western counterpart adrift, that it would be lost without its nemesis. The presence of even a false alternative obliged the masters of the diffuse spectacle to think historically. With its victory, the diffuse spectacle integrated into itself the practices of state secrecy of its rival, to the point where it deceived even itself.

Clark opposes a deep attention to the image as a foil to both the absence of historical thought, and—paradoxically—as a challenge to the apparently image-drenched world of the disintegrating spectacle. "Sure, I count myself an enemy of the present regime of the image: not out of some nostalgic *logocentricity*, but because I see our image machine as flooding the world with words—with words (blurbs, jingles, catchphrases, ten thousand quick tickets to meaning) given just enough visual cladding."[11] Clark himself contributes to the critique of the disintegrating spectacle as one of the members of the group Retort, whose text *Afflicted Powers*, while by no means Situationist, nevertheless can be read as drawing in part upon Clark's earlier work.

Retort's signal date is 2003, when some eight hundred cities hosted anti-war demonstrations. "It was a world-historical moment. Never before had such masses of people assembled, against the wishes of parties and states, to attempt to stop a war before it began." What appeared is "a digital multitude, an image of refusal," but set to become just one more image, "another image-moment in a world of mirages."[12] In 2003 the anti-militarist strain of popular revolt reappeared—and again failed to stop the wars.

Where Clark values Pissarro's anarchist vision as a small token of a worker's movement that eschewed a vanguard, Retort extends this critique to the vanguard form of the anti-western jihadists. While it might tempt some on the left to welcome attacks on the empire, Retort is quick to show that the limits and dangers of this kind of vanguard are the same as the Jacobin one and its Leninist inheritors. The fatal flaw hinges on usurping the political and setting oneself up as its armed image.

As for the 9/11 bombers: "They were exponents of the idea (brilliant exponents, but this only reveals the idea's fundamental heartlessness) that control over the image is now the key to social power." Spectacular power is vulnerable to a raising of the stakes, to being beaten at its own game. Or so it appears: "But the present madness is singular: the dimension of spectacle has never before interfered so palpably, so insistently, with the business of keeping one's satrapies in order."[13]

The colonization of everyday life proceeds apace, an "invasion and sterilizing of so many unoccupied areas of human species-being." What is somewhat blandly referred to as *globalization* turns in on itself, "mapping and enclosing the hinterland of the social."[14] What the disintegrating spectacle leaves in its swirling wake is a world of loosely attached consumer subjects, and a weak form of citizenship which the ramping up of nationalist rhetoric does its best to mask. Weakly attached citizens-consumers still need to heed the call up, from time to time, to make *sacrifices* to preserve the state. Neither the popular forces nor even the state itself seems to manage any form of historical thought. The state comes to believe its own disinformation.

The Situationist project is often dismissed as if it were a claim to penetrate the veils of false consciousness and reveal the essential truth it masks. What Clark's dilation on the history of revolution and representation affords is a more subtle view, in no way reducible to such ideology critique. As Clark writes: "supposing we take Debord's writing as directed not to anathemizing representation in general (as everyone has it) but to proposing certain tests for truth and falsity in representation and, above all, for truth and falsity in representational *regimes*."[15]

A first test would hinge, as in his examples from David and Delacroix to Courbet, Manet and Pissarro, on the materiality of the encounter. A second test might turn on the social form of the relation within which an image is produced. The dilemma of modernity is the split in the results it achieves in these two tests. The avant-gardes of modern art end up channeled into a preoccupation with the materiality of the encounter, even while modern experience is rife with popular social movements that express desires that escape from the regime of representation and produce other kinds of relation. The spectacle emerges not least as the means of absorbing the expression of both desires back into the representation of the commodity. And yet the very persistence of the spectacle indicates that desire still exceeds it, and on at least these two fronts.

What matters is the remaking of counter-strategies that do not necessarily reveal the real behind the symbolic curtain, but rather attempt to produce a different kind of social practice for expressing the encounter of desire and necessity, outside of power as representation and desire as the commodity form. Clark: "Why should a regime of representation not be built on the principle that images are, or ought to be, transformable (as opposed to exchangeable) — meaning disposable through and through, and yet utterly material and contingent; sharable, imaginable, coming up constantly in their negativity, their non-identity, and for that reason promoted and dismantled at will?"[16] In short, why should détournement not be the practice by which the encounter with the world is discovered and produced?

For Debord, the spectacle emerges out of a key moment, when the Second and Third Internationals come to stand in the place of proletarian power, when the proletariat has to be killed in order to be represented, and represented in order to be killed. Clark extends the historical frame back to the nineteenth century, to show that the spectacle emerges out of not this one but a whole series of encounters between the expression of popular power and the power of representation. From there, perhaps it's a question of extending forward as well. It is not as if the social democratic and Stalinist forms of usurpation of popular power are the last.

One of the most salient points of departure for critical thought and action in the early twenty-first century may well be the account rendered by former Situationists of the failure of the popular movements of their time. This might at least forestall the curious nostalgia that animates contemporary leftism, which is so often so indiscriminately fascinated by the *red decade* in France from 1966 to 1976, by the various forms of neo-Maoist philosophy that linger in its wake, and by the Italian Autonomist movement, which arose with a vengeance around 1977 to take up the banner of waning militancy in France.

Situationists and Post-Situationists were consistently hostile to such currents, which might provide a certain useful counterweight to an ahistorical nostalgia for the remnants of such thought. But before turning to the seventies, there is another path that passes from the French Revolution, through its consequences, to the

Situationist International and beyond. If Clark restores to view the life of the image and an anarchist vision, then Raoul Vaneigem brings back to our attention the poetry of utopia, and of that moment in modernism for which Clark has so little sympathy: the Surrealists.

6 The Revolution of Everyday Life

Comrades whom you have offended make the bitterest enemies.

Baltasar Gracián

It was the start, if not of a beautiful friendship, then of a harmonious one, at least for a time. Raoul Vaneigem and Guy Debord met in 1960. Henri Lefebvre introduced them. They sealed their friendship Situationist style. Vaneigem: "My psychogeographic dérives with Guy Debord in Paris, Barcelona, Brussels, Beersel and Antwerp were exceptional moments, combining theoretical speculation, sentient intelligence, the critical analysis of beings and places, and the pleasure of cheerful drinking. Our homeports were pleasant bistros with a warm atmosphere; havens where one was oneself because one felt in the air something of the authentic life, however fragile and short lived. It was an identical mood that guided our wanderings through the streets, the lanes and the alleys, through the meanderings of a pleasure that our every step helped us gauge in terms of what it might take to expand and refine it just a little further..."[1]

Among other things, they discussed the books they would write. Debord was nothing if not encouraging. He wrote to Vaneigem in 1965 that his manuscript is "perhaps the first appearance, in book form, of the tone, the level of critique, of those revolutionaries called 'utopian', that is to say, of the basic propositions for the overthrow of the totality of society."[2] Vaneigem's book got into print a little sooner than Debord's *Society of the Spectacle*. Famous in English as *The Revolution of Everyday Life*, it was at first rejected by various publishers, including Gallimard. Then an article appeared in the press that claimed the Situationists were an influence on the Provo agitations then rocking Amsterdam. Raymond Queneau asked Vaneigem to resubmit it to Gallimard, and so it ended up with one of the most prestigious houses in France. If there was an author who anticipated the mood of May '68, it was Vaneigem with his "lucidity grounded in my own desires."[3]

In contrast to Clark's melancholia, Vaneigem thinks of May '68 as the revolution that never ended, a "genuine decanting, from the kind of revolution which revolutionaries make against themselves, of that permanent revolution which is destined to usher in the sovereignty of life."[4] Its significance lay less in the confrontation with the state than in the transformation of everyday life. It would not be a revolution within the economy, but a revolution against the economy. It would germinate in the pores of the old world and burst through the dead skin of politics. "One day, though, we'll have to admit that May 1968 marked a complete break with the majority of patriarchal values..."[5]

All of which was finally too much for Debord and some of the others in the Situationist International, who retained a rather more Jacobin idea of revolution. After an exchange of not particularly edifying diatribes, Vaneigem resigned in 1970: "How did what was exciting in the consciousness of a collective project manage to become a sense of unease at being in one another's company?" He wrote to his former comrades that he had no desire to see them again until after the revolution, much like Hölderlin's Hyperion, who would not trouble himself with friendships that are mere fragments of a new life yet to dawn. [6]

Vaneigem left the Situationist International, which dissolved two years later. He did not stop writing. Often deploying pseudonyms, over the ensuing decades he periodically issued manifestos restating a small number of themes. Some of his best books were on heresies, as they brought together his unique talents.[7] He studied Romance philology at the Free University of Brussels from 1952 to 1956. Then he taught at the École Normale in Nivelles, a small town in the Walloon region of Belgium, from 1956 to 1964, where a liaison with a student got him fired. He survived on editorial and hack writing jobs thereafter.

If Debord's debut book of 1967 was a détournement of Hegel, Marx and the Marxisant writings of the moment, then Vaneigem's reaches back to one of Marx's precursors, Charles Fourier.[8] Marx and Engels had an ambivalent relation to Fourier. Henri Lefebvre: "Like Fourier, Marx desired and projected the new life." But they kept him at a distance, grouping him with utopian writers with whom he had little in common. They admired him chiefly as a satirist. And yet "Marx owes much more to Fourier than is generally admitted."[9] In drawing up his list of theoretical topics to deal with without pedantry or delay, Vaneigem listed an homage to Fourier, something he never quite carried out, unless one considers his whole life to be such.[10]

Charles Fourier (1772–1837) and G. W. F. Hegel (1770–1831) were both writers shaped by the French Revolution. Hegel perhaps had more enduring impact, for while Fourier had a number of disciples, most were more like Judas than the Apostles. They betrayed his larger vision. He was somewhat selectively read as a socialist prophet. His French followers joined forces with the Jacobin left in 1848 and went down with them. A statue in bronze of Fourier by Émile Derré went up at the Place de Clichy in 1899, but his influence was decidedly on the wane by that time.

André Breton's *Ode to Charles Fourier* (1947) opens with the author reminiscing about the day ten years earlier when he noticed that someone had placed a flower at the foot of Fourier's statue. In 1941 the Germans melted down the statue and used the copper for the manufacture of munitions. Breton: "They've preferred the good old method." Gone is "the immortal pose of the thorn-extractor."[11]

Breton, like his contemporary Theodor Adorno, was exiled by the war in America. Unlike Adorno, Breton did not think the concentration camps obliged him to forswear the poetic, but rather to delve even deeper into it, via Fourier's "extreme tact in extravagance." Caught between the futility of art for its own sake and the utility of art to Stalinism, what remained of the Surrealist movement turned to Fourier in the bleak years of the war and the fragile promise of the peace that followed. Breton: "Fourier they've scoffed but one day they'll have to try your remedy whether they like it or not." Breton revived interest in Fourier not so much as a socialist prophet of associative labor, but as the poet of liberated desire.

In March '69, Pierre Lepetit, a teacher at the École des Beaux Arts, joined forces with some friends of the Situationists and restored Fourier's statue on the Place de Clichy, or at least a plaster replica.[12] René Riesel, René Viénet and Alice Becker-Ho witnessed the installation. Lepetit's statue bore the legend: "In homage to Charles Fourier from those who manned the barricades on the rue Gay-Lussac," the spot where the Situationists took their stand against the police in May '68.

The Fourier of liberated desire was somewhat at odds with the militant asceticism of the French postwar left. Roland Barthes mentions a study group on Fourier formed at the occupied Sorbonne in 1968 that was denounced as *bourgeois* by the militants. Fourier's revolution was always in a minor rather than a major key, a revolution of everyday life rather than of the state. Barthes: "Marxism and Fourierism are like two nets with meshes of different sizes."[13]

Fourier, with his weird fetishes and manic obsessions, is an easy prey for the new priests of psychoanalysis.[14] Barthes rescued him from travesty by drawing attention to Fourier as a writer. He famously characterizes Fourier as a *logothete*, an inventor of a language. He anatomizes Fourier's technique, which isolates itself from everyday language, articulates new rules for its assemblage and regulates the production of text, resulting in the fantastic repetition that characterizes his writing, which like that of the Marquis de Sade contains scene after scene with variations on the same game.

Raymond Queneau thought Fourier's calculus of the passions was more sophisticated than Hegel's dialectical logic. Walter Benjamin saw something machine-like in the meshings of his utopia. Italo Calvino imagined him, and not unkindly, as writing a vast computer program.[15] Roland Barthes' Fourier is the designer of wilder systems, which can never quite complete themselves and yet thrive on the very attempt. Time and again writers find ways to connect Fourier to their own passions. He has been successively a socialist prophet, a free-love utopian and then a writer's writer.

A useful corrective to these Fouriers is that of Fredric Jameson, who finds instead an ontological Fourier, in which a new cultivation of the passions (superstructure) organizes freely associating labor (infrastructure). Jameson reconnects the older, socialist reading of Fourier as prophet of free labor with the surrealist reading of Fourier on liberated desire, while still paying attention to writing as a formal procedure which structures the relation of one to the other as an open-ended practice of systematizing without a system.

As Jameson reads Fourier, that which can be desired is the very basis of social structure, and not just of social structure, but of nature itself. Fourier is the most vigorous resister to the thought that something of desire has to be forsaken, that the condition of life is the tragic one of sacrificing desire on the altar of the real. Fourier is no moralist. Jameson: "The ethical or moralizing habit is above all what resists the great thought of immanence, what hankers after the luxury of picking and choosing among existents…"[16]

Where Debord perfected a style of almost absolute negation, Vaneigem learns from Fourier how to affirm the world: "I first read the selected texts, published by the Editions Sociales, in the early 1960s. I then read the version of the *Nouveau monde amoureux* edited by Simone Debout. One of the things that made Fourier a genius was that he revolutionized the world and the perception we have of it without labeling himself as a revolutionary. He expressed no judgments made on a moral basis. He acknowledges a world of domination. He takes the society as it is—with its desires and hidden passions. He creates the conditions that would lead to their harmonization and refinement. Thus, what in a logic of civilization would be a frenetic race for success (upward social mobility) and behaviors focusing on producing exclusion, is replaced, in a logic of harmony, by ludic imitation."[17]

What Fourier and Vaneigem have in common is their refusal of necessity. Fourier: "The passions are proportionate to the destinies." Vaneigem: "Love is the science of pleasures that organizes destinies."[18] Fourierist writing connects the totality of nature to the events of everyday life via the ubiquity of the passions. While there is always something outside the system, Fourier keeps extending the system sideways to include it, even if, in the process, something else falls out of its reach. The passion that drives Fourier to systematize is always reaching toward what it excludes with fresh gestures of welcome. This is his capricious and capacious beauty.

The limit to the Jamesonian reading is that while it frees Fourier from partial readings via labor, desire or language, the Fourier who spent his days trying to change the world is absent. Vaneigem has the merit at least of attempting to synthesize Fourier on the association of labor, on free love, and as visionary poet, with the praxis of everyday life. Vaneigem: "If cybernetics was taken from its masters, it might be able to free human groups from labor and from social alienation. This was precisely the project of Charles Fourier in an age when utopia was still possible."[19] It is not that Fourier is like a machine or a computer. Quite the reverse: the machinic and the algorithmic could be fragments of a Fourierist playground ready for *self-assembly*.

For Vaneigem it is a question of how poetry can be an activist mode in the world: "Poetry is an act which engenders new realities."[20] Far more than the other Situationists, Vaneigem takes seriously the latent potentials of the Surrealist project: "Surrealism's failure was an honorable one."[21] Vaneigem's roots are more in the revolutionary Surrealism of his native Belgium than the Letterist movement Debord encountered in Paris. Via Vaneigem's détournement of the Surrealists and the Surrealists' of Fourier, a neglected strand for Situationist thought and action emerges. While Debord and Vaneigem were fellow travelers in their Situationist wanderings, in the end they belong to different camps. The nets through which they strained to understand—and change—modern history use meshes of different dimensions.

In the century after the French Revolution, and particularly after the emergence of the art market in the 1850s, the bourgeoisie tried to build a new transcendent myth out of the ruins of religion, an autonomous sphere of Art as redoubt from economy. The struggle for new mythological forms can be traced from David's *The Death of Marat* to Manet's *Olympia*. Vaneigem: "The 'spectacle' is all that remains of the myth that perished along with unitary society: an ideological organization whereby the actions of history upon individuals themselves seeking, whether in their own name or collectively, to act upon history, are reflected, corrupted and transformed into their opposite—into the autonomous life of the non-lived."[22] Where Clark traced the tactics of realist painters in and against the spectacle, Vaneigem records those of the romantic and Surrealist writers.

Three strategies confront the challenge of the bourgeois world's autonomous art. One was a radicalizing of aesthetics from within: Stendhal, Nerval, Baudelaire. A second was the struggle to abolish art as a separate world and realize it in everyday life: Hölderlin, Lautréamont. The third was a systematic critique of aesthetics from that world from which it separated: Fourier and Marx. Dada came closest to a synthesis of the available strategies, but the defeat of the German revolution of 1919 doomed it to failure, too. Dada offered an absolute but abstract break with bourgeois art and life. Surrealism, at its worst, was a kind of reformist version of Dada, obscuring its negativity, restoring partial forms of revolt.

The Surrealists struggled against, and eventually collapsed into, the autonomous sphere of art. Vaneigem: "Hence Surrealism became the spectacularization of everything in the cultural past that refused separations, sought transcendence, or struggled against ideologies and the organization of the spectacle."[23] And yet, not least through Breton's intelligence and discretion, "the Surrealists made a promise which they kept: to be the capricious consciousness of a time without consciousness."[24] Vaneigem appreciates Breton's expulsions of unworthy members, even as he slyly notes "his tendency to choose people's aperitifs for them."[25]

At their best, the Surrealists resisted both specialized art and politics, and hewed close to the discovery of the potentials of everyday life. While some capitulated to the art market, Benjamin Peret, Antonin Artaud, André Breton and Jacques Prévert waged a campaign against Surrealism as ideology. They extracted themselves from the allure of the Communist Party, whose deadly policies Peret saw firsthand as a volunteer in republican Spain. Vaneigem: "The foundering of this project under the helmsmanship of Stalinism and its attendant leftisms was to reduce Surrealism to a mere generator of what might be called the special effects of the human."[26]

Still, they pioneered a psychoanalysis freed from therapeutic pretensions. They remained guardians of dreams, even if they could not quite bring themselves to call for their realization in everyday life. From early on, René Crevel documented the persistence of non-life in the totality of human affairs: "All our life we circle around the suicide that legislators have condemned so that the earth might not be deserted."[27] Crevel took his own life in 1935. His suicide note said simply, "disgust." When they turned away from Stalinism, Breton and friends were left with nowhere to go except the rewriting of everyday alienation as cosmic mental theater, either on the epic scale of Artaud, or as Crevel's chamber pieces.

Vaneigem gives the Surrealists more credit than does Debord for what they preserved through the dark times of the late thirties. They kept alive fragments of a project of emancipation, the trace of a theory of passionate moments, moments of love, encounter, subjectivity. Yet they turned such moments into an absolute, an illusory totality. They fell for the cult of woman, and for a hierarchy of spiritual over carnal love. Breton in particular failed to live up to Fourier's lack of judgment about homosexuality, or so-called deviance in general.

The Surrealists constructed a new canon: the atheist priest Jean Meslier, the romantic extremist Comte de Lautréamont, the criminal poet Pierre-François Lacenaire, and the desiring machinery of Charles Fourier, among others. But they abandoned Dada's quest for collective poetry and total negation in favor of the specialized domains of avant-garde politics and art. Vaneigem: "The discovery of Fourier might perhaps have underpinned an overall recasting of the movement, but Breton would always prefer Fourier the visionary, Fourier the poet of analogy, to Fourier the theorist of a radically new society."[28] At war's end there was not much left of Surrealism as a radical project. "They were Don Quixotes tilting against housing projects."[29]

Vaneigem finds the backbone of the movement in its poets, not its artists, who were usually to the right and quickly absorbed into the art market. They offered, moreover, not particularly interesting détournements of previous modernist advances: Joan Miró redid Paul Klee; Max Ernst redid Giorgio De Chirico. Even the best Surrealist writing on the everyday—Michel Leiris—descended into a sort of queer empiricism.[30] "Never opting firmly either for a poetry made by all or for the venality of the ruling system, Surrealism took something of both and produced an impoverished cultural hodgepodge."[31] One suspects Clark would not entirely disagree.

The Situationist program was a rectification of the Surrealist one. The poetry of everyday life had to be brought in contact with the critique of political economy, where each extended the other. The Situationists wanted to abolish both the *separation* of labor from desire and the *spectacle* in which all that could be desired returned in the form of mere images of commodities. To spectacle and separation, Vaneigem offered a third object of critique: *sacrifice*. If Debord's critique was of political economy in the era of the reign of the image, then Vaneigem's was a critique of *general economy* — of mythical as well as real exchanges — in the era of a generalized political economy. Sacrifice is a key transaction between the finite and infinite realms.

Fourier is quite uncompromising about the new myths of the bourgeois order, not least its emerging political economy: "According to this science all industries are useful as long as they create legions of starving men who sell themselves at bargain prices to conquerors and shop bosses."[32] Its one advance was to reverse the ban on luxury and wealth propagated by the moralists. "It is true that the economists permit us to love wealth, but they don't make us wealthy."[33]

The sacrifice that is labor is not rewarded with anything equivalent to it, as Marx might say, but moreover, it can never be. On the contrary: "They encourage us to submit passively to civilization, with its system of incoherent and loathsome work."[34] Work which, more often than not, does not make wealth for the worker, and sometimes not even for the boss: "There are over a hundred different kinds of bankruptcy: such is the perfection of reason under modern philosophy."[35]

The infirmity that is work has the deformity of leisure for company: Fourier: "And so on Sunday they go to cafes and places of amusement to enjoy a few moments of the sort of carefreeness that is vainly sought by so many rich men who are themselves pursued by anxiety."[36] The worker seeks the playful idleness of the weekend bourgeois, but cannot really afford it. The bourgeois can afford it, but is hardly in a playful mood with the hundred kinds of bankruptcy buzzing around his head. Such might be Fourier's reading of the faces of Manet's café-concert scenes. The workers sacrifice their bodies; the bourgeois their souls. Or so it may at first appear in the bourgeois theology of labor.

To everything there is a place and to everything there is a time under heaven. There is a time and a place to be born, to die; to build, to destroy; to weep, to laugh; to get, to lose; to give, to take; to buy, to sell; to work, to rest — and to sacrifice. Each is particular and separate, fragmenting time and space into disparate, disconnected moments. There is a time and a place for every particular thing. But what of *everything* in the sense of the totality, the unity of time and space—what is the time and place for that? Paradoxically, the totality too has its separate time and space, that of the sacred. The sacred is a separate time and space with the odd quality of being that of the whole. It is the separate moment for what is not separate. The sacred is the place and time for a very particular kind of sacrifice, for the giving up of something of this world of particular things to the world of the totality, imagined as that which is universal and eternal. If once the place of the sacred was the church, now it was the café, or the art Salon.

For the errant Surrealists Michel Leiris and Georges Bataille, the sacred persists as a problem for the modern world, which has lost its contact with this other realm of totality and no longer knows how to offer itself. For Vaneigem, it's more a question of discovering what kinds of gift could be freely given that might break with the whole logic of sacrifice. "The urge to play is incompatible with self sacrifice," and once the rules of the game become the rites of a ritual, it becomes an offering in exchange for something else.[37] Vaneigem extends the Marxist critique of exchange from the secular to the spiritual economy.

For Marx, an exchange between owners and non-owners of property cannot be an equal exchange. With nothing to exchange but labor power, the non-owner of property does not get the full value of labor returned in the form of wages. For Vaneigem, the labor of the non-owner is also a sacrifice, a real giving up of time, effort, not to mention a renunciation of desires. In exchange for this material sacrifice, the owners of property offer imaginary ones. "To the sacrifice of the nonowner ... the owner replies by appearing to sacrifice his nature as owner and exploiter; he excludes himself mythically, he puts himself at the service of everyone and of myth."[38]

Fourier had a rather complicated picture of the succession of historical stages. Vaneigem boils it down to what one might call three modes of sacrifice: ancient slavery, medieval feudalism and modern capitalism. Rather than modes of production, they are perhaps modes of destruction, general economies of the immolation of human happiness. Vaneigem is not interested in the social product; he is interested in what is destroyed in its making. He is not interested in the objects extruding from an economy; he is interested in the subjective potential sacrificed to it. His three modes differ in how the sacrifice of free agency is extracted.

In the slave mode of sacrifice, the labor of the non-owner has in the last resort to be compelled by force. The slave sacrifices everything and the owner nothing. In the face of slave revolts, Christianity proffered an ingenious solution that would be crucial to the feudal mode of sacrifice. It created a reason for the non-owner to offer a voluntary sacrifice. The sacrifice of particular labors and desires in the temporal world could be returned in the form of eternal salvation. But wait! There's more! As if that offer wasn't enough, Christianity throws in a free set of steak knives: at the end of times the just will be resurrected and the golden age return. The non-owner will be the closest to God—eventually.

For the moment, however, the non-owner is furthest from God, at the bottom of a hierarchy, underneath the priests and overseers, who in turn are underneath the lords and cardinals, who in turn are underneath the kings and popes. The non-owner makes a modest, particular sacrifice of time and effort. The owner—whether of temporal or spiritual power—makes a symbolic sacrifice to the totality itself. The non-owner is given over to the particular task; the owner is given over to that which orders all particular labors. We all have to make sacrifices, but some sacrifices are more equal than others.

One of the signs of the declension from critical theory to hypocritical theory is the repudiation of Marx's atheism and a credulous respect for all things biblical. Some even go so far as to venerate Saint Paul! Marx, the old mole, who wrote his dissertation on Epicurus and Democritus, would probably grumble and quake from the underworld if it existed. Vaneigem too takes his distance from atheism: "Without God, suffering became 'natural', inherent in human nature, it would be overcome, but only after more suffering..."[39] But he at least charts a path through those heresies of the ancient and feudal world that refused or resisted the sacrifices that the Christian church institutionalized.

Heresies can have quite different relations to sacrifice. One strand to heresy exposes the false sacrifices of the non-owner, but calls in their place for real ones. This is the path that extends from the religious ascetics to the revolutionary militants. Or, heresies can refuse the language of sacrifice altogether. As Vaneigem shows in his studies of heresy, this is the path of Simon of Samaria in the ancient world and of the Movement of the Free Spirit in the feudal world. It is also the path of Fourier: "Duty is man's creation; attraction comes from God."[40] He too is a heretic rather than an atheist.

The Surrealists wavered between modernizing sacrifice and abandoning it. Crevel: "The man who stutters with pleasure will soon seek divine laws, laws greater than those adopted for the petty economy of this expectant globe."[41] Leiris: "Asceticism in fornication, unselfishness in possession, sacrifice in pleasure, these were also the ideals whose antinomian appearance exalted me."[42] Vaneigem continues Crevel in this rather than Leiris.

Fourier and Vaneigem point out a path between the return to the clutches of the church on the one hand and an atheism that collapses into the bourgeois dogmas of sacrificial labor on the other. Vaneigem: "From the ruins of heaven, man fell into the ruins of his own world."[43] Fourier and Vaneigem treat atheism as a failed project, one that did not break the spell of sacrifice, but rather detached sacrifice from the spiritual and attached it to the profane realm. Labor becomes a universal sacrifice to what is supposedly the common wealth, but where the non-owner makes the concrete sacrifice of labor and the owner makes an imaginary sacrifice to the totality of the economy.

One of the manifestations of this imaginary sacrifice is patronage, whether of the church or of art. One of the virtues of Fourier is that he was not arrested at the intermediate stage where art replaced religion as the separate sacred space for sacrifice to the totality. Fourier intuits that the economy itself becomes the sacred whole. In Vaneigem's reading, Fourier is a kind of secular heresy against this "mercantile totalitarianism."[44] Fourier: "We must love work say our sages. Well! How can we? What is loveable about work in civilization? For nine-tenths of all men work procures nothing but profitless boredom."[45] Fourier refuses the "martyrdom of attraction." Desire is not to be sacrificed to work any more than it was to God, and Art is no more compensation than faith. As Vaneigem intuits, Fourier's critique is a powerful one, whose uses if anything multiply in our mercantile times.

7 Détournement as Utopia

Far better the jobs we don't grow bored with, where variety com-
bines with salience and refreshes our taste.

Baltasar Gracián

Perhaps it was because Fourier's is a kind of self-taught *low theory*
that he was not tempted into the compensatory realm of art or
literature or philosophy, but rather directly attacked the relation
of aesthetic experience of everyday life to the totality of nature.
Fourier came from the provincial center of Besançon, a town
dominated by the church, the army and local government. He was
raised in the somewhat Balzacian world of a prosperous merchant
family that expected him to take his place in the business. He had
as good an education as a small town could offer, and won school
prizes for everything (except obedience). His pious mother feared
too much education might make him another Luther or Voltaire,
and she was not entirely wrong. Fourier became a class traitor. He
took seriously that to which his class paid lip service, he inverted its
cherished beliefs, and he betrayed its venal secrets. He claimed that
at the age of nine he swore an oath against trade just as Hannibal
swore to destroy Rome.

If Besançon was Fourier's education in the ways of the merchant
class, Lyon introduced him to late-eighteenth-century class conflict.
The silk industry was in decline, sharpening the struggles between
the weavers and the silk merchants. He was in Lyon when the
French Revolution came. For a brief moment Fourier shared in its
illusions: liberty, equality and fraternity and all that. The revolution
destroyed his attempt to set himself up in business. His cotton bales
were requisitioned and used as barricades. Drafted by counter-

revolutionary forces, he nearly lost his life in the defense of Lyon. He barely managed to escape revolutionary justice. Conscripted again, this time he soldiered for the other side.

The revolution he experienced wasn't glorious. All he saw was speculation and graft, hunger and death, boredom and arbitrary justice. The revolution may have been made in the name of the people, it may even have mobilized the people, but in the end it was business as usual. Vaneigem: "All struggles for freedom obey a law of business expansion."[1] Whatever sacred mysteries are imputed to the revolution as *event* by latter-day pseudo-Jacobins, this is its quotidian consequence.

Situationists and bourgeois liberals are in uncommon agreement that the red terror is a refutation of Leninism. Only Vaneigem is consistent in seeing the Jacobin terror as a refutation of the bourgeois philosophers as well. This is his fidelity to Fourier, or more properly speaking his *solidarity* with him. Bourgeois thought is convicted by the violence it refuses even to acknowledge as its own. Fourier: "Agitators promise to make people happy, rich and idle; but once they have gained power, they oppress the multitude and reduce it to a more complete state of servitude in order to consolidate their own position as idlers or as managers of those who work."[2] The new Sparta had, like the old one, turned out to be a slave state. What grows out of the barrel of a gun, besides corpses, is investment opportunities.

Fourier was hardly alone in this repugnance, of course, but unlike so many writers of his generation he did not take refuge in the past. In refusing to bow down at the altar of labor subordinated to capital, he did not return to the altar under the tortured Jesus. These are the same thing, modes of sacrifice, and sacrifice itself is the thing to repudiate. Fourier: "If they wanted to attack the Catholic religion, they should have opposed it by one which provided contrary excesses: it sanctifies hardship, so they should have sanctified sensual pleasure."[3] His was a heresy that broke with the imperative to sacrifice of both Christian and bourgeois thought, and he points to the way out of many of the aporias the Surrealists found themselves in by attempting to modernize sacrifice rather than abolish it.

Bourgeois liberalism at its most mindless insists that utopias lead to bloody revolutions, and of course they have this, as usual, completely backwards. It was the miserable experience of the bourgeois revolution that led to Fourier's utopia. The simultaneous devaluing of all values, old and new, created the opening for a recasting of the cosmos out of whole cloth. Not the least of Fourier's cunning is his ability to find value in the damaged intellectual goods left from the chaos of revolution. His writings are an extraordinarily skillful détournement of exactly this intellectual inheritance. Fourier's thought proceeds by way of what Vaneigem, following Bertolt Brecht, calls a reversal of perspective.[4] In place of reasons of faith and faith in reason, Fourier based his doctrine on the passions.

As much as he denounced Rousseau, Fourier took freely from him, but mostly from *Émile*, *The Confessions* and *New Heloise*. Like Lautréamont after him, he read Buffon and other naturalists, but his roots were more in the neoclassical seventeenth century, in Molière and La Fontaine. These were his pawns in a game against logics of sacrifice, both new and old. Vaneigem: "détournement is an all-embracing reinsertion of things into play. It is the act whereby play grasps and reunites beings and things hitherto frozen solid in a hierarchy of fragments."[5] Vaneigem sets some of the pieces Fourier deployed in motion again against the sacrificial order of the late twentieth century. Perhaps confronting the even more terrible and total logic of sacrifice that persists in this next millennia will take a détournement that draws from them both.

In the early twenty-first century the idea gained force that pretty much everything can be sacrificed to the disintegrating spectacle, from which nothing much should be expected in return. Far from the care and management of the *biopower* of its subject populations, the state's role is rather to sacrifice the health and education of present and future populations by cutting taxes on finance capital and freeing the latter for yet more speculative investments, from which not much should be expected beyond a few menial jobs. Nor should the state invest in infrastructure for future industrial expansion. No Haussmanns are to re-engineer American cities to absorb surplus labor and capital and build platforms for new forms of accumulation. Even the ground under American feet could be sacrificed to powerful blasts of chemical-infused water to extract natural gas with few safeguards. The failure of past sacrifices to the spectacle calls forth a cargo cult of unprecedented dimensions, in which everything left is to be fed to the maw of Moloch, simply because it is unimaginable that there could be any other course of action but to offer still more gifts to appease these bored Gods. Such is the end game of all civilizations, as Fourier well knew.

Eric Santner: "Why does the beast need to be starved? Why does the 'flesh' of the body politic need to be reduced, reduced, reduced? The answer we hear over and over again is: for the sake of the 'Job Creators.' The one Creator God has effectively been dispersed into a pantheon of new idols, those to whom we must all sacrifice so that they may show favor on us and create new worlds of economic possibility. Job creation has become the new form of grace or gratuitousness otherwise reserved for divinity. Our duty is to make sacrifices and above all to be vigilant about not calling forth the wrath of the Job Creators lest they abandon us and elect others as their chosen people (other nations who make bigger and better sacrifices). The old culture wars concerning hot-button social issues have simply assumed new guise. Tax increases have come to be regarded as a sort of job abortion, the killing of unborn economic life."[6]

What would it take to imagine a life free from such sacrifice? Fourier's writing is intensely visual. His imaginal architecture, the phalanstery, has all the symmetry and serene poise of a Nicolas Poussin landscape, and yet also the fantastical qualities of a Claude Lorrain.[7] The Harmonians who occupy these spaces seem to relish their time like the gallant youth of Antoine Watteau. A visit to Paris in 1789 gave Fourier tangible models for the architecture of his new world, not least the fairy palace that is the Palais Royale and the covered galleries of the Louvre. Fourier's tastes tended toward the classical, to the dominance of form over movement.

Fourier took a measuring stick with him when he wandered the streets, charting urban improvement plans of mathematical proportion. According to Vaneigem, he and Debord took ether instead, for more measureless encounters with a labile space and time. Vaneigem dissolves Fourierist order into romantic arabesques. Perhaps a more contemporary détournement of both Fourier and Vaneigem might revisit the question of form and dynamics, paying more attention to the play of Fourier's systematic writings, but without dissolving that play into Vaneigemesque gestures. Fourier is a contemporary of the romanticism that effloresced in Germany and England, but is not quite of it. Perhaps this very untimeliness points toward new approaches to the problem of form.

Barthes emphasizes the solitary character of Fourier's writing, but this is misleading. In the years in which he consolidated his ideas Fourier was far from a loner. He seems to have had both lasting friendships and passing affairs. Later, he would discover the company of lesbians, which allowed him to have enduring platonic relationships with women. At work, he donned the mask of the reliable, punctual businessman. He was no nay-saying Bartleby; he was a model employee.[8] He was easily bored, so the life of a commercial traveler suited him well. Travel informed his passion for geography, and he loved to meet new people, learn their stories, share the intimacies of the road, and move on. From his travels he knew first hand the real poverty of Europe. Unlike many of the writers of his time, his work was based on conversations with people from many occupations and regions. His utopia is informed by an ethnography.

Fourier had a gift for confidences. He admits his desire to Désirée Veret, a young feminist, but acknowledges that the attentions of an old man could be of no interest to her. In exchange for such frankness, she writes of her experiences to him. Of sex with the English, she notes: "They make love like they make machines."[9] It is not hard to imagine Fourier alone in his garret, scribbling his sexual utopias with a hard-on in his hand. One wonders if there are stains on the manuscript pages. And yet there is a certain understanding of the desires of others that could only come from fieldwork, or perhaps participant observation.

Fourier's world is a pantheist universe of plural passions. If all cosmologies are analogical, then his is built on a harmony that is at once planetary, mathematical and musical. By denying divine providence, the Enlightenment sent civilization on a course of political revolution that did not result in a harmony below to match the — now abolished — heaven above. Vaneigem: "God has been abolished but the pillars which supported him still rise towards an empty sky."[10] From what he knew of the everyday life of desire, Fourier reconstructs the fabric of the cosmic order.

Fourier takes Newton's celestial mechanics to be the only major scientific discovery, and boldly offers to fill in what it lacks. In the absence of a science of energy, growth and life, he adds to Newton a poetics of that which the science of his time was incapable of systematically thinking.[11] For Fourier the planets themselves are animate. Like humans, they have twelve passions, and communicate with twelve aromas. Planets, like humans, can have one or more dominant passions. Some are monogynes (one dominant passion), some are digynes (two dominant passions), and so on. The universe is dynamic and alive. There is "copulation between the planets."[12] Unlike humans (or perhaps not so unlike), planets each have a male north pole and a female south pole. They are androgynous and bisexual. Fourier's whole universe is queer.

The universe is bound together by planetary passions, and so too could be the earth, if humans did not play so crudely on the twelve-tone system of planetary harmony. "The creatures of various degrees of the polyversal keyboard all have use of the twelve radical passions, but they differ in their exercise of them."[13] Like the planets, the being of humans is relational rather than atomistic, each swings in the gravity of the others. The universal gravity of social life is not reason but the twelve passions. Five of the passions are derived from the senses: sight, sound, touch, taste and smell. Then there are four spiritual passions: ambition, friendship, love and family. The penultimate passions are social ones: the composite, the cabalist and the butterfly.

The composite passion is a kind of vertical axis and the cabalist a horizontal one. The composite passion connects enthusiasms of the most material kind to more rarified sensations, and vice versa. Food, for example, becomes the vehicle for Fourierist *gastrosophy*, an elaborate tending to both sensation and meaning. The cabalist passion is horizontal and connective. Jameson: "Nothing is more remarkable, among the multitudinous slogans this Utopia floats from its banner-head, than this positioning of the conspiratorial schemer as the heroic center of social construction itself; nothing better illustrates the sublime indifference of Fourier to conventional moral judgments (and not only the sexual ones)."[14]

Politics in the cabalistic sense is usually at best a necessary evil for radical thought, something to be endured in order to articulate one demand to another. Or, politics is doubled with a fantasy category of "the political" and recoded as a sort of spiritual Jacobinism of the moment of pure revolt. Fourier affirms the game of politics as a pleasure in its own right, and one that cuts across the liberal distinction between public and private realms.

The butterfly passion seeks variety. Fourier is particularly attentive to the question of boredom. Both bourgeois and radical thought tends to privilege the spectacle of the monogyne who pursues one mania relentlessly, writing book after book, for example. Fourier's world has room for varying and combining the passions. In one of their rare statements on the Communist good life, Marx and Engels draw on Fourier's account of the butterfly passion in action. Why not go fishing in the morning, write philosophy 'til dusk, and party 'til midnight?

Unityism, or harmony, is not so much a thirteenth passion as the sum and totality of them all. It is "unlimited philanthropy." God's method is the association of the passions. Morality, whether of the Christian or Enlightenment kind, is a futile struggle against the passions. "It is erroneous to believe that nature is sparing of talent; she is prodigal beyond all our desires and needs."[15] Fourier's divine order calls for no sacrifices, real or imagined. The coordination of the passions unleashes natural abundance.

The *equality of man* is the most enduring bit of bric-a-brac to descend from the revolutionary period. Becker-Ho: "In the process of its formation as a social class, an ideology of equality between men was of great use to the bourgeoisie. Nevertheless, it is the law of the strongest that prevails everywhere: by force of arms, money, sex, as well as intelligence. Only the dangerous classes dare proclaim it loud and clear though: for where there is in fact no equality or justice among men, then by the same token there can be none between the sexes."[16] As we shall see later, Becker-Ho steps outside of bourgeois legality, to find leverage against it in its margins. Fourier détourned this tenet of bourgeois thought in the most direct manner. He simply reversed it.

Fourier's social universe is based on difference rather than equality. He considers bourgeois philosophers to be the utopians, imagining they can wish away the differences among the passions.

Fourier is completely at odds with the neo-Jacobin thinking of Alain Badiou or Jacques Rancière, for whom equality is a founding political principle. Fourier's thought is anchored to a quite opposite idea: that of the series. Everything in the natural and the social world comes in a series. A series of horticulturalists, for example, growers of tulips, of roses, of chrysanthemums, bound together by affinity, but also by rivalry and contrast. Social organization is not premised on a universalizing abstraction, but rather on enumerating and linking particular practices.

The bourgeois philosophers promise the wealth of nations, but not their happiness. Civilization proceeds by political revolution, but seems still to make very slow progress. Take the centuries it took to abolish slavery. "Like a sloth, civilization moves forward with an inconceivable sluggishness through political storms and revolutions. The new social theories put forward by each generation only serve, like brambles, to draw blood from the people who seize upon them."[17] Social theory either denies the passions or, in acknowledging them, seeks only to contain them.

While Fourier did not believe in equality, he believed in the abolition of unnecessary suffering and poverty. His *phalanstery* offered not only a right to agreeable work and sustenance for all, it also offered a certain minimum of sensual gratification: "society should grant a minimum of satisfaction to the two senses of taste and touch." Or in other words, nobody should go without food and sex.

"While the sense of taste goes into open rebellion, the sense of touch protests silently. But if the ravages it causes are less obvious, they are no less real."[18] The source of revolution is hunger; the source of everyday discontent is sensual hunger. The satisfaction of these basic needs is only a first step. His project for the development of a life beyond so-called civilization has three stages: First, material plenty for all, and the enrichment of the five senses. Second, liberty for the four group passions. And finally, justice for the passions of the series. Relationships should be the major preoccupation of life.

Fourier is famously acute in his critique of the bourgeois family, which he sees as essentially a business. "Prohibition and contraband are inseparable in love, as in merchandise." The bourgeois family leads not to duplicity but to *quaduplicity*, where husband and wife deceive not only each other but also their respective lovers. That the married couple consider each other's passions their property is only the beginning of the family's perversity. The property relation then extends as well to the children. What one might call the family spectacle arises from its foundations in a property relation, not least that of parents over children: "Poor in pleasure, they want to be rich in illusion. They claim for themselves rights of property upon the affections of the weakest."[19]

For Clark, utopia is "the invention of early modern civil servants."[20] But what he finds in Pissarro, Vaneigem finds in Fourier: that passion and order are not opposed. If civilization has discontents, then so much the worse for civilization. Fourier: "All repressed passion produces its counter-passion."[21] De Sade is the ultimate product of manifold repressions. But it is not a question of a simple liberation from repression into freedom. Of the four spiritual passions (ambition and friendship, love and family) civilization puts too much stress on the fourth alone as the pillar of order. Putting an end to civilization means a refinement of the associative potentials of the other passions. From there, the passions of the series can also lead to further enhancements of being.

The passions of the series were known to so-called primitive society, but not to civilization. "This is the secret of lost happiness that must be recovered."[22] The three social passions, the composite, the cabalist and the butterfly, produce only libertines and eccentrics in this world, not to mention Situationists. The twelve passions are common to all, but they are not equally present in all. Fourierist social organization is a geometry based on a probability. Given a unit of social life big enough to have all the types represented, mutuality can then be composed out of them.

Fourier's followers tended to concentrate on this as a geometry of labor, where each could pursue their various passions and yet the sum that resulted would be a prosperous and productive one. The disintegrating spectacle has no interest in labor. Labor is in exile, behind Chinese walls, real or imagined. The Fourier one might counterpose to it is perhaps the Fourier of the passions. This Fourier frees the passions from their sacrificial relation to the commodity form. What Vaneigem takes from Fourier, and what in the age of the disintegrating spectacle one might take from both, is a systematic reversal of perspective, a heretical détournement of spectacular commonplaces, which imagines both labor and everyday life outside the logic of sacrifice, even of Lenin-worshiping neo-Jacobin kinds.

8 Charles Fourier's Queer Theory

> To turn sorrows into pleasures is to know how to live.
> Baltasar Gracián

If most civilized philosophies are just castles in the air, then why do they not at least have orgies going on inside them? There are not a few pedants who prostrate themselves before this or that philosopher's airy erection, who admire its *rigor*, who have slaved so hard to peer into its many rooms that they cannot but defend its *stature*, even if it means they have to explain away said castle's torture gardens. Fourier too may be a castle in the air, but he takes pains to equip his with parade grounds and covered walkways. He even keeps the noisy spaces for kids away from the quiet ones for grown ups. Violence, for Fourier, is a failure of *design*, of both built space and social relations.

Rural life with his nieces in Talissieu at first seemed designed to please Fourier, but in the end proved to be somewhat trying. It is hard to know how much of a good time his nieces were really having with the dashing young officers who came so often to call. Fourier claimed to have stumbled upon a young officer with a hand up one young lady's skirt while his other niece watched them. Fourier felt they should be free to fuck whomsoever they wanted, but their hypocrisy galled him. When he confronted them they feigned to be offended by the mere suggestion of anything improper. He also suspected the young officers were not as gallant as they claimed and would abandon the young women when they proved inconvenient.

In any case, it all went badly in the end. These circumstances did inform the writing of what may well be Fourier's impossible master-piece, the *New Amorous World*. It would not see the light of day until 1967. Perhaps it can be read then as a sort of belated Situationist classic. Vaneigem: "I was so fascinated by it that I re-printed some fragments of it (with an introduction) while at Payot's."[1] Those efforts not withstanding, it is still a little-known queer theory classic.

Fourier's fragrant mix of elaborate social imagination and porn was something of an embarrassment to his later followers. It was not without precedent, however. Fourier sets his new sexual order on Cnidus (or Knidos), the Greek city famous for Praxiteles' statue of Aphrodite removing her clothes. It was where Newton discovered a fine statue of Demeter, and also the setting for a work by Montesquieu on chaste and sincere love. The courtly love tradition had imagined ideal household constitutions for the romantic life. Something like it can be found also in Rabelais. Both Restif de la Bretonne and the Marquis de Sade imagined universes arranged around sexual pleasure and, like Freud after them, saw sexual passion as the antithesis of the social.[2] What is distinctive about Fourier is that he imagines the social as entirely composed out of the passions. He refused the erotic Jacobinism of universal monogamy (still to be found in Badiou, for instance). His passionate social order is not one of a universal but singular love, but rather one of the diversity and difference of the passions.

Vaneigem: "Sensual intelligence will bring about the classless society."[3] This is a Fourierist sentiment. At heart Fourier wants to be an erotic umpire of passionate games, not a political economist. His most beautiful writings, on the *New Amorous World*, are a unique kind of philosophy of the orgy, or systems-theory porn. As a pornographer Fourier is interested in the tableaux, the staging, the ritual, rather than the actual fucking.

The world of Harmony satisfies a sexual minimum for all. Every monogyne can get his or her rocks off. Fourier is no egalitarian. He is barely interested in describing such paltry pleasures. It's the baroque world of the omnigynes that attract him, with their polymorphous play on the whole twelve passions. Fourier considered himself an omnigyne, and hence his porn had to arouse all twelve of the passions, not just the passion for "touch-rut."

Philosophy is too concerned with ambitious or major politics, and not enough with amorous or minor politics. If Marx plumbs the limits of political philosophy in political economy, Fourier finds it in an amorous economy, but one where amour is neither private nor at odds with the world. Vaneigem attempts a curious synthesis of these two critical filters, but one where the Fourierist mesh is the finer. In modern civilization, "the space-time of private life was harmonized in the space-time of myth. Fourier's harmony responds to this perverted harmony. As soon as myth no longer encompasses the individual and the partial in a totality dominated by the sacred, each fragment sets itself up as a totality ... In the dissociated space-time that constitutes private life—made absolute in the form of abstract freedom, the freedom of the spectacle—consolidates by its very dissociation the spatial absolute of private life, its isolation, its constriction."[4] In place of which Fourier imagines a new harmonization of desire and the social, and a new built form, the phalanstery, in which public and private are no longer spatially separated and no longer need a phantasmal mediation via the spectacle.

Why is love the passion the philosophers want to admit the fewest possible bonds, when one is supposed to love one's brother, be a citizen of the world, and so on? *Sexual politics* means something quite specific in Fourier's world. There's hardly any point in politics in its civilized senses. In a decentralized world of plenty, there's nothing to fight over, no point to empire. Capital, labor and talent cooperate rather than struggle against each other. Politics is the domain of the cabalist passion, of intrigues and factions, rivalry and collaboration, but the stakes are largely symbolic. Some are richer than others in Harmony, but here social stratification is not a mere mask for class. The real contest is for prestige and renown.[5] Sexual politics is a game of sensual largesse. Its currency is attraction, but the point of the game is not to hoard and covet, but to dispense and distribute the favors of the favored.

The *quadrille* is a dance that requires a refined coordination of the dancers. Fourier imagines an erotic quadrille of sixteen persons. For this quadrille "orgies are prepared by the minister and female pontiff who arrange delightful reunions and cumulative sympathies that heighten each other."[6] Pleasures accumulate and ramify in memory, ours and others. It is an economy of reputation, where liaisons are structured to produce harmonious results. The quadrille heightens all the particular passions through their combination, added to which is the pleasure of unityism, which heightens all the other passions as well.

Rather than random encounters, the new amorous world is one of "harmonic polygamy."[7] Fourier: "The result is very brilliant orgies that furnish charming illusions and precious and durable souvenirs."[8] Participation is not a sacrifice, but a heightening of pleasure. As in the quadrille as a dance, each adjusts to each other, pleasures the other, only some will distinguish themselves more than others. "All men and women who have worn a cross in the court of love advance in steps proportionate to the number of foci they have formed."[9] Its perfection would be the omnigyne quadrille, composed of thirty-two persons whose distribution of passions is the same as the thirty-two planets.

Fourier is a little coy about revealing how the quadrille really works to readers shackled by civilized morality. It's clear that what he calls pederasty and lesbianism are included as expressions of the passions. But perhaps what's more interesting is that he understands difference in desires not so much along the straight/curious/gay continuum, as within a more complicated space of possibilities. It's more about which, and how many, of the passions are dominant.

For instance, a pentagyne straight woman, who has five dominant passions, might require encounters with five monogyne men, each of which corresponds in his dominant passion to one of hers. Of course monogynes rank low in the scale of erotic reputation in the quadrilles. The omnigynes, fully alive to all twelve of the passions, are most likely the ones in demand, acquiring reputation, and eventually playing the roles of conductors of the dance. Fourier upends the moral judgments of civilization. In the erotic quadrille, the sluts rule.

Civilization treats sexual space as a hierarchy of values, with straight monogamy at the top and random fucks at the bottom. The realm of sanctioned sexual practice is a hot topic, but it is really just about where to draw the line. Serial monogamy might be okay for some, a period of random dating among the young before they *settle down*, perhaps. Maybe it's okay for people to have sex outside marriage once the kids are out of the house. Maybe one incident of *cheating* can be forgiven, but not if it's a habit.[10] Maybe gay people can be allowed in the hierarchy of sanctioned sex if they form monogamous relationships like everyone else. And so on. In civilization, the realm of the acceptable distinguishes itself from two things. At one end is the prude, who denies and represses sexuality. At the other end is the slut. If virginity is not as prized by the civilized as it once was, fucking around is still not acceptable, particularly for women. It's random, infectious, a threat to civilized order.

Fourier dispenses with this whole stigmatizing of the space of sexual possibilities. There are no straight-gay, prude-slut or order-random axes to his sexual universe. There are only the twelve passions, and variability as to which and how many of the passions are active. Harmony is the game of combining the passions. It's true that his world is hierarchical, and it is tempting to say that the sluts are on top, but that isn't quite it. Omnigynes are favored in Harmonian sexual politics, but all sexuality is played out in the form of elaborate games. What's valued is the richness of passionate attraction, and the philanthropy with which talent is dispensed.

The most extraordinary sentences, a porn of the relation, not of the act, follow from this, viz.: "The two foci first elect the four cardinal sub-foci of the quadrille; these are the four who are loved in title of favoritism and unityism. Then each one elects, from fourteen loved ones, seven that are pivotal in high scale and seven in low scale. Next are elected four ambiguous in low scale; the surplus from the twelve major and the twelve minor keys, of which seven are pivotal in each octave."[11] This is what is truly remarkable about Fourier: the ability to imagine a relational pornography, where all social contacts are pleasurable and engage as many of the passions as possible. It is a heretical reversal of perspective of liberalism. Rather than sacrifice the body to labor in order to sustain a survival in which some modest pleasure might be endured at the margin, the whole social field can engage all of the passions all of the time.

Something like it happens every other Saturday in a dungeon in Brooklyn. They are men, women, and some unclassifiable. They are black and white, and some none of the above. They are gay and straight, and some neither. They are young and old, beautiful and ugly. They are not the same, but they all have passions, and they all gather and remove their clothes before venturing into a darkened labyrinth. Here a man whips another with a switch. There a woman fucks a man up the ass with a dildo. In the back room is a group scene, too dark to tell of genders or preferences. A cry of pleasure draws five men, cocks in hand, to watch from the shadows, some in the hope of joining in, others simply to watch and come in their own hands, making an offering, if only they knew, to Barbelo, reigning Goddess of one of Vaneigem's favorite heresies.[12] It is hardly what Fourier had in mind. It's not far removed from the seraglios that he knew were the necessary other side to bourgeois morality. Fourier was most likely a solitary wanker. But he might have appreciated the emergence, in such spaces, of tacit rules that enable the meshing of the passions. Readings in decadent literature led him to suspect an erotic charge even—or especially—to the "the secret bambocciades of respectable women."[13]

Harmonian sex is highly regulated. The court of love meets every night. A high pontiff presides, and arrayed beneath her are various other ranks, who enforce the amorous code of conduct. Not infidelity but insincerity is the chief failing that concerns them. Membership is voluntary, so there is nobody to coerce, but recognition in this world is not easily achieved. The main currency of this hierarchy is sexual philanthropy. Saintly rank is bestowed upon those who share their sexual favors with those most in need.

Besides the arranging of the sexual encounters within the court's jurisdiction, the pontiff and her associates have to arrange for the entertainment of travelers. Fourier imagines a host of wanderers and knights-errant, searching the world for rare pleasures. Those with particularly rare fetishes may travel far to join gatherings of their kind. Fourier foresaw a federating globally of the partisans of each branch of passion, with sects devoted to each particular sexual mania. A global association of heel-scratching fetishists might travel the world in search of ardent supplicants willing to offer their heels. Roland Barthes: "For Fourier, and this is his victory, there is no normality."[14]

Everyone wears insignia to mark their whims, although these may of course change.[15] The officers of the court of love, mostly older women, would conduct interviews to determine who wants what and who might best provide it. The court would jot it all down on a card index system. Strangely enough, indexing is one of the few things characteristic of the post-revolutionary era which

Fourier regards favorably. His phalansteries are also all equipped with the telegraph, and form a distributed network, each in communication with each other. Between the card index database and the telegraph network, Fourier imagines Harmony within a dense space of communication—a world wide web.

The *New Amorous World* is a reversal of perspective of the hierarchies and cultic practices of the Catholic Church. In Fourier, its *indulgences* are likewise bestowed by an ecclesiastical order, only one devoted to satisfying pleasures rather than repressing them. The tithes required of members would be more of the order of handjobs for the elderly than a grain requisition. The saints would be paragons of a new kind of virtue, bestowing mercy fucks on the sick and infirm. Excommunication remains the ultimate sanction. Membership in any court is voluntary on both sides.

Fourier thought that if everyone had their minimum sexual needs meet without unnecessary anxiety, it would prompt desires for new kinds of platonic love. Young people in Fourier's world could choose to be bacchantes, or they could choose to be vestals. While the vestals withhold their bodies, it isn't as a sacrifice. In any case, certain lapses are permitted, and it is temporary anyway. One of Fourier's more refined passions is the composite, which laminates sensual and social passions together. The vestal becomes an object of adoration and longing through the delay in choosing whom to fuck.

Fourier's is an amorous order for women, the elderly and perverts—all those scorned by civilization. It honors sexual philanthropy and amorous nobility. Its highest ranks in Harmony are open only to those attracted to both sexes. In Harmony, love is an affair of state. The Situationists were fond of quoting Saint-Just: "Happiness is a new idea in Europe." For Vaneigem at least, what this meant was something more like Fourier than the Committee of Public Safety. Affairs of state would be amorous affairs. War would be more like a game, a war of position in which rival courts would take prisoners for the prisoners' gratification rather than their own.

Fourierist sex takes place in broad daylight, preferably in public, preferably in the context of a carefully directed orgy. What civilization treats as something furtive and nocturnal will be brought into the light. A celestial mirror in the sky will reveal any secret lovers hiding out in the woods. Stendhal's *On Love*, written around the same time, circles relentlessly around the emotional stress of unrequited desire.[16] Fourier's solution is practical. A whole class of officers of the court of love will offer themselves to those not otherwise favored.

Fourier's world may seem impossible, ridiculous. But is it more so than this world that actually claims to exist? Charles Beecher: "It is not given to all of us to imagine a world populated by anti-lions and anti-crocodiles. Nor is it given to all of us to see as clearly as Fourier saw into the contradictions, the wasted opportunities and the hidden possibilities of our own lives."[17] At the very least one can read the symptomatology of civilization in Fourier in negative. Fourier: "civilized social order is an absurd mechanism, the parts of which are in conflict with the whole."[18]

This brings us back to Vaneigem's most famous line, about those who "without understanding what is subversive about love and what is positive in the refusal of constraints, such people have a corpse in their mouth."[19] Here Vaneigem brings Fourier to bear as a critique of the militant asceticism of the Leninist strains of the French postwar left. Lenin too had his utopia: vigorous, ascetic, and drawn from Nikolai Chernyshevsky's *What Is to Be Done?*[20]

Fourier's utopian thought had its absurdist side and, most notoriously the *archibras*, the human tail with a hand and eye at its end. Genetic engineering has not exactly made that possible, and even our pornographers have neglected to explore its theoretical possibilities. On the other hand, Fourier has a strange predictive power. His analogical method enabled him to develop possible permutations on the given in language which bypassed the rhetorical centers of gravity of his time, and not a few of which illuminate, in their own strange light, the spectacle of disintegration.

The seas did not turn to lemonade, but as Fourier predicted, the planet is surely warming. Species dangerous to humans are quickly becoming extinct. For better or worse, more amenable ones have indeed been engineered. Elements of Fourier's sexual universe came to pass, from the global conclaves of fetishists to the hook-up culture of young vestals and bacchantes. This disintegrating civilization refuses to award a social and sexual minimum, and is if anything reversing the progress in that direction that the labor movement, feminism and the counter-culture had, in their contradictory ways, advanced.

And yet, for its treasured hirelings, the disintegrating spectacle has had to deploy Fourierist techniques to stimulate the passions as a way of extracting useful labor. The full-service *campus* for top technical and creative employees would put the marble-encrusted workshops of the phalanstery to shame. The movement toward so-called *game-ification* tries to mobilize the cabalistic passion for rivalry as a productivity tool.[21] This is the world that the failure of the revolution of May '68 has led to.

Vaneigem: "The evening that we left the National Institute for Pedagogy, which we had occupied in May 1968, I proposed to the gang to go bar-hopping along the left side of the street where we wandered. It seemed to me that we were following on the footsteps of the combatants of the Paris Commune. The farther we dérived into the mists of a frozen drunkenness, the more we felt the ephemeral and faltering sympathy, given to us by the bar owners, turn into hatred ... We had frustrated in them that same hope we were supposed to fulfill. Had it been at the time when the Versaillese patrolled, we would have been put up against a wall and executed, so as to soothe their thoughtlessness. I was then able to measure the extent to which the disenchantment of a promise of life, when not held, could turn into a reflex of death and destruction."[22]

May '68 launched two critiques of the society of the spectacle.[23] Whether knowingly or not, these two critiques had their roots in Marx and Fourier respectively. They were never effectively combined, and both were recuperated in their own fashion. Wage labor was bought off in the usual fashion, with more of the same, at least while it retained the power to demand it. The more Fourierist critique of the alienation of everyday civilized life was met with more subtle attempts to enmesh the passions in the maintenance of the spectacular order. Perhaps the real failure of May '68 was the inability to combine these two critiques in practical ways. Here is where the Situationist International still leaves a useful legacy, for while Debord and Vaneigem took the double critique in quite different and perhaps in the end incompatible directions, the space mapped out by what one might call Post-Situationist practices is rich with productive variations on this double theme.

Fourier thought that social progress and the ends of eras took place accordingly as women progress toward freedom. Engels agreed, as did Vaneigem, as might modern feminism. So too might the Post-Situationist writers of the journal *Tiqqun*, whose oblique debt to Fourier resides in their program "to embrace a form of life … more faithful to our penchants than our predicates."[24] The disintegrating spectacle certainly offers boundless images of women, or rather not of women, but of a certain iconic double, of and for women—let's call her The Girl. If Manet tried to picture particular women caught in the tensions of an emerging spectacle, then The Girl is the image on their reverse side. She is not what is caught in the spectacle; she is the concentrated image of the spectacle itself. And now she is everywhere. You can find her in any magazine. The disintegrating spectacle is not presided over by the Law of the Father but by the figure of The Girl.

The Girl is a new kind of asceticism, a sacrifice of a kind unknown to Fourier. She doesn't deny or repress sex. Rather, she makes it something abstract: not sex but sexuality. *Tiqqun*: "The present sexual misery in no way resembles that of the past, because these are now bodies without desire, burning up inside because they can't satisfy these desires they don't have."[25] In the disintegrating spectacle, sexuality is everywhere, a hollowed-out form that connects not bodies to bodies but bodies to commodities. On the other hand, love is nowhere. It becomes privatized; it is what is supposed to found couples outside of the spectacle, but only so that they might build the storage space within which to accumulate its decorative veneers.

Contrary to appearances, feminism has succeeded far less than a certain *femitude*. Women were not freed from the domestic; the domestic expanded to encompass the whole of everyday life outside the home. Contrary to appearances, there was no sexual liberation. Sexuality was not freed from repression. Sexuality was freed from sex. Whole new kinds of preventable sexual misery reign, beyond those anatomized by Fourier. Sex is sacrificed to sexuality; love to privatization. And yet, while Fourier's diagnosis of the sacrifices entailed in civilization may be a little out of date, his concept of sacrifice and his critical-poetic mapping of other possibilities are alive and well, as Vaneigem has been so good as to remind us. Vaneigem: "He drew from his own subjectivity the project of a society capable of furthering the desires of each and harmonizing them. He does not content himself, like the philosophers, to dress the old world in new clothes. His solitude was peopled by a multitude of beings that prefigure the new global society, one whom the servile masters and slaves of the arrogant old world persist in not seeing before their eyes that she is born."[26]

Vaneigem finds Fourier a convenient foil against both the asceticism of supposedly militant practice and against the game leaders who in the sphere of play might presume to organize everyone's fun for them. The problem of a critical practice might be "to enter the collective project with the calculated innocence of Fourier's phalansterian players, rivaling each other (composite passion), varying their activities (butterfly passion), and striving for the most advanced radicality (cabalist passion). But lightheartedness must be based on conscious, 'heavy' relationships. It implies lucidity regarding everyone's abilities."[27]

This might be particularly so within transformative situations. Vaneigem: "One of Fourier's great merits is to have shown the necessity of creating immediately—and for us this means from the inception of generalized insurrection—the objective conditions for individual liberation. For everyone the beginning of the revolutionary moment must mark an immediate rise in the pleasure of living—a consciously experienced entry into the totality."[28] Against the holy family of Jacobin-Leninist-Maoist political nostalgia, wedded to the pomp and circumstance of high theory within the academy, one might, in the name of Vaneigem and Fourier, go looking for low theories, practiced in the thrall of everyday life, and not shy about inventing critical practices out of any and every situation, for the hell of it.

Voyage to Oarystis (2005) is Vaneigem's own utopia, his textual city, designed for seven thousand inhabitants. Visitors must first stay at a sumptuous hotel on its borders, a place so grand that a mature curiosity is required to move on to Oarystis itself. The city is traversed by aerial and aquatic passageways, as well as terrestrial ones. Function and folly entangle in all its forms. It is a fungible landscape, fashioned after the tastes of a people who confront the last struggle—with boredom. They frequently change their names to suit their moods.

The centerpiece is Fourier Place, bisected by the Grand Canal, fed by Lake Montaigne. A statue to Freud is both honored and despised, and Hegel Street appears to be a dead end. Art is erratic in Oarystis, always being changed or replaced. Every surface is covered by poems, art or philosophical theses. The toilets are named after dictators such as Napoleon and Mao, and are public, so their infamies can be discussed during elimination.

Waste and recycling functions are all below ground, where everyone works three hours per week on essential tasks. Everyone except the Friends of Paul Lafargue, who are engaged in the even more difficult effort of not working at all.[29] Most Oarystians feel the need for the alternating rhythms, the fast pace of work below and the slow strolling up above, as what Fourier called the butterfly passion is common among them.

The Oarystians don't tell lies — unless they are amusing. They are free to exercise their desires, so long as they do not oppress others. Not every matter is settled. The vegetarians campaign to outlaw consuming meat by putting it to a vote in Fourier Place. Various leagues, factions and phalanxes petition the city with their common passions. Screens display the various motions and votes, as well as all information about the stocks of goods available in the city at a given moment.

Oarystis, with its escalators and rolling walkways, is a labyrinth for a great game, where each must navigate within the chaos of their own desires and aversions. Oarystis decomposes the hierarchy of public and private selves, the defensive need for an interiority. Here, "what is tangible, what is invisible, the shadow of our dreams, the tentacles of a forgotten desire, the suppuration of an ancient memory, and quite simply, hence, everything that is in me, everything that is not in me, everything that could or should have been in me, what I would or would not want to experience, all this forms an inextricable terminal of nervous and organic filaments that is called reality."[30]

No system of knowledge, no matter how arcane, is useless in Oarystis. It's just a matter of weaving them into the patterns of desires. In the Quarter of the Illuminati are the makers of delirious systems, impossible geometries, infinite virtualities. Here are the builders of invisible palaces, the technicians of immortality, the vivisectors of desire, the manufacturers of parallel universes, the gatherers of storms. The last survivor of the city's founders is a climate architect, and he spends his time in the Climate Variation Dome, experimenting with different arrangements of the seasons.

Visits to Oarystis can last no more than fifteen days, and Vaneigem's guests must return to their—to this—world just as they are beginning to become oriented in the city. Their mission, and ours, is to build Oarystis where we are.

Even in Oarystis, Vaneigem never quite manages to reconcile the Fourierist critique of the sacrificial labor of militant practice with a Marxist critique of the society of the spectacle. It was René Viénet who came closest to their synthesis, which he turned into a powerful counter to the lingering fascination with Leninist asceticism in the west. Viénet says goodbye to the politics of sacrifice, at the same time as he negates separation and spectacle.

9   The Ass Dreams of China Pop

Those who are first are entitled to fame, and the children who follow are left to file lawsuits for their daily bread.

Baltasar Gracián

René Viénet (b. 1944) was a docker's son from Le Havre. He came to Paris to study Chinese, but he was curious also about the Situationists. As Debord writes in a letter to him: "The simplest manner of approaching all the questions enumerated in your letter to the S[ituationist] I[international] is to come see for yourself. We can lodge you, feed you, even offer you a shower, for about eight days at the following address."[1] He became a member of the Situationist International in 1961.

He went to China in 1965, the year France opened diplomatic relations with the People's Republic. He wrote letters to Debord on his impressions, making the Situationists one of the few groups of the time whose views on Maoism were informed by direct reports. He was expelled from China in 1966. He had a somewhat stormy career as a Sinologist on his return, not least because of his virulent opposition to the apologists for Mao.

Enragés and Situationists in the Occupation Movement (1968), the more or less official account of Situationist involvement in May '68, was published under his name. Viénet's text is particularly clear on the role of the movement's would-be recuperators, the Stalinoid apparatchiks of the various factions who wanted to install themselves as its representatives. This text, in spite of its obvious merits, was but a warm-up for a series of remarkable films Viénet made in the seventies, where questions of politics and representation find their most telling answer in the practice of détournement.

Can Dialectics Break Bricks (1973) uses as its raw material a kung fu movie by Tu Guangqi (1914–80) called *The Crush* (1972) and recasts its struggle between vicious warlords and oppressed villagers as a struggle within the left between Stalinists and Situationists by dubbing in new dialogue in French. Meaghan Morris: "Tu came after World War Two from Shanghai to Hong Kong, where he made cultural nationalist Mandarin language films; a right-winger who worked for the Asian Film Company, established in 1953 with American money, Tu helped remake and reinterpret—indeed *détourner*—successful left-wing dramas and themes from a right-wing nationalist perspective. If that is so, there is definite poetic justice in the French fate of *Crush*."[2]

Crush is set in Korea under Japanese occupation, while the hero who appears on the scene looking for a relative is Chinese, and hence naturally has superior martial arts skills. Both China and Korea were occupied by the Japanese at one time, and both had Communist regimes at the time *Crush* was made. The film is already an allegory about Communism as an occupation. What Viénet does is divert the allegory from the service of Nationalist struggle against Maoism to that of a Situationist critique of the Stalinist and Maoist wannabes of the red decade in France.

Viénet's détournement seems at first sight to work by the simple expedient of changing the dialogue, but he has also moved some scenes around, subtly making the moving images serve his own purposes.[3] While in *Crush* the hero's position is never in doubt, Viénet makes him a more ambiguous figure, caught between desires. He does this by changing the role of the central female character in a way that makes her more interesting.

Dialectics opens with the villagers practicing their martial arts on a chilly morning, in a place "where the ideology is particularly cold." A student arriving late gives the password: "live without dead time!" This contrasts with the slogan of the dreaded bureaucrats, a litany of sacrifices: "work, family, fatherland!" The bureaucrats arrive to break up the morning kung fu practice of the revolutionaries and warn them of what is to come: "I don't want to hear any more about class struggle. If not I'll send in my sociologists! And if necessary my psychiatrists! My urban planners! My architects! My Foucaults! My Lacans! And if that's not enough, I'll even send my structuralists!" The structuralists were generally indifferent to the events of May 1968. Lacan looked on in bemused silence. Foucault was out of town. Althusser, the structural Marxist, stuck to the official Communist Party line, even if expressed in his own theoretical language: don't do it, comrades, the conjuncture is not ripe![4] For all the prestige they accumulated in the seventies, these thinkers were outflanked by events. "Mediation is their game," as Viénet puts it. Their language games open as a cul-de-sac in compensation for the loss of the streets.

Like the original it détourns, *Dialectics* hinges on a character of superlative kung fu skills. He seems to waver between rival forms of power. In Viénet's version those forces are the Stalinists and the Situationists. The favors bestowed upon the Stalinist recuperators seem tempting. The decisive event is perhaps the hero's meeting with the courtesan. In *Crush* this character is a *good girl*, but Viénet creates a different impression in the spectator with some small changes. His female lead is a courtesan in the service of the bureaucrats, but she is not one of them. "They offer crumbs," she says. "We want it all!" The glittering prizes for cooperation are not what they seem: "A bit more pay is a bit more poverty." Like many veterans of 1968 adrift in the 1970s, she is in mourning for what did not come to pass, and is looking for solace elsewhere: "The only thing I have left is the experience of love."

The only thing left in the twenty-first century appears to be the crumbs. A sparkler lights the way as a large and expensive order of booze finds its way to the table, making it easy for the models or near-models to find their way to the men whose largesse this is. The sparkler and the bottles are held high by the *bottle girl*, whose job it is not just to serve the table, but to reel in big-spending clients and keep up a steady friction on their credit cards. Says Kim, a twenty-six-year-old graduate of a fine liberal arts college: "you're a bottle waitress, and that means you're half a stripper and half a pimp. If you don't book a client, you're fired. Most places I worked, I had to sign a confidentiality agreement about celebrities." Her services have certain boundaries: "I do have to flirt with them, booty-dance with them, call them, hang out with them, occasionally procure girls and party favors for them, all the while in teeny outfits. So I suppose it's a form of social prostitution." But then what's a girl to do? "I figured: I'm cute, I'm young, I can make a shitload of money, so fuck it!"

Kim is not exactly an innocent player of this game: "Last Spring I went to meet R at the Oak Room at the Plaza Hotel, he was already slurring and three martinis in when we found this sweet young girl in a Jackie O dress reading Baudelaire at the bar." This Jackie O was straight out of an Ivy League school and new to the city. "R started to tell her how he went to Princeton (he did not) and I suggested she join us for a drink, then dinner at Daniel, then more drinks downtown, then a table at a club in the [Meat Packing] district where I could get commission for bringing R. I knew how to deal with him, she did not." When he tries to kiss Kim, she slaps him down a bit. When he tries to kiss the Jackie O girl, she does not know how to fend him off. "He of course pushed farther reaching down her dress. I was just happy it wasn't me tonight and demanded he give me more money for blow. She tried to get me to protect her, he alluded to her being a lesbian and wanting to sleep with me. I played along and ordered another bottle of champagne. She was slurring and wobbling more and more, he was pretty much holding her up as he pawed at her." Kim ditches them both and goes off to trawl for new clients. "I never heard from or saw her again, though I found her Baudelaire book at the bottom of my purse."[5] Such night life would not have surprised Baudelaire, although the absence of a recalcitrant urban proletariat ready to greet these characters of the night the next morning might.

Viénet's films recall a moment when history appeared on a different path than that toward sparkly spectacles. For Viénet the stakes are high. "Whatever is lost in partial confrontation becomes part of the repressive function of the old world." But it is not simply a question of the unfulfilled desires of May '68, and as we shall see Viénet has good reason to stress this: "the falsifiers sang socialism above all the charnel houses."[6] The slogan "those who make the revolution by halves dig their own graves" is not mere overblown sixties rhetoric. It is quite literally true.

Under the big kung fu fight scene, Viénet offers this title: "For this sequence, consult *Enragés and Situs in the Occupation Movement*, Gallimard edition pages 2–7 and 231." These pages point specifically to the problem of recuperation: that the struggle was as much against the left as the right; that if the revolution can't be made consistently then it ought not to be made at all. Viénet's vision is of a mass of popular desire that is constantly wearing away at the old world, but which is captured and channeled into mere innovations in oppressive technique. Under the big chase scene, this subtitle: "On this wall a slogan was just erased: 'Run comrade, the old world is behind you.'" Against the right, Viénet turns the Marxist filter; against the left, the Fourierist one.

Viénet had been to China, had seen the Cultural Revolution begin, and was well aware of the costs of failed revolutions. Latter-day apologists for the Cultural Revolution prefer to speak grandly of the Political as a concept rather than the messy business of politics, and they prefer the terrain of great leaders coming into being as subjects on some astral plane to the everyday life on the backs of which this was built. Rey Chow: "My most vivid childhood memories of the Cultural Revolution were the daily reports in 1966 and 1967 of corpses from China floating down into the Pearl River delta and down into Hong Kong harbor … There are also memories of people risking their lives swimming across the border into Hong Kong and of people visiting China with the 'little red book' but also with supplies of food and clothing. This was a period of phenomenal starvation in China."[7]

In Tu's film, the Koreans prevail with the help of the superior fighting prowess of the Chinese hero, but at a great cost of life. *Crush* is an imaginary defeat of what to the Nationalists was a real enemy. Viénet underscores the purely spectacular nature of this victory. *Dialectics* also ends with a massacre, but his voice actors break character to declare they are "sick of dubbing dialogue tracks so they're pretending to be dead. It's hard work, it seems, and doesn't even pay the cab fare." Unlike Debord's détourned films, Viénet's always have an undercurrent of earthy laughter.

Hard work indeed, although it did not stop Viénet making a second détourned film, technically simpler, but formally more ambitious. *The Girls of Kamare* détourns Norifumi Suzuki's *Terrifying Girls' High School* (1973), with a bit of Teruo Ishii's *Female Yatuza Tale: Inquisition and Torture* (1973) thrown in, plus a few cutaway shots made especially. Both of the détourned films are examples of the *pinky violence* genre films that became popular in Japan from the sixties onwards.[8] These low-budget films mixed sex and sadism but stayed within Japan's quirky censorship laws. They were a response to declining cinema attendance during the rise of television. Viénet's détournement of the dialogue is much simpler this time: he simply added French subtitles.

If *Dialectics* mourns the moment of 1968, then *Kamare* recalls the moment of 1961: "People of France you knew it already, and it doesn't take a Japanese film, to speak to you about the Algerians thrown in the Seine in October, 1961."[9] This happened during the ugly endgame of the struggle to free Algeria from French colonial rule. The National Liberation Front had been bombing police stations in Paris before it decided to stage a big demonstration for Algerian independence. The police responded by beating demonstrators senseless and throwing them in the river. The colonial war brought home to the streets of Paris is the context for the political turn of the Situationist International. Those who protest the Situationists' abandonment of art in the sixties forget that France was in a state of civil war at the time.

The Situationists were hardly starry-eyed about Algerian independence. "[Ahmed] Ben Bella fell as he had reigned, in solitude and conspiracy, by a palace revolution. He was ushered out by the same forces that ushered him in: [Houari] Boumédienne's army, which had opened the road to Algiers to him in September 1962."[10] This revolution had always been at one and the same time the attempt by the masses to achieve self-management and that of the bourgeoisie to create the conditions of a capitalist economy, if necessary via the state.

Put crudely, the Situationist line was that Fanon, Castro and Guevara are the false consciousness through which the peasants carry out the task of overcoming colonial leftovers. Ben Bella, Nasser, Tito and Mao are the ideologues of the takeover of these movements by petit-bourgeois or military and urban strata. The bureaucracy assumes the function of an absent bourgeois class. Once it achieves state power, the bureaucracy can shed its more political wing, leaving the military or technocrats in power, as in Algeria. The post-colonial revolution is an ambiguous phenomenon at best, even if the "only people who are really underdeveloped are those who see a positive value in the power of their masters."[11]

The kinky eroticism of Japanese reform-school girls supposedly water-boarding one of their number takes on a strange resonance against the background of ongoing colonial war. Viénet: "we learned torture during the colonial wars. The enemy within would do well to remember that." In 2002 Bruce Jessen and Jim Mitchell, retired air force officers and psychologists, were looking for a new business opportunity. They found a great client, the CIA, for whom they designed an interrogation program that culminated in water-boarding. Jessen and Mitchell boasted of receiving up to two thousand dollars a day to supervise the use of their techniques at a secret interrogation site in Thailand. The two psychologists had previously trained American pilots to survive behind enemy lines and to resist interrogation if captured. It transpired that neither had any interrogation experience, nor were they qualified to declare the procedure medically safe. They still managed to rake in millions of dollars in consultancy fees for their services.[12] Once again, the talents learned in colonial wars have an afterlife, this time as a business opportunity.

To the names insulted in *Dialectics, Kamare* adds Roland Barthes, Louis Althusser and Simone de Beauvoir. Unlike *Dialectics, Kamare* borders on incoherence. Unlike the straightforward narrative of *Crush, Horror High School Women* barely makes sense. It does provide the raw material for one fabulous Vaneigemesque set piece. To a scene in which two schoolgirls fuck in a toilet, Viénet appends his manifesto for the cinema, which one reads off the subtitles to the sound of fake squeals of pleasure and seventies soundtrack-funk: "What there is of lived experience in this film I have no intention of making apprehensible to spectators who do not honestly prepare themselves to relive it. I await its becoming lost, then found again in a general shift of consciousness. Just as I flatter myself that current conditions will be effaced from the memory of men. The cinema must be remade. All the production and distribution specialists will not prevent this."

Viénet's school girls, like Pissarro's peasant women, make awkward stand-ins for the desires that reside in the everyday. Women's bodies do the work not only of being the screens on which the spectacle projects the passing show of all that can be legitimately desired. They have to function also as the locus of hidden desires as well. Pissarro shows that, alongside the desire that the peasant woman be some locus of rustic charm, she also indicates the moment of idleness within the labor that, unlike the industrial worker, she controls for herself. The women in the films Viénet détourns possess a certain fantastic castrating power. But what he would rather have them point to is the capacity to order their own passions. The delinquent now takes the place of the peasant as the one in possession of the body's own powers, but it is still a woman's body.

Kamare brings to the surface something rather less obvious in *Dialectics*. Namely, that the source of the capacity for détournement, the distance that enables the appropriation of these cinematic trifles to quite other purposes, is Viénet's own lived experience. This is what separates détournement from so much of the cut-up, remix and mash-up culture that superficially looks so much like it. It's the enduring significance, not just of May '68, but of the moment of negation in general. Where remix bows down before the power of recuperated desire and merely makes a fetish of it, détournement has no such reverence. But nor is it a brute iconoclasm of the kind Clark imagined on the steps of the National Gallery, where he contemplates the destruction of a work by Nicolas Poussin.[13]

Rather, it is like a kung fu move that uses the power of spectacle against itself, leveraging it over into the service of autonomous desire. Or as Viénet says: "One escapes banality only by manipulating it, by détourning it, by delivering it up to the delights of subjectivity. I did more than my share in playing out my subjectivity, but no one should give me any grief about it before having considered what the objective conditions, that the world brings into existence each day, make possible in favor of subjectivity." As always Viénet balances the bravado of his manifesto with sly humor. In films so devoted to the negation of the commodity he nevertheless pauses to plug books from the publisher he works for—even if he advocates stealing them.

Viénet moved the scenes around in *Dialectics*, but with *Kamare* he adds a little as well. This is perhaps another kind of détournement, not one of eliminating the inessential from the détourned element, but adding that which completes its line of thought. The pinky violence films stop short of the sex act itself, and they stop short of connecting their violence to historical situations. While sex and violence will become key dialects of the disintegrating spectacle, sex is always to be disassociated from the politics of desire, and violence is always to be disassociated from the desire for politics. *Kamare* joins the dots, in brief flashes of bodies fucking atop volumes of Red Guard writings from China's Cultural Revolution, writings which embody all the tensions between popular revolt and its co-option by state power. The title of the anthology, *Révo. cul. dans la Chine Pop* (1974), in which Viénet had a hand, could be read as *The Ass Dreams of China Pop*.[14]

10   Mao by Mao

Always speak well of the enemy.
Baltasar Gracián

As if his talents as a Situationist writer, filmmaker and trouble maker were not enough to recommend him to posterity, René Viénet was also a student of Chinese. Expelled from China in 1966, he edited the Chinese Library for Editions Champ Libre, and in that capacity published a famous book by Pierre Ryckmans called *The Emperor's New Clothes*. Ryckmans was a Belgian sinologist who taught for many years in Australia, where one of his former students would even go on to become prime minister. Writing as Simon Leys, he became the Orwell of the east, the first westerner with a real working knowledge of Chinese society to publicize the violence and terror of the Maoist state.

For there is another sixties, the sixties of anti-colonial struggle. While the Situationists had been committed to the anti-colonial cause ever since Debord and Bernstein signed the "Manifesto of the 121," they were hardly starry-eyed about the prospects. The collapse of the international Communist movement, so evident in the split between China and Russia, was actually welcomed by the Situationists. The east's concentrated spectacle was the "pseudo-negation and real support" of the diffuse spectacle of the west, and as it broke up into warring factions, the path to a real transformation of the diffuse spectacle was revealed. Debord predicted the triumph of the diffuse spectacle in 1967, some twenty-odd years before the fall of the Berlin wall, but it was Viénet who had the telling critique of the most influential version of the concentrated spectacle, based on his knowledge of Mandarin, his brief but firsthand experience in China, and his grasp of Situationist theory and practice.

As Viénet wrote in his introduction to the 1971 Champ Libre edition of *The Emperor's New Clothes*: "The plaster statues of Mao will perhaps make less noise when crumbling down than the steel bust of Stalin thrown to the ground in Budapest in 1956 and, because of the distance, perhaps one might only collect the fine, white powder that the eastern winds will deposit on the heads of western Maoists. There, again, a theoretical calculation permits us to get to know the nature of these consequences even before they are gathered for analysis: Chairman Mao's thought is *biodegradable*."[1] How strangely right he would turn out to be.

While many were seduced by the visage of Mao in the sixties and early seventies, the Situationists saw it as the face of the "accelerating disintegration of bureaucratic ideology." The concentrated spectacle was proletarian society turned on its head. The essential thesis, shared by Viénet and Debord, was that the Cultural Revolution was a symptom of a split within the Chinese ruling class over economic policy. Deposed by his rivals for the failure of the Great Leap Forward, Mao staged a comeback through control of the ideological apparatus. The conflict was one between the Maoist faction, "masters of absolute ideology," and the fragile, underdeveloped economic base. Mao mobilized the Red Guards to fight his faction wars, but authentic class struggle arose unbidden, when workers started acting for themselves, mounting strikes, seizing arms and staging anti-Maoist demonstrations.[2] The result was a "confused civil war." The Situationist theses on China were quite classically Marxist, and basically right, even if, when first formulated in 1967, the end was not quite in sight.

Viénet returned to something like the Situationist position on China, and to the cinema of détournement, with two 1977 films. *Mao by Mao* is a short work he co-produced, in which the life of the then recently deceased Great Helmsman is told in his own words, using quotes culled from various Red Guard publications.[3] It is best watched as a warm-up for Viénet's *One More Effort, Chinese, If You Want to be Revolutionaries!*[4] The two titles of this film, pinched from the Marquis de Sade and the Marx Brothers respectively, neatly sum up Viénet's tastes, and even his philosophy. The fake film company that produced it is the Despair of Billancourt, the site of the biggest factory in France, the Renault car plant, whose striking workers held the fortunes of May '68 in their hands. The film is dedicated to Li Yi Zhe, the nominal author of a famous Democracy Wall critique of the Maoist state.

In *Mao by Mao*, the rise to power of the film's namesake appears as the inevitable outcome of a dialectical logic. Or so the voice-over might lead one to believe. If the usual practice of détourned films is for the soundtrack to undermine the image, here the reverse occasionally takes place. The images critique Mao's words. They show that which, even in the official visual record of the times, the narrative elides. The effect is subtle and requires at least a passing acquaintance with Chinese politics to work. *Duck Soup* offers no such delicacies. It has all the qualities Debord once attributed to Viénet: "one feels the assurance of the revolutionary, and also the pedantry of the specialist. In short, that is Viénet, when he happens to write. There is humor and also naiveté that would like to be cynicism."[5] While hardly generous, Debord is here quite perceptive.

Duck Soup opens with a florid sequence in which Chinese Communist Party leaders appear like movie stars in a trailer for some Hollywood A-movie, a neat analogy in which the Chinese version of the concentrated spectacle appears as a low-tech version of its western counterpart. Viénet will later compare the Red Guards to television, agents of enforced passivity sent into every home, not via radio waves but with heavy footsteps. Viénet has the cheek to include a shot of himself waving to the crowd, only the volume he is holding is certainly not Mao's *Little Red Book*.

Before leaping into its bloody saga of modern Chinese power, *Duck Soup* presents old newsreel images of working people from the colonial and civil war periods, to the soundtrack of popular sentimental songs. The songs chosen were mostly banned by the Communists. While the proletariat becomes the official hero of the spectacle after the Maoist seizure of power, what is expunged is the affect of the old songs, their sadness, their longings.

Crucial to Viénet's version of the story is Harold Isaacs' contention in his — Trotskyist, but still serviceable — *The Tragedy of the Chinese Revolution* that the Chinese proletarian revolution was defeated in 1927, when Stalin ordered the party to collaborate with the

Nationalists, and the Nationalists destroyed them. "Stalin made some mistakes," notes Mao himself, in *Mao by Mao*, with world-historical understatement. Mao came to power by deposing those who followed Stalin's line, and his peasant army triumphed in 1949 by winning a civil war, not a revolution. The party was nevertheless thoroughly Stalinist, "even though Stalin has never done them any favors." Sino-Soviet relations were, in a word, colonial.

While "assholes like Sartre" were making apologies for the Soviet Union, the proletariat of Budapest rose up in 1956 against the Hungarian branch office of the Stalinist regime. Mao was sufficiently unnerved to launch the Hundred Flowers campaign, soliciting criticism of the regime in order to defuse it. But the torrent of discontent was not the fealty he expected, and his critics were quickly silenced in the following Anti-Rightist Campaign.

Repression only gets you so far. Mao counted on Russian aid to get the economy moving, and this was not particularly forthcoming. The 1958 Great Leap Forward, famous for its backyard furnaces where peasants were urged to smelt their own hand tools into useless iron, was a desperate attempt to make up the shortfall from Moscow. The failure and famine of the Great Leap Forward led to Mao's demotion.[6] Liu Shaoqi and Deng Xiaoping were in charge, but Mao did manage to install Lin Biao as Minister of Defense. Mao bided his time in luxury resort hotels, plotting his comeback.

Duck Soup has a contrapuntal structure, oscillating between the power struggle at the top and everyday life, as if sifting both coarse and fine-grained history. In this it differs somewhat from Debord's cinema, which does contain privileged moments of everyday affect but lacks Viénet's palpable empathy for everyday popular life. Viénet characterizes the dense net of social control practiced by the Maoist regime by juxtaposing pictures of Chinese youth, a syrupy Serge Gainsbourg make-out tune, and court documents in which a twenty-six-year-old teacher who "promoted a bourgeois lifestyle based on pleasure" is condemned to death. The sequence includes a still of a young woman which one cannot help thinking of as having an undeclared resonance for Viénet. Debord, as we shall see, also included snapshots of loved ones in his films.

Mao's counter-attack, when it comes, issues from his stronghold in Shanghai and seizes the ideological high ground. The official language of the concentrated spectacle is Maoist, and even his opponents present themselves within this language, and this leaves ample room for Mao to turn the tables. With Liu Shaoqi in Pakistan, Mao and Lin Biao arrest their other rivals. Mao swims the Yangtze River to show that he still has it, even if, as Viénet claims, it took four frogmen to keep him afloat. It still makes for terrific newsreel footage. Liu is demoted, but hangs onto power. But when Mao mobilizes the Red Guards, the leadership are confronted with a million of them massed in and around Tiananmen Square.

The Red Guards are literally *mobilized*, traveling the country on the Exchange of Revolutionary Experiences and unaware of the extent to which they are a "choreographed rebellion." Following the general line of the Situationists on such matters, *Duck Soup* characterizes the Red Guards unequivocally as a fascist movement. Fascism and Stalinism are the decadence of the worker's movement. They are the detachment of the representation from that which it represents, its becoming a power over the represented.

Viénet is not so concerned about the Red Guards' destruction of monuments. These are relics of past oppression, and the people always have the right to let their rulers know that one day all oppression may be just a memory. Rather, it is the working over of independent intellectuals by the Red Guards that is the tragedy. They attack China's equivalents to critical Bolsheviks like Victor Serge.[7] The Red Guards quickly descended into pogroms and factional feuding. Viénet's approach is not without its nuance, however. That they were so readily mobilized speaks at one and the same time to the effectiveness of the Maoist state but also to the depth of dissatisfaction within it. While manipulated as tools of Mao's factional war, they were a dangerous weapon. "Mao knows, even if they don't, that there was always a chance they might turn to open rebellion."

Strikingly, both Mao and his opponents within the state apparatus used variations on the same ideological language in their struggles with each other. Even as the state descended into civil war, the ideological façade did not crack. The "proprietors of ideology (Mao and his sidekicks) wanted to re-appropriate the economy. All of the bureaucrats wanted absolute and exclusive control of ideology. For ideology, as everyone knows, is the lever of power." So nobody really wanted to question that ideology. The party still traded in the "myth of an undying comradeship forged in revolutionary struggle." Viénet spends some time debunking this myth, retailing the folklore of the bitter fights among rival leaders, setting the stage so that when some very high-ranking bureaucrats later turn up dead one's mind immediately turns to conspiracy theories.

Events come to a head when what will later be known as the Gang of Four, acting in Mao's name, attack the venerable Communist leader Zhao Enlai. This was over-reaching, for Zhao was a consummate political player, with many allies in the army. Zhao forges an alliance against Mao, Lin Biao and the Gang of Four. The military seizes control of factories. Anti–Red Guard militias are mobilized. The Red Guards are packed off to the countryside.

The film's contrapuntal break returns to the everyday with a free translation of "On Socialist Democracy and the Legal System," by Li Yi Zhe. This was the pen name of four activists whose critique of the Cultural Revolution appeared as a wall poster in Guangzhou in 1974. The text provides a mordant critique of the days when Mao's Red Guards "put politics in command," as the phrase had it. Li Yi Zhe: "Politics was the watch word in every sphere. A word designed to reward apathy and punish enthusiasm." A time when everyone was supposed to be studying the revolutionary thought of the Chairman. "Study? It was more like telling the rosary." A time when everyone was supposed to aspire to revolutionary glory. "And all the talk of the revolution exploding in the depths of the soul. Not so much an explosion as a wet fart." A time when delirium was used as a tool of power, and everything "plunged into a pea soup of religiosity. Until everything began to stink of God." The three principal members of Li Yi Zhe went to the labor camps in 1977.[8]

Outflanked by Zhao and the army, Mao cut his old "comrade in arms" Lin Biao loose. He dies in a plane crash. Things are turning against Mao. He is down, but not out. Mao will be there to greet Richard Nixon when he arrives in 1972, and to show him the ballet version of the *Red Detachment of Women* (1964), one of the eight model plays his wife and Gang of Four member Jiang Qing has inflicted on Chinese culture. But behind the scenes the old possessors of economic power are aligning against him.

Viénet tells the old joke about three prisoners asking each other the reason for their imprisonment. "I was for Deng Xiaoping," says the first. "I was against Deng Xiaoping," say the second. "Oh, it's different for me," says the third. "I *am* Deng Xiaoping." Deng will return to the scene in 1973 and begin his rise to power over the Chinese state.

Zhao Enlai lasts until 1976. Viénet wonders whether he was poisoned, a wild conspiracy theory, lent credence by the extraordinary ways some of his comrades died. The passing of Zhao is the pretext for vast demonstrations. He was known for occasional acts of compassion, and was the least irrational and most refined of the party's overlords. All the same it is not really Zhao that people are mourning, but their own lives. Mao's death in 1976 finally leads to the end of the Gang of Four in what for Viénet is essentially a military coup. Mao's portrait still presides. The concentrated spectacle lives on in his name, only his official portrait is slightly different. A wart appears on his chin.

In twenty-first-century China one can find citizens who are not even sure who Mao Zedong was, even though the Chinese Communist Party boasts some seventy million members.[9] Perhaps this is the time for a different kind of story. Zhang Yuchen (b. 1947) was a toddler at the time of the Liberation; he was born in Shangdong province. His older brother got a job in a state factory in Beijing, so the whole family moved to the capital, and Zhang attended school there. He was a teenager when the Cultural Revolution started, and had what would turn out to be the great good fortune of joining, not the Red Guards, but a construction brigade. Like a character in *The Sims*, he rises from construction brigade worker to brigade leader.

After the Cultural Revolution he was able to study—the universities are returning to some semblance of life—and with his degree go on to become an official in the Beijing construction bureau, which has oversight of all major building projects in the city. He rose through the ranks of the bureau before going into business in 1991 with a wealthy partner from the south who wanted to break into Beijing real estate.

His first major project, Baixan villas, was built on farmland to the north of the city. He sold five hundred of the California-style bungalows. After the success of his Baixan villas development, Zhang came up with the even more ambitious Chateau Zhang Lafitte. This palace on the outskirts of Beijing is copied from François Mansart's Chateau Maisons-Lafitte, twelve minutes out of Paris, but with two additional wings, copied from the royal apartments at Fontainebleau, and a garden modeled on Versailles— buildings that would have prompted Charles Fourier to take out his measuring stick with glee. Zhang: "It cost me $50 million, but that is because I made so many improvements compared to the original." Beijing's *high net worth individuals* can rent rooms there, which might persuade them to buy homes on the grounds. "Buyers want the right environment so they feel they are fully realizing their identity." An environment protected by private security in period livery.

The eight hundred farmers of Yangge village used to cultivate this thousand acres as a collective until Zhang *persuaded* Changping district officials to let him develop it. First, the officials converted it to a *green zone*, then they leased it to Zhang at an annual rent of $300 per acre. Zhang: "The whole project is exactly in line with Beijing's policy to maintain the land as green space." Officials granted Zhang easements to build the Chateau and a thousand luxury homes on 170 acres of it, in exchange for nearly ten million dollars. As part of the deal he pays the elderly villagers a stipend, and the younger ones can apply to work on his grounds, waterways, golf course and vineyard.

The new industries that the money was supposed to start never materialized, and villagers insist that this latter-day enclosure of their land is in breach of contract over many issues. Still, Zhang is nothing if not well connected. Politburo member Jia Qingling, fourth-ranked leader in the whole of China at the time, came to visit. Giant color photos of him inspecting the vineyard grace the wine bar. "Today's leaders have exactly the right kind of thinking," enthuses Zhang.[10] Not surprisingly, Zhang is himself a party member. This was the real destiny of Mao's party, one perhaps not entirely predictable from Viénet's 1977 films, but one that is legible there all the same. In them, détournement at least does its job of negating power's capture of the available signs and the rendering of them as historically mute.

All of Viénet's films embody the qualities that Clark thinks of as those most critical to détournement. In place of reverence, Viénet manipulates his sources with a wry insouciance. The result is not a pleasing pastiche, but a confident assertion of historical consciousness. He cuts between the key instances, and discards that which is of scholarly interest only. Elements of very different styles come together, like in Viénet's recipe for dialectical eggs, where the yolk and white are cooked separately before being combined in one dish.[11]

The whole effect is to cut a template for what it might mean to become the author of historical time itself, while being careful not to have the work stand in for such an authoring, which could only be collective, collaborative, and far removed from the space and time of cinema. Viénet's anti-cinema is not as well known or well regarded as Debord's, and this is a pity, for Viénet's earthy humor and genuine sympathy for popular affect are a useful counterpoint to the more astringent beauties of Debordian cinema, and help us disentangle the elements of personal style in Debord's films from their conceptual advances.

Aside from his merits as a filmmaker, Viénet tried valiantly to put an end to the romance of the Cultural Revolution within the western political imaginary. But Maoist China is only one version of the historical nostalgia that has seized the imagination of leftist intellectuals in the twenty-first century. The other is surely the Autonomist movement in Italy, from 1969 through the seventies and beyond. This is a different story, and its central actors are often not far removed, in theory and practice, from Situationist positions. Yet at the risk of factionalism, certain Situationist or Post-Situationist works might offer a critical distance, a historical reframing, of those events as well.

11 The Occulted State

Know how to wait ... Stroll through the open spaces of time to the center of opportunity.

Baltasar Gracián

A woman with two small children tries to board a plane at Ronald Reagan airport. Security officers stop her when they discover that the child's sippy cup contains more than the permissible three ounces of liquid. At once, uniformed agents gather, superiors are notified. The boarding halts. The child's sippy cup becomes an object of extreme suspicion. It is as if the greatest power ever to bestride the world could be brought low by the most modest formula.[1] As Gianfranco Sanguinetti once wrote: "cowardice becomes, for the first time in history, a sublime quality, fear is always justified."[2]

What happens next is obscure, even on the security tape. Perhaps the woman throws the contents of the sippy cup on the ground. Perhaps they accidentally spill. Uniformed goons encircle her and make her get down on her hands and knees and clean up the spilled liquid—twice. (The first time she missed a bit.) Shortly after, the authorities revoke the ban on liquids, describing it as an ineffective piece of *security theater*. It is all in the name of the *war on terror*. A war that, as Vice President Dick Cheney once casually said, can never end.

 "War, in a word, is modernity incarnate," as Clark and the Retort group write.[3] Given that these were times when, during a hunting expedition, Cheney shot a friend in the face, and it was *the friend* who thought he should apologize, then naked displays of pure power legitimated by nothing much more than their own balls-out bareness were the norm. The state of emergency, or the state of exception, was revealed once again to be merely the normal state of affairs. Retort again: "Ultimately, the spectacle comes out of the barrel of a gun."[4]

That the state is founded on something other than justice, law or the social contract would hardly surprise the Situationists. As Debord writes to fellow founding member Pinot Gallizio in 1958: "Yesterday the police interrogated me for a long time concerning the journal and the Situationist organization. This is only the beginning. One of the threatening principles that appeared quite quickly to me in this discussion: the police want to consider the Situationist International as an association dedicated to bringing disorder to France."[5] Ever since he moved to Paris in his youth, Debord came into contact with the state mostly via its police. He did not work for any state media or cultural agency. He was not involved in the folderol of its political parties. As Debord would later quip: "It is known that I was a professional, but of what?"[6] Of making trouble. In his experience, the state was the police.

After the assassination of his friend and patron Gérard Lebovici in 1984, journalists took a certain relish in claiming to have been privy to certain details of secret police files on Debord. They claimed that he had been under surveillance for some time. This led him to remark: "What a strange and unfortunate land, where one is informed of the work of an author more quickly and confidently through police archives than through the literary criticisms of a free press or through academics who make a profession out of knowing the issues at hand."[7] Debord specified, in a literary testament like that of the vagabond poet François Villon, that statements he had made to the police should not be included in his collected works. Not because any statements he made there would cause him any embarrassment, but because of literary "scruples about the form."[8]

Debord admitted to using false names and documents in Italy in the seventies, but he had his reasons. This was a time of the *strategy of tension*, in which a rising tide of working-class militancy was diverted by a shadowy game of bombings and other terrorist acts by secretive groups, followed by repressions and reprisals from police agencies of the state. Things reached a peak in 1978 when the

Red Brigades kidnapped Aldo Moro, who had twice been prime minister and was the architect of the so-called *historic compromise* which was supposed to bring the left into the government. Moro was found dead in a parked car. Debord: "It was a mythological opera with great machinations, where terrorist heroes by transformation become foxes so as to ensnare their prey, then lions so as to fear nothing and no-one so long as they retain it, and stool-pigeons so as not to draw from this blow the smallest harmful thing to the regime they aspire to defy."[9] The right blamed the Communists for the Red Brigades. The Communists blamed the far-left Autonomists. The Autonomists blamed each other.

Debord thought he saw the hand of the state in these murky events. He encouraged his young friend Gianfranco Sanguinetti to expose it: "I have known a man who spent his time among the *party girls* of Florence and who loved to keep bad company with all of the hard-drinkers of the bad neighborhoods. But he comprehended everything that went on. He demonstrated his comprehension once. One knows that he will do it again. He is, today, considered by some to be the most dangerous man in Italy."[10] Sanguinetti had, with Debord's assistance, pulled off a brilliant hoax in 1975, and Debord encouraged him to action again. Sanguinetti's response to the Moro kidnapping was even more paranoid than Debord's. On hearing the news, he retreated to his country house and made sure he was seen by the local people, to generate possible alibis in case he was suspected of involvement in the Moro affair. Sure enough, his house was searched by the police, who of course found nothing.[11]

Sanguinetti did not initially credit Debord's theory of secret police involvement in the Moro affair, but he came around to it. He published a short book called *On Terrorism and the State* in which he wrote that: "It is its own secret services which organize and pull the strings of terrorism. Is this not, then, the main secret of the Italian State?"[12] This was an extraordinary thesis at the time, and it got Sanguinetti into even more trouble.

It retrospect it doesn't seem all that far fetched. A war on terror — led by a general no less — aided the consolidation of a state in crisis. The big losers, in Sanguinetti's account, were the Autonomist left. Both the state and its official enemy, the Communist Party, were united in condemning the Autonomists for sympathy, if not complicity, with the armed struggle, pushing the Autonomists onto the defensive. Sanguinetti: "The poor Autonomists, who, for their part, never had much of a clue either about terrorism or about revolution, have thus ended up, like a coveted prey, in the game-bag of the Stalinists and the judiciary."[13]

The most famous of the Autonomists, Antonio Negri (b. 1933), was arrested in 1979 and charged with being a leader of the Red Brigades and for involvement in the kidnapping of Aldo Moro. In exile in France from 1983, he built on his political writings a sustained philosophical critique. He returned to Italy and to prison voluntarily in 1997, in part to honor the hundreds of other political militants still in jail, often on trumped-up charges. He was released in 2003. With Michael Hardt he co-authored a series of original post-Marxist works, starting with *Empire* (2000). His work would become one of the most influential leftist currents of the early twenty-first century.

Not the least merit of the 1970s texts of Sanguinetti is that they provide an alternate window into the hothouse of Italian political economic life in which the Autonomist strain of thought was formed and to which it remains, for better or worse, inextricably linked.[14] And while in the pages of *Tiqqun* Debord is described as "an execrable middleman for all that was explosive in the Italian situation," the analyses he sponsored might still have something to say to those who would make of Italy a sacred memory.[15] Debord and Sanguinetti's critique of the Italian left pleases no one, and that alone may be its sole merit.

From a wealthy Tuscan family with leftist pretensions, Sanguinetti joined a newly formed Italian section of the Situationist International in 1969. He was around twenty years old. The Italian section took part in the struggles of 1969, which like those in France combined elements of a general strike, an insurrection, perhaps even a nascent civil war. Sanguinetti then lived underground in Paris until his expulsion from France back to Italy in 1971. When in 1972 Debord published *The Veritable Split in the International*, his texts on the dissolution of the Situationists, he made Sanguinetti the co-author as a tribute to a friend and comrade. Sanguinetti was arrested in 1975 and spent a few months in prison, and was turned back at the French border in 1976 when he attempted to leave the country again. His experience of the state, even more than Debord's, was mainly of its policing function.

Sanguinetti's analysis of terrorism, while salutary, is nevertheless somewhat unsatisfactory. His identification of terror directly with the state feeds into a conspiratorial approach to thinking about state power, as if by uncovering the secret machinations of the state one could somehow apprehend its truth. Something like this was the aim of the five hundred people who gathered at the Embassy Suites hotel in Chicago for a combination trade show and political convention for the 9/11 Truth movement. Given that Zogby polls show 42 percent of Americans doubting the conclusions of *The 9/11 Commission Report*, and 49 percent of New Yorkers believing that some leaders "knew in advance" about the 2001 attacks on the World Trade Center and the Pentagon, they are not alone. The Truthers are out there.

The talk at Embassy Suites compared 9/11 to the Reichstag fire, the Tonkin Bay incident, the assassinations of President Kennedy and Martin Luther King, Jr. In his keynote address, syndicated radio host Alex Jones rehearsed the main argument of the movement, that on September 11, 2001, a "controlled demolition" brought down the towers of the World Trade Center in New York City, not the impact of hijacked passenger jets.[16] This is the central tenet of the 9/11 Truth ideology. To them it seems more plausible than imagining that, where 9/11 is concerned, the state has nothing to hide.

Sanguinetti distinguishes between offensive terrorism by non-state actors and defensive terrorism by the state. He judged Italian terrorism of the period to be defensive terrorism on the part of the state. This refreshing claim can be turned aside from the path of conspiracy theory and used for new tactics in thinking through the inscrutable surface effects of power at work. Perhaps the origins of terrorism are not so easily decided. Perhaps the origins are not even all that relevant. Perhaps the state can make use of what appears to be offensive terrorism, coming from a non-state actor, as a way to consolidate power and pre-empt social movements. The state that makes a spectacle of responding to a need for security need not answer to any other desires. As the rather more sanguine Debord remarks: "Such a perfect democracy constructs its own inconceivable foe, terrorism. It wishes to be judged by its enemies rather than by its results."[17]

In the disintegrating spectacle of the twenty-first century, truth is as strange as fiction. In his 2007 novel *Spook Country*, William Gibson writes of a *cold civil war*, all but invisible, waged within a state of Byzantine complexity and obscurity.[18] His elaborate spy plot includes the usual agents and counter-agents, but curiously enough mixes in the owner of an advertising agency with the improbable name of Hubertus Bigend (b. 1967). The son of a minor Situationist, Bigend has grasped that the secret is to the spectacle as art once was to culture. The secret is not the truth of the spectacle, it is the aesthetic form of the spectacle. Gibson intuits something central here to Situationist experience, if not its theory: that the spectacle of appearances has another side. That which is good appears; that which is concealed *is better*. And for no other reason than that it is concealed.

The secret is not the truth of the spectacle. The division between the spectacle of appearances and the secrecy of non-appearances is itself an aspect of the falsification of the whole that the spectacle affects. While the spectacle renders all that appears equivalent, the division between the secret and the spectacular implies a hierarchy—the main game of power. Appearances are exchangeable for appearances; secrets exchangeable only for secrets. For Debord and Sanguinetti, it is not knowledge which is power, but secrecy.

A counter-power is then not so much a counter-knowledge as a strategy that is capable both of revealing secrets when it is tactically advantageous, but also of fabricating them. Against the power of the secret as the founding power of the state, Situationists and Post-Situationists alike pose the glamour of the clandestine as a kind of counter-power. The refusal to appear within the spectacle is also a refusal of the division between the spectacular and its secret. Which in turn makes the Situationists (and certain Post-Situationists) appear as dangerous to the state. The paradox is that this apparent danger, while only apparent, becomes in spectacular society a real danger.[19]

Another Hotel Room: this time the Budapest Hilton, and this time the organizer is the International Republican Institute, a nongovernmental group which may or may not be in receipt of US government money. Retired Army Colonel Robert Helvey leads a seminar on the techniques of nonviolent resistance attended by about twenty leaders of Otpor, the Serbian opposition movement. Helvey's approach is based on that of Gene Sharp, author of *From Dictatorship to Democracy* and other works, which in turn draw on the insight of Montaigne's friend Etienne de La Boétie.[20]

The key to de La Boétie's thought is that if people withdraw their obedience to the state, the state cannot stand. Or as Debord says in the same vein: "This is how, little by little, a new epoch of fires has been set alight, which none of us alive at the moment will see the end of: obedience is dead." And yet the outcome is far from certain. The withdrawal of consent from one state may just as easily serve another. Debord: "Yet the highest ambition of the integrated spectacle is still to turn secret agents into revolutionaries, and revolutionaries into secret agents."[21] An exchange of one clandestine form for another.

All the disintegrated spectacle might add to this transaction is that they might not even know it. There might be two ways of becoming an agent of the state. One is to be knowingly co-opted; the other is by descending into the spectacle of violence. Whether the Italian Red Brigades were manipulated by the first method or not, they certainly became agents of the state via the second. Regardless of their allegiances and ideologies, both the secret agent and the armed revolutionary use the same forms of organization: the form of hierarchy and secrecy. Sanguinetti: "All secret terrorist groupuscles are organized and directed by a clandestine hierarchy of the very militants of clandestinity, which reflects perfectly the division of labor and roles proper to this social organization: above it is decided and below it is carried out."[22]

Given that agents of the state invariably have much greater resources at their disposal, it is no accident who gets to infiltrate and manipulate who. But in the disintegrating spectacle, this may not even be necessary. Regardless of the inconvenience, a terrorist attack on the state provides the very pretext the state needs to consolidate its power, and in more recent times, perhaps, to go on the offensive, preempting popular self-organization in advance.

Nothing succeeds as well as a terrorist attack in making the people feel as though they have a common enemy with the state. In the disintegrating spectacle, the state offers nothing but the spectacle of its own necessity. Debord: "Until 1968 modern society was convinced it was loved. It has since had to abandon these dreams; it prefers to be feared."[23]

The spectacle incorporates within itself images of its own overcoming. Debord: "It is known that this society signs a sort of pact with its most avowed enemies, when it allots them a space in the spectacle."[24] It is personified by certain kinds of anti-celebrity, images of the integral action that would further disintegrate the spectacle, but which actually sustain it to the extent that they are mere images.

Anti-celebrities appear as dangerous to the spectacle in spite of being useful for it because the spectacle does not control them. They do its work for their own reasons. Since no other reasons besides the logic of spectacle are supposed to exist, their very existence is both useful and troubling. After the assassination in 1984 of his friend Gérard Lebovici, Debord found himself becoming cast as just such an anti-celebrity, who must be dangerous precisely because of his refusal of service to the spectacle.

The enemy that the spectacle can recognize is, once again, as in certain times past, the terrorist—the *spectacular* negation of the middle-class ideal. An act of terror aims above all at the production of the image. It is the spectacle for those who do not own their own news network or movie studio. It is a hijacking of the vehicle of the image itself. While terrorists appear as, and may even believe themselves to be, enemies of the state, their role is quite different. They are the—apparently—external principle of necessity for the state. They provide it with its reason to exist. They may act of their own volition. They may be agents of another state. They may be agents of the very state they are attacking, or merely its dupes. It doesn't actually matter. They provide the state with a reason to exist, and can usually be assured of its full attention. The state is more concerned with threats to itself than to its subjects.

"The top secret world … has become so large, so unwieldy and so secretive that no one knows how much money it costs, how many people it employs, how many programs exist within it or exactly how many agencies do the same work." In the United States alone there are at least 1,271 organizations and 1,931 companies at 10,000 locations employing 854,000 people who produce 50,000 intelligence reports per year. As one of the few super-users with security clearance enough to know something about all of it says: "I'm not going to live long enough to be briefed on everything … The complexity of this system defies description." A certain James Clapper declares: "There's only one entity in the entire universe that has visibility [over it all] and that's God." And he is the Director of National Intelligence.[25]

By 2011 the United States Department of Homeland Security had the third largest state workforce, after Defense and Veteran's Affairs. It is getting a new $3.4 billion dollar complex in Anacostia, the largest government complex built since the Pentagon. Some of the new buildings for the expanding universe of the security state are "on the order of the pyramids" says a contractor who worked on them. Most of these *intel factories* are staffed with analysts making $40–65k per year, some straight out of college, often with little training or language competence, who churn out reports, most of which use the same intelligence and arrive at the same conclusions. It is rather like graduate school. Debord: "It is in these circumstances that we can speak of domination's falling rate of profit, as it spreads to almost the whole of social space and consequently increases both its personnel and its means. For now each means aspires, and labors, to become an end. Surveillance spies on itself, and plots against itself."[26]

In the disintegrating spectacle, the state even renders spectacular the production of its own secrets. As Sanguinetti saw as early as the seventies, when it loses its grip on historical thought, the spectacular state succumbs to the spectacular economy whose depredations it was supposed to at once enable yet guard against. Capital missed the last chance to save itself from itself. The disintegrating spectacle originates in that moment when capital defeats not just the proletariat but also its image, be it Social Democrat, Leninist or Maoist. It is reduced to the security theater of opposing images of images. It frees itself from all impediments to its total war against the earth itself.

12   The Last Chance to Save Capitalism

Don't turn one foolish act into two. Often we commit four blunders to correct one.

Baltasar Gracián

There is a certain vanity in thinking that every aspect of our everyday life is of intimate concern to power. Certain states are less and less concerned with the well being and productivity of their subjects—their so-called *biopower*.[1] The state of the disintegrating spectacle reveals itself as concerned mostly with its own sovereignty. What if power, too, was not much more than a spectacle of appearances? Sanguinetti's greatest work did not just make an argument about the nature of power as appearance, it acted as the means by which power exposed itself in a less than flattering light.

In 1975 Sanguinetti sent out a curious document to a hundred or so prominent people in Italian public life, under the pseudonym Censor. The text contained the Machiavellian argument to the effect that creating the appearance of the Communist Party joining the government does not negate the rule of bourgeois power, but could actually enhance it. The text apparently addressed itself to the real power elite—the ruling class—and took a distinctive form: "One reason we chose the ancient form of expression, the pamphlet, rather than a more systematic text, is that we do not want to renounce the pleasure of speaking with swords drawn."[2]

Censor called for the ruling class to at least attempt to be truthful amongst itself. It ought not to be duped by the specter of the power of the Communists. This was merely a phantom, which the ruling class had itself invoked to strengthen the state during the cold war. But there was no need for power to believe in a phantom that was largely its own creation. The real danger was elsewhere, but before examining it, Censor expounded on the distinctive features of Italian capitalism of the seventies, features not unlike those Debord identified as the *integrated spectacle*.

As a consequence of its own development, capitalism expanded state power, which took on a nominally democratic form, but in the context of expanded secrecy and disinformation. The perimeter of the state may have become more democratic, but only so that its core may become more clandestine. Its principal means of dealing with conflict was to incorporate it at the margin. Censor: "The state is the palladium of commercial society, which converts even its enemies into proprietors."³ Like the wooden image of Pallas Athena, whom the Romans called Minerva, that the Greeks took from Troy and which Aeneas brought to Rome, the state is that ancient thing that protects capital from the enemies of its own making, the forces which its very development casts before it.

Development had one aspect that troubled Censor, namely that it made the economy an autonomous sphere. He offered a critique of it apparently from the right. Left to its own devices, the autonomous development of the economy might generate the forces capable of overthrowing the state. Censor called for the ruling class to think and act historically and politically rather than to believe in its own ideology of a self-regulating economy.

The organized labor movement—or at least its titular head, the Communist Party—was no longer the enemy. The project of postwar reconstruction had already incorporated it in a subordinate and peripheral role of maintaining labor discipline, in the name of building a modern, democratic economy and society. Certain forces within the Communist Party had threatened insurrection in 1948, but the party itself put down this revolt, thus confirming its allegiance to the bourgeois state. Censor: "The Trojan horse should not be feared, except when there are well-armed Archean troops inside."⁴ Much more damaging to the state was the behavior of the Christian Democrats. Censor saw them principally as the party of the middle classes who aligned their interests with the bourgeoisie. The party was riddled with private interests who treated the various organs of the state as so many personal fiefdoms.

The main danger to the state came from neither the apparent strength of the Communists nor the unreliability of the Christian Democrats, but from a new kind of worker's movement. The working class had defected from its own party, the party that in Debord's estimation had become a spectacular representation of the proletariat already in the 1920s. After May '68 the working class could no longer be co-opted via its representative. The workers' response is as the courtesan says in Viénet's *Dialectics*: "They offer crumbs. We want it all!" The workers did not know what they were fighting for, but what they wanted was to fight. They had started to question private property itself—the one thing crucial to the state. Censor: "Private property thus constitutes the fortress wall of society, and all other rights and privileges are the advanced defense."

The internal weakness of the state made this movement particularly dangerous: "on high reigns apathy, boredom and immobility; below on the contrary, political life begins to manifest feverish symptoms." One such symptom was the Autonomist left, outside the Communist Party. But for Censor this was just the fever. The spontaneous action of the working class was the real disease. This was causing something of a panic among the ruling classes: "The bourgeoisie is afraid of being right, and afraid of being afraid. It soon perceived that it was right to be afraid."[5]

Censor stressed the usefulness of the Communist Party in imposing discipline on the working class and keeping refractory elements in line. But this view was not shared by the ruling class, deluded by their own fiction that cast the Communists as the leadership of the working class against the state rather than as the police agent of the state against the working class. The ruling class thought the price the Communists demanded for their services outweighed the guarantees they could offer of their own effectiveness. And perhaps rightly so, as the Communists quite underestimated the danger to themselves of rebel workers who no longer saw the unions and the party as their representatives. And so, from 1968 on into the seventies, Italy descended into an undeclared civil war, in which "the only things still functioning in Italy were the unions and the police."[6]

The hot year of 1969 was the time when the possibility of a general insurrection seemed genuinely close. What averted it was a wave of bombings, variously attributed to anarchists or fascists, but behind at least some of which was the hand of the secret services of the state. Against this, not only the Communists but also much of the Autonomist left felt the need to rally around opposition to clandestine violence. But for Censor, the continued use of the terror tactic was dangerous. If the complicity of agencies of the state were to come to light, this risked alienating the very people that the strategy had neutralized, and re-establishing the conditions for worker's revolt. As Censor wryly observes, in the spirit of Gracián: "If no good policies have ever been founded on truth, the worst policies are founded on the improbable."[7]

Re-founding ruling class power on firmer ground meant a less disingenuous policy. The state had to reinstate legality or disappear. But the state couldn't count on anything but its secret services, and the continual use of force was weakening the state. Alluding to Machiavelli's *Prince*, Censor argued that a state that used force too much and too often did not appear stronger for it, but weaker. And in any case, terrorism was less of a threat to the state than the mutiny of the working class.

The real threat was not bombs but, as La Boétie would say, disobedience. The ruling class had discounted the threat of the working class because the new movement lacked leadership and organization. Organized labor and Communist leadership was co-optable; *disorganized labor* was not. This was much more dangerous: "all revolutions in history began without leaders, and when they had them, they were finished."[8] From their analysis of the Paris Commune onwards, this is the first and last axiom of Situationist politics.

The state had to stop its short-term defensive tactics. As Clausewitz had already shown, the relation between offense and defense is asymmetrical. Censor: "our state, continually defending itself against phantom enemies — red or black according to the mood of the moment, all poorly constructed — never wanted to confront the problems posed by the real enemy."[9] The army was not going to defend the state; it was as useless as the postal service. The secret service risked losing its secrecy, and thus its power. The murder, or rather *theatrical killing*, of the leftist publisher Feltrinelli, for example, was a dangerous move. As Gracián might say, it was not wise policy to cover up a foolish act with a dozen more.

The real threat remained disorganized labor: "this crisis is total because, intensively, it is life itself ... that has succumbed to the contagion." It is not a crisis *in* the economy but a crisis *of* the economy. The workers gained wage rises but were disenchanted with the flimflam that was all these wages could buy. Censor: "we poisoned the world, and we gave the people a special reason to revolt against us every instant of their everyday life: we poisoned life itself."[10]

It might still be possible to head off the danger from disorganized labor by bringing organized labor—the Communist Party—into the outer perimeter of the state. This was the policy of the historic compromise, although as Censor points out it was neither historic nor a compromise. There is nothing historic about a merely expedient tactic that could later be reversed. There is no compromise when only one side—the Communists—gives anything up.

On the international plane, the cold war had subsided into a period of *peaceful coexistence* between Moscow and Washington, between the diffuse and concentrated variants of the spectacle. For Censor this too was a mere tactic. Both sides faced troubling dissent internally. In the West, most clearly in France and Italy; in the east, the Czechs and Poles were creating their own forms of spontaneous withdrawal of obedience. This was the backdrop to Censor's proposal for a fuller incorporation of the Communists into a Western state. The integrated spectacle would replace the diffuse form, drawing organized labor not just within the orbit of the spectacle, but completely inside the state, or at least appearing to do so, while the core of the state's functions became occulted and withdrawn.

Censor called the ruling class to action. Power could not be delegated to others any longer. The maintenance of the state could not be entrusted to the secret police alone. As for the utility of the army, those who think it better to govern with rifles than with Communists overestimate how many of their soldiers are good shots. Power could not be entrusted to the Christian Democrats, who were content to squabble over the spoils of each particular office and leave the state as a whole to its ruin. Power could not be left in the hands of managers, who were no better than overpaid wage earners, unable to grasp the historic process. Nor was it acceptable to cash out and become mere rentiers, passing on the mess to whoever is cashed up. (The Saudis at the time, then Japan, then Chinese sovereign wealth funds.) The diffuse spectacle was undermining the very authority of the class that had created it, and was in as much trouble as the concentrated spectacle in the east. The ruling class risked being overcome by its own creation.

It simply had to be faced that capitalism did not deliver on its promises. The manufacture of abundance had led only to an abundance of boredom. The ruling class lost sight of anything of real value. Far from securing power, abundance threatened it. Censor: "We have thoughtlessly dispersed so much false luxury and comfort that the entire population is quite rightly dissatisfied."

While the ruling class struggles against disorganized labor and its negation of property and the state, it had also the positive historical task of affirming something of value outside of mere abundance. This may be an even bigger challenge. Censor: "this abundance of fabricated objects requires the demarcation of an elite more than ever—an elite that is sheltered by this abundance and takes what is really precious: otherwise, there will soon be no place on earth with anything precious left in it."[11] Prophetic words. Has not the ruling class of the disintegrating spectacle been thoroughly corrupted by the spectacle itself? Even those powers it withdrew into a clandestine core became corrupted by the high-end trade of the spectacle's exclusive other currency—the secret.

In Lampedusa's classic historical novel *The Leopard* (1958), the aristocrat Tancredi justifies going over to the side of Garibaldi's bourgeois revolution in these terms: "Unless we ourselves take a hand now, they'll foist a republic on us. If we want things to stay as they are, things will have to change."[12] Censor pointed the way to the seizure of initiative by the ruling class as the seventies gave way to the eighties. Sanguinetti's pamphlet received creditable coverage in the news media, including much speculation about its author. It was thought to be either the work of some kind of modern-day Tancredi who still retained the patina of classical knowledge, or perhaps of some junior state functionary who had actually learned something at a modern university. When Sanguinetti revealed the hoax, scandal followed, but one aspect of the affair is often overlooked. Sanguinetti produced the aura of authenticity for his document by making it appear as if it were a secret that had been revealed. The secret quality of the document was what made it appear as if it had, not truth, but power.

Sanguinetti's *Real Report* still works as an allegory for the relation between power and the secret in the age of the disintegrating spectacle. Unlike Censor's Christian Democrats, the US members of Congress of the early twenty-first century cannot be bought; one rents them by the hour. They squabble over the particulars while the state as the guarantor of the property interests of the ruling class as a totality becomes nobody's business. Terror still forms a convenient alibi, if not always a terribly effective one. And yet there are major differences between the integrated spectacle of the seventies and the disintegrated spectacle of the early twenty-first century. For one thing, what is left of organized labor is thoroughly integrated into the state.

Perhaps these days one could call this *disorganizing labor*: Emmalee Bauer, using work time to sit at her desk and write about not working. Or Steven Slater, a Jetblue flight attendant who became a working-class hero with a spectacular exit from the workplace. After an altercation with a passenger, who hit him in the head with the lid of the overhead storage bin, he told the passenger off over the intercom, grabbed some beer, activated the emergency chute and slid to the tarmac. Slater made it all the way out through airport security and all the way home before police caught up with him. They found him in bed with his boyfriend. Slater then found himself before the judge on charges of criminal mischief, reckless endangerment and trespassing. Jetblue suspended him, but a fan base sprang up on social networking sites to raise money for his defense. Psychologist Alan Hilfer says, "Despite the celebrity he is enjoying, he will not easily find a new job unless his new job is being a celebrity."[13] A job he held as long as such things last.

In the twenty-first century, the state as the centralized power over the double form of spectacle and secret gave way to a disorganized and decentralized distribution of such powers. Debord: "the liars have lied to themselves."[14] The diffuse spectacle of the postwar years merely incorporated the image of that which would negate it, the image of organized labor and its bureaucratic sock puppets. The outbreak of a fresh form of negation, that of disorganized labor, led to the full incorporation of the organization of labor into the integrated spectacle. With the failure of disorganized labor to turn local and sporadic expressions of boredom into a strategy for dismantling spectacle power, the integrated spectacle emerges triumphant.

It is not as if workers are thus magically rendered content with their poisoned world. Workers respond with boredom, indifference, absenteeism, petty theft on the job, and now and then by popping the escape chute. In the absence of the great game of struggling against that which refuses it, the integrated spectacle begins to disintegrate of its own accord. It becomes the marvel of none other than its own deliquescence. Its motto: That which appears is all there is; all there is, is that which appears. The tricky qualities of appearances, however, are the domain of the ineradicable stain on spectacular perfection, of what one might call the devil's party.

13   Anti-Cinema

Do, but also seem. Things do not pass for what they are, but what
they seem.

Baltasar Gracián

There is a strange amnesia about the seventies. The sixties are a
subject of persistent nostalgia. Everyone of a certain age claims to
have *been there*. Nobody much makes such claims about the seventies. In the seventies, the acid test gave way to the heroin epidemic.
Politics as street festival became bombing and kidnapping. The
notorious slogan of the Watts uprising (1965), "burn, baby burn,"
became a lyric to the dance number "Disco Inferno" (1976). If you
remember the sixties, you weren't there; if you forgot the seventies,
maybe you have something to hide.

The Situationist International dissolved itself in 1972. It cannot
be brandished as yet another example of what was wrong with the
times.[1] The great break into lived time of May '68 had come and
gone. For Debord, Paris lost its charms. He would spend much of
this decade, and the next, in voluntary exile from Paris, circulat-
ing between Florence, Arles, Seville and the Auvergne. These were
quietly productive times. He found new cities, each with their own
field of possibilities. He even found something to do in the countryside.[2] He found some sterling collaborators, whose witting and
unwitting contributions to thinking a way out of these times has not
yet received its due. And he made some remarkable films. Debord
had made films before, but these seventies films stand out as both
conceptual elaborations of the problem of living in the lackluster
light of the society of the spectacle, and practical demonstrations of
how to move in and against it.

Debord's films were always ahead of their time. They antici-
pate, and in many respects exceed, the achievements of materialist
cinema. They manage a synthesis in advance of a politics of form
and a politics of content. They draw attention to their mode of production but don't make a fetish of this gesture or expect miracles
of it. His is a cinema that you have in the absence of certain more
important things to do, which will interrupt your program presently. Debord's films, and the Letterist cinema from which they
emerged, were widely plagiarized. Tom Levin: "An inordinate
amount of Debord's concerns reappear in later works by Godard
… One even encounters the same 'stars': years before she became
the leading actress in numerous films by Godard as well as his wife,
Anna Karina appeared as the actress in a Monsavon commercial
détourned by Debord."[3]

If the key to Viénet's films is insouciance, then *insolence* is the
key to Debord's three mature films of the seventies, an insolent
disregard for the proper handling of images. Nothing about their
provenance is to be respected; not their context, their ownership,
their genre. This insolence is not an indifference to what images
mean. Debord is not interested in setting them free to frolic in some
postmodern indeterminacy. Nor is he interested in subjecting them
to endless *interrogations*, ferreting out secret codes of significance.
Both of these attitudes are too respectful. In and of themselves,
images sublimate neither poetry nor power. Rather, he starts with
a casual disregard for the value that professional makers or owners
or interpreters claim of them. Images are merely moves in a game,
tactics in a strategy, the goal of which is the critique and overturning of a world in which images are just objects of contemplation.
The people make meaning, but not with the media of their own
choosing. The task is a social production of recovered meaning
or fresh-minted meaning, with what images one can beg, borrow
or steal.

Images themselves are not the enemy. Writing is as much a part
of the spectacle as cinema, and the same problems attend to both.[4]
How can a text, a film, a representation take sides against itself?
Rather than making representations of what is wrong with this
world, or of what a better world of the imagination might be like,
how can representation be a partisan for another kind of world-

making? Could this be an anti-cinema that hastens cinema toward its end? A purely individual and moral choice to not make cinema would be of no consequence, for cinema has not yet exhausted its potential.

The time of cinema is not yet over. But perhaps it can be hastened to its end, and that is what Debord almost succeeded in achieving. In the wild, viral, endless world of the cutting, mixing, mutating, mutilating of cinema in the disintegrating spectacle, Debord's anticipation of the dissolution of cinema is partly realized. And partly not. There is still an extraordinary gift in his films which points to how much further the ebb tide has to go.[5]

Who says the spectator is always a passive receptacle of spectacle? At a 2008 Christmas day screening of *The Curious Case of Benjamin Button*, James Cialella got so enraged at a father and son who would not shut up that he took out a .38 caliber gun and shot the man. "It's truly frightening when you see something like this evolve into such violence," said police spokesman Lt. Frank Vanore.[6] One only regrets that Cialella injured a fellow spectator for obscuring his enjoyment of the spectacle, rather than taking aim at the screen for obscuring his life with his fellow spectators.

In the passing show of images that populate Debord's late films, very little is ever explained to the spectator. In *Society of the Spectacle* (1973) in particular, the images flit by in a seemingly absurd order. Occasionally they seem to correspond to Debord's voice-over, but often the link is obscure. They certainly don't make much immediate sense in relation to each other. It is not as if there is a complete disconnect between sound and image of the kind advocated by Isidore Isou as *discrepant cinema*.[7] Rather, Debord has taken Isou's initial break between sound and image and conceived of a way to reconnect them in a different way. The crisp rhythms of the edits accumulate as the film progresses. Clusters of images that together don't make much sense reveal themselves in the light of later ones. Surprising complexity and consistency emerges if one accepts a central premise: that the spectacle attempts to negate the possibility of making history, but history remains as a residue within the spectacle in fragmented form.

Martine Barraqué edited *Society of the Spectacle* (1973) and its sequel, *Refutation of All Judgments* (1975). They are best treated as one work rather than two. As Barraqué notes, *"Refutation* was entirely made out of footage that had not been included in the *Society of the Spectacle."*[8] *Refutation* is an extraordinary precursor to the answer-video of the kind that pop up like wildfire on the internet in the early twenty-first century. In appending it to *Society of the Spectacle*, Debord makes a complete work that subsumes not only the actual reactions to the film but any possible reaction into the work itself, in advance.

Barraqué came to Debord via the patron Debord acquired in the seventies, Gérard Lebovici (1932–84), the publisher, film producer and film agent, about whom there will be more to say later. Barraqué was already working as an assistant editor for François Truffaut (1932–84) and makes two brief uncredited appearances in Truffaut's *Day for Night* (1973), playing a film editor. Among others, she would go on to edit *The Green Room* (1978) and *The Last Metro* (1980) for Truffaut, but Debord's *Society of the Spectacle* was her first credit as an editor. Of Truffaut and Debord she says: "they were both (I was in the middle of them) curious about one another." Perhaps it is time to be a little curious about Martine Barraqué, too.

Her significance in realizing Debord's films is honored in the credits. She gets a whole title card to herself. It would be amusing to compare her Debords and Truffauts to see if Barraqué left a comparable stylistic signature on them. While Barraqué also lent a hand to Debord's later film, *In Girum Imus Nocte et Consumimur Igni* (1978), it was edited by her former assistant Stéphanie Granel, and it has a rather different pace and structure to it. While both Barraqué and Granel doubtless worked under Debord's direction, highlighting the contribution of his editors might be a modest attempt to prevent the subsumption of Debord under the usual *auteurist* view of cinema production as Truffaut and other *masters*.

Society of the Spectacle uses selected text from Debord's 1967 book of the same name, read by Debord himself in an even tone quite at odds with the tradition of voice-over delivery for the cinema. The soundtrack was recorded in Debord's apartment. The images were cut to the soundtrack. The images come mostly from four sources: stills from popular magazines, newsreel documentation of current events, advertisements, and extracts from classic feature films. As Barraqué explains the process: "We had lists of documents that we had to search for, keep and file once found, and that we would use in future work. The documents could be old news, we had a lot of still images that he cut-off from magazines (that his wife must have read, and that he used to cut images from), that he kept and that I had filmed in order to have them in the film as 24 frames per second images. It was a very detailed work. He could come to the editing room at 2 p.m. and by then I already had the images sorted so that he would look at them. We went through the images together, and then he decided the order in which they would be presented. Afterwards, we would look for the paragraph that would be juxtaposed to the images."

The relationship between image and text in Debord's late films is not representational. The images do not usually illustrate the text, nor does the text explain or refer to what is onscreen. The relation between the two is critical. Cinema's limitations can be turned to advantage. It is something like a jujitsu move, using the weight and power of the enemy against itself. The spectacle tries to abolish the qualitative space and irreversible time of history. In its place it offers mere representations of time and space, images that have a formal equivalence, any of which can be exchanged for another. The worth of any image is measurable in other images, but only in other images. Any image can follow any other. Time loses its irreversible, historical quality and becomes as homogeneous as the TV schedule — a sitcom followed by a movie, or a movie then a sitcom.

By freeing images from these constraints, Debord does not want to further reduce them to meaninglessness. His approach is quite the opposite. It is to take the images of the spectacle as a true representation of a falsified world. A fine example would be his proposition in *Refutation* that spectators do not get what they desire; they desire what they get. An English television ad shows a man going to a tailor to be measured for a tailor-made cigarette. Once the customer decides on the exact length that suits him, the tailor offers him a Senior Service cigarette which, it turns out, his desire exactly matches. To commit a historical act a people needs its desires, but to merely watch the spectacle act in one's place one merely desires the needs it is offered.

The spectacle classifies the world by genre and organizes it by narrative. All images, sounds and stories are formally equivalent in the spectacle. Any element of it can be measured in the currency of another. A Marilyn Monroe image might be worth four Mao Zedongs or twenty anonymous pin-up pictures. All the elements of the spectacle can be arranged in a hierarchy of value, and the spectator is encouraged to make distinctions between them.

This is the essence of middle-class café or dinner party conversations, not to mention a certain kind of college education about aesthetics: Is Welles a greater filmmaker than Truffaut? —discuss. In *Day for Night* (1973) Truffaut imagines his younger self stealing lobby cards of Welles' *Citizen Kane* (1941) from a cinema. For Debord that might be as good an emblem as any of spectacular value. Truffaut steals Welles to create his own personal values and market value. Debord, as we shall see, will use Welles for quite different reasons.

From the archives of the spectacle itself, Barraqué built an archive specifically designed to catalog images for Debord's purposes. "I had a very, very long list of documents that I had selected, classified and archived by (say) group: history, fashion, scoops, decoration, (what else?), politics, and speeches. So, whenever he would ask 'Do you remember this? Could you find this again for me?' My assistant and I, knowing where we had classified them, would be able to fetch them very quickly." Using this archive, Debord cuts the image away from both narrative and genre, but not to make it just a free-floating sign. Rather, it is to produce, out of the tension between the senses it brings with it from its previous context and the senses Debord imposes by embedding the image in a critical context, a new ensemble of significance.

In *Refutation* another ad shows the American south before the civil war and declares that nothing remains of this civilization but its iced tea. Advertising appropriates the residue of what was once historical time and hitches the thought that arises from it to the commodity. In this case, the idea of the passing into history of a whole way of life. Debord's procedure here is simply to strip the pitch from the idea and insert it into a new context. His wager is against the spectacle's confidence in its ability to subsume qualitative action to the commodity form. While the spectacle has to subsume history always and forever, history has to erupt into the spectacle and destroy it only once.

What separates Debord's seventies films from his earlier ones is the sophistication with which images produce critical friction through their relation to each other independently of their relation to the voice-over. This is where the crisp rhythms of the editing of *Spectacle* and *Refutation* really stand out. For instance, in *Spectacle*, Barraqué cuts together images of women on the beach with images of an iceberg as seen through the periscope of a nuclear submarine, followed by images of that submarine, then of Cuban leader Fidel Castro in a TV studio, then Castro haranguing a crowd. The logic of the images connects what it is that is to be desired within the spectacle, the power that maintains the spectacle, the counter-power of another form of the spectacle. For Debord the cold war clash between the concentrated spectacle of the socialist east and the diffuse spectacle of the capitalist West masks a commonality of interest in maintaining spectacular domination. One side gets half-naked women to look at; the other gets a charismatic dema-gogue—which have more in common than might at first appear.

Not that the diffuse spectacle of the West is without its own pin-ups of power. Barraqué cuts images of The Girl next to a polit-ical leader (Pompidou), a car show, more of The Girl. Here the rostrum camera pans along a series of bikini-clad women several times, as if there were an endless succession of them, just as there is an endless succession of factory-made images, cars, leaders. Henri Lefebvre: "Everything happens as though the image (myth, ideol-ogy, utopia, or what you will) of the total woman had replaced the image or the idea of the total man after the latter had collapsed."[9] That women's bodies become the surface of desire, the mediators between the commodity and fetishizing, will become a whole genre of critique. What is interesting is the way Debord connects this to a broader critique of the spectacle. Clark discovers something already beginning in Manet: that pictures of The Girl become a privileged kind of image in the spectacle.[10]

Scenes of industrial waste, a car driving past mountains of garbage, a smoggy panorama of a contemporary city, are then linked to scenes from the 1965 Watts riots. A black woman is manhandled; a bloodied black man lies on the ground. Here Barraqué co-joins the two *externalities* of spectacular society. On the one hand, pol-lution; on the other, the proletariat. This is followed by riot police rehearsing against a fake street riot, which they easily defeat, then scenes from May '68, then Mao Zedong meeting President Richard Nixon and his Secretary of State Henry Kissinger. The link is between the police function of the state and the spectacular function of the leader. Nixon's pact with Mao isolated their mutual enemy, Russia. But for Debord, the real struggle was between the state of spectacular society—both east and west—and their respective peoples. The spectacle's overcoming of history is spectacular, but history's overcoming of the spectacle will be historical.

Some poignant images of Marilyn Monroe alternate with French socialist politician François Mitterrand, leaflets thrown to a crowd, the Nazi rise to power, more riot police, the Vietnam War, the Nazi rally at Nuremberg, Soviet leader Leonid Brezhnev at a Moscow May Day parade, tanks, traffic, industrial food. The range of available celebrities model the range of available desires, be they sexual or political. Either way they propose an end to historical time, which nevertheless leaves behind fragments of its furtive, fugitive existence. In both east and west, spectacular political power is built on the ruins of failed attempts to seize it. Whether fascist, communist or capitalist, the spectacular falsification is in some respects the same, and should be treated with the same insolence.

A cake factory, motor racing, Mao Zedong and Lin Biao, Josef Stalin, Hungarians destroying a statue of Stalin in the 1956 uprising, a pin-up girl, a box factory: One of these things is not like the others. As the film progresses, its rhythm changes, and more and more images of the subjective moment in history, the seizure of historical time, appear. But the spectacle erases history, turning it into mere images, the significance of which fades.

Perhaps Mao's face is still well known only because Andy Warhol made a portrait of it. But who remembers Lin Biao? The general who led the People's Liberation Army into Beijing in 1949 became Mao's second in command and designated successor during the Cultural Revolution, before he died in that mysterious plane crash. Lin Biao was most likely assassinated in the power struggles of the time, but it is characteristic of the occulted state that nobody who knows would speak of it, and anyone who speaks of it does not know. Debord's *Society of the Spectacle* was made at a time when Mao exercised an extraordinary fascination over the French left.[11]

In Debord's films Mao, Castro, the Soviets are all versions of the concentrated spectacle, and as such images of domination.

Pre-war Shanghai divided by colonial concessions is followed by tourists on a bus and a boat. The city becomes an image of itself. Pleasure boats and seaside apartments follow the riot police who guard against outbreaks of history that might render such spectacular distractions moot. The subjective moment in history can only be represented within the spectacle, and these representations appear as isolated moments, contained within narratives that neutralize them. Debord retrieves them from these constraints, whether documentary or fictional, and puts them together.

Rather than moments of historical time neutralized by spectacular narrative and isolated by genre—here comes everybody! Cavalry charges, the storming of the winter palace, the Spanish civil war: situations of irreversible action in time. Spread throughout the film is the particular sequence of moments in which historical time accelerates, and the conflict of forces pushes it toward new qualities: Paris 1871, St. Petersburg 1917, Barcelona 1935, Watts 1965, Paris again, 1968. The sequence continues in *Refutation* with the *carnation revolution* in Lisbon, 1974.[12] It is a sign of the further progress of the spectacular erasure of historical time that one could be forgiven for not knowing that some of these events even happened, just as attempts to leave the twenty-first century, in Thailand or Greece or Tunisia or Egypt, run the risk of erasure from history.

American Phantom jets on an aircraft carrier; The Girl again—a refrain of the earlier moment where Barraqué links The Girl with a nuclear submarine. Again, these images appear with a picture of Alice Becker-Ho, to whom Debord was married in 1972. *Society of the Spectacle* begins with love and ends with friendship. Dissolved in 1972, the Situationist International no longer exists, so it is back to the forms of discreet sociality out of which it in part emerged. Here two series confront each other. One series is spectacle/spectator. The other is a little harder to define, but is composed of history as the collective and subjective being in an irreversible time, and being in discreet relations of friendship or love which also entail irreversible moments.

Barraqué interrupts the rhythmic succession of clusters of images at key moments for fragments of scenes from movies, complete with their original dialogue and music. While the news-reel footage was simply purchased from archives, getting hold of feature films involved a certain amount of deception and secrecy. Barraqué: "And it was lots of fun! Going, calling, telling people that the director I worked for and the film were very important, but that he was currently scouting for locations in Italy (and then in America, etc.). So that we didn't know the exact date that he could come in to watch the films, and so that I needed them for—at least—three days: the time it took for me to insert the rigs in the copy, have an inter-negative made, wait for the results, then removing the rigs from the copy, and then give it back to the distributor. Still, I was able to obtain all that was needed. We therefore stole—without paying any copyrights (not a dime to any of them)."

The feature films are détourned to a different effect to the news-reels. As Debord writes, these stolen films are deployed for the "rectification of the 'artistic inversion of life.'"[13] They are like blocks of affect, of potential feeling that can be retrieved from the cinematic inversion and "put back on their feet," as the vehicles via which to make one's own meaning, one's own sense. Debord and Bar-raqué use Nicholas Ray's *Johnny Guitar* (1954) for its ambivalent, tender yet fraught memories of love; *The Shanghai Gesture* (1941) for the confused and excited sensation of adventure; John Ford's *Rio Grande* (1950) for the giddy élan of historical action; Orson Welles' *Mr. Arkadin* (1955) for the pathos of authentic friendship; Sergei Eisenstein's *Battleship Potemkin* (1925) for the moment of collective decision. In each case an insolent disregard for narrative and genre frees the fragment for redeployment.

Cinema, like the novel, was of interest to Debord to the extent that it posed a certain problem with time. His interest in cinematic time is in its historical and affective dimensions, not the conceptual and ontological time of the philosopher Gilles Deleuze. As Debord wrote in a 1959 letter after some remarks on the novel: "It seems to me that the question of time is posed in an analogous manner by the cinema, which is another form of the representation of the temporal flow of things. Here, as there, what's interesting lies in those moments at which the alienated satisfactions of the spectacle can, at the same time, be rough sketches (in negative) of a planned development of affective life, that is to say, of the affective events inseparable from thought and action."[14]

Many of the fragments Debord détourned from various films have a particular quality, a distinctive emotional tone that corresponds to a situation in which an irreversible action is beginning. Johnny and his old flame Vienna warily reunite in very different times. A general commits troops to battle just as he learns that the enemy knows of the attack, dooming it from the start. Sailors gather under threat of a firing squad and in an instant coalesce in mutiny. But where cinema under both the concentrated and diffuse spectacle seeks to neutralize these moments, strapping them down to predictable narrative arcs and the expectations borne of genre conventions, for Debord they can serve as proxies for a quite different kind of sense. This is not to be confused with the idea that spectators make their own meaning, that their viewing is active, subversive of dominant codes and so on. It is not that people make new meaning, but that they could make new social relations. The appropriated images are still only proxies, blocks of sense mobilized to open up a possibility outside of themselves.

It's the Russian civil war. A Red partisan with a machine gun fires on an advancing infantry formation of the White army. She keeps firing, but they keep coming, a look of desperation in her close-up. "Some cinematic value might be acknowledged in this film if the present rhythm were to continue, but it will not."[15] The film is the Vasilyev Brothers' *Chapayev* (1934), one of the classics, if there is such a thing, of Stalinist cinema.[16] In this image, the woman is the active subject, a reprise of Delacroix's *Liberty Leading the People* with updated weaponry. It is an image that is not without its problems, caught as it is in hierarchies of gender, and can only have tactical value. Debord uses it for what it is worth, expends it, and moves on.

Debord's insolence toward cinema does not devalue all of it. Rather, he claims his desire to make of it what is needed. It doesn't always matter which war or which love is portrayed. It's the diagram of forces, the picturing of the game of time, that matters. But cinema, like any art, represents the world too well. Lived time disappears in art, and art at best can only mourn its passing. Cinema is a kind of memory, an abstract memory, not of particular events, particular people, but a memory of the possibility of life before it becomes mere representation. A life about which cinema can say nothing, show nothing, which cinema can acknowledge only in passing. Johnny Guitar asks his lost love, Vienna: "How many men have you forgotten?" And in this game, Vienna gives as good as she gets: "As many women as you've remembered."

The Dancing Kid tosses a coin to decide whether to kill Johnny or let him play Vienna a song on his guitar. She catches the coin in mid-air. Johnny's song for Vienna puts her into a reverie, but she catches herself: "Play something else," she commands. Those times are gone and cannot be relived. Cinema cannot bring life itself back to life. It's the same with historical time on a grand scale. General Sheridan orders John Wayne to catch and kill the Indians, even if he has to cross the border with Mexico to do it. If he is caught he will be court-martialed. If he is court-martialed, Sheridan will have him judged by others who were with them both at Shenandoah.

This prompts Sheridan's reverie: "I wonder what history will say about Shenandoah?" They might say of this civil war event that, with its scorched-earth destruction of the South's economic power, it signaled the beginning of modern warfare. To the practice of which Sheridan later added his genocidal campaigns against the Indians. But for Debord there's something else as well. The experience of lived time, irreversible time, on a small or a grand scale, is that which escapes the spectacle, and hence remains a resource against it. And yet the spectacle cannot help itself. It is drawn again and again to the memory of that which it erases.

Those who experienced lived time together are bound thereafter by it. They may no longer be lovers, comrades, or even friends, but something remains, something unsaid, something unspeakable. Orson Welles as Mr. Arkadin tells a parable about a graveyard where the dates recorded on the tombstones are not the lifespan of the deceased but the length of time the dead kept a friend. He then proposes a toast: "To friendship!" The friendships commemorated on the tombstones may be as brief as many of the memberships in the Situationist International. Raoul Vaneigem joined in 1961 and resigned in 1970. T. J. Clark joined in 1966 and was excluded in 1967. René Viénet joined in 1966 and resigned in 1971. Gianfranco Sanguinetti joined in 1969 and was the last remaining member with

Debord when the Situationist International was dissolved in 1972. These things have their time, and the memory of lived time is a resource against the dead time of representation. Friendships, like montage, both connect and sever.

Mr. Arkadin recounts a second Aesopean parable, in which the scorpion asks the frog to carry him across the river.[17] "But you will sting me and kill me!" says the frog. "Why would I do that? I would drown if I did that," says the scorpion. So the frog carries the scorpion into the river. Half way across, the scorpion stings the frog. "But why? Now we will both die," says the frog. "It's in my character!" says the scorpion. Mr. Arkadin offers a toast: "To character!"

As Barraqué remarks, "Especially with *Mr. Arkadin*, when he is telling the tale of the scorpion—you can see how it completely follows his line of thought, the plan of transforming this *Society of the Spectacle* from the book into a film." The scorpion is the practice of détournement, which stings the image as much as the word, as it crosses the river that separates the sign from its interpretation. "It's in my character!" says détournement.

Johnny rides through the desert and finds Vienna's saloon. When he enters, he finds it empty, the barman and croupiers standing ready. A man shows Gene Tierney around a crowded casino. "The other place is like kindergarten compared to this," she says. "Anything could happen at any moment!" Barraqué adroitly joins scenes from different films which both present the moment a situation opens, with its finite but barely known field of possibilities. Of course, in cinema, only one possibility can occur. The narrative moves on, and cinema is usually impatient to move it on. Barraqué finds the exact bounds of the event in the relentless mechanic time of the cinema. Interpretation can open the situation again, open toward an infinite realm of possibilities. But this is not what interests Debord. Rather, his attention to the situation is to the finite and specific options for action any given situation contains.

Power can't be seized the old way. The revolutionary movement is over. Some might think it dies in Paris in '68. For Debord it died in Barcelona in 1935, when the Communists defeated the revolutionary movement in the name of winning the civil war, which was lost anyway to Franco and his Nazi backers.[18] A civil war general, on learning that Franco's forces know about their attack already:

"Too late. That means we're done for. This time we fail. Too bad. Yes, too bad." The failure of the workers' revolutions is that they relied on the same thought, the same methods, as the successful bourgeois revolutions before them. The fruit of bourgeois enlightenment, from its specialized forms of knowledge to its hierarchical forms of organization, cannot be turned against it.

In *Spectacle*, Debord shows an etching by Jacques-Louis David of *The Tennis Court Oath* (1791), signal event of the French Revolution. The image is designed to draw the eye to Robespierre in the middle, one hand raised, the other on his heart as he takes the oath. David was close to Robespierre, and a powerful figure in the arts during the Revolution. Imprisoned upon Robespierre's fall from power, he would later ingratiate himself with Napoleon I and create for the latter his *empire style*. Debord shows Robespierre, then in close-up the political specialists beneath him, making their little deals on the quiet. Then he cuts to a woman and child in a window above, spectators at the making of history. It is the very form of bourgeois power which now has to be opposed, just as it is the form of its cinema that must be opposed. *Society of the Spectacle* and *Refutation of All Judgments* are about not just the clamor of images but also the silence of power, a silence which, since the seventies, has become deafening.

14 The Devil's Party

Fortune against envy; fame against oblivion.

Baltasar Gracián

"Shipwreckers have their name writ only on water."[1] Debord takes it to be Shelley's epitaph, but it is also Debord's. His last film, *In Girum Imus Nocte et Consumimur Igni* (1978), perhaps his master-piece, has an aquatic mood. The eddies and currents of the river as it flows into the sea are so many situations that form and dis-perse on its surface, to be replaced by others, and still others. *In Girum* has a slower rhythm, a more somber mood than *Society of the Spectacle*. The emphasis shifts toward a more fine-grained denuncia-tion of the colonization of everyday life by spectacular images of the commodified world.

Against this, Debord can only posit the remembrance of lost friends and the implacable onrush of a historical time, which will return no matter how much the spectacle denies its existence. Martine Barraqué: "And oddly, while working on the last film (what I am telling you is quite harsh, right?) I had the impression of working with a veteran of war. That he could not write anything else that was new — that everything kept turning round and round in the usual ways because he had already said it all."

In girum imus nocte et consumimur igni. The palindrome of the title means something like: We go into the circle by night; we are consumed by fire. If water is a figure for a particular quality of time, fire is another. The momentary conflagration, the clash of forces, the cavalry charge, or the fatal bullet which, Debord once noted, killed an uncommon number of his friends.[2] Fire is the other elemental time, and if we all are borne along by a liquid current, there are those few, those happy few, who are the friends of fire; the devil's party, orbiting the flame, like moths to enlightenment. By the time of *In Girum*, the party of fire is a diminished band, the everyday situation no longer seems quite so resonant with a wider historical current. In the disintegrating spectacle negation no longer works against it from without. All that remains is the spark of a memory, to be recalled, over and over, until it torches time again.

In Girum détourns scenes from movies as *Spectacle* does, and sometimes the same films, but to different effect. *Shanghai Gesture* appears again, but this time Debord chooses not Gene Tierney but Victor Mature playing Doctor Omar, who describes himself as "a doctor of nothing ... it sounds important and hurts no one, unlike most doctors." Doctor Omar even has the temerity to steal a line from the Roman playwright Terence: "I am a thorough-bred mongrel. I am related to all the earth and nothing human is foreign to me."[3]

He is the first of a series of characters appearing in *In Girum* who might be described as being of the devil's party, agents of deception and division. While Robin Hood and Zorro make appearances as rather more straightforward fantasies of redemption from within the spectacle, Debord is drawn to the more ambivalent and dangerous trickster figure. Robin Hood and Zorro uphold the true society against the false one. Like Censor's tract, the devil's party undermines the true and the false order alike by appearing to be in possession of the secret of the relation between them.

Most of the films détourned in Debord's seventies films are from his youth. A certain veiled autobiographical quality resides in them. Two seem to have particular resonance in this regard. Director Marcel Carné (1906–96) and screen-writer Jacques Prévert (1900–77) collaborated on two great films during the occupation, *Les Visiteurs du soir* (1942) and *Children of Paradise* (1945). Carné and Prévert were leftists before the war. Drawing from Surrealism and popular cultural forms, they were leading exponents of a style sometimes called poetic realism.[4] Their wartime films were big productions, sanctioned by the pro-Nazi film apparatus, but were neither Nazi propaganda nor simply coded resistance allegories. These films and their makers fell rapidly out of favor with postwar audiences and taste-makers alike. It didn't help that Arletty, who stars in both, was accused of collaboration. (Arletty: "My heart belongs to France, but my ass belongs to the world.") These films later became a particular foil for new-wave filmmakers such as François Truffaut. That Debord would borrow scenes from them in 1978 comes with more than a few layers of significance.

Debord ignores the narratives and discards most of the major characters. He concentrates on the character of the Devil from *Visiteurs* and of Lacenaire from *Paradise*. "I come from far away. Forgotten in his own country, unknown elsewhere, such is the fate of the traveler," says the Devil. He is the principle of division, the agent of historical time. Of the comrades of his youth, Debord will say they were "people quite sincerely ready to set the world on fire just to give it more brilliance."[5] Or as the Devil says, "I dearly love fire! And it loves me." In *Visiteurs*, the Devil sends his emissaries, Dominique and Gilles, into the world to create division through a little gender-queer sexual intrigue. As Gilles sings: "sad lost children, we wander in the night." Or as Dominique explains the game: "Other people love us, and they suffer for us. We watch them and then we go away. A fine journey, with the Devil paying the expenses."

"I declared war on society long ago." From *Paradise* Debord takes mostly the character of Pierre François Lacenaire (1800–36), a real historical figure, the criminal-poet-philosopher, who was the model for Raskolnikov and fascinated many writers from Stendhal to André Breton. In his *Memoirs*, Lacenaire wrote, "I come to preach the religion of Fear to the rich, for the religion of Love has no power over them."[6] The Lacenaire of *Paradise* says to some uncomprehending bourgeois: "It takes all kinds to make a world — or to *unmake* it." Later he will pronounce his own panegyric: "I've become famous. I've pulled off a few little crimes and created quite a sensation." Like the real-life Lacenaire, he would have preferred a literary success, but will settle for lasting infamy. "I have no vanity. I have only pride," he says. If, as Adorno says, "every work of art is an uncommitted crime," then to Lacenaire every crime is an act of commitment. Or as Vaneigem says of Lacenaire: "Intrinsic to the logic of an unlivable society, murder, thus conceived, can only appear as the concave form of the gift."[7]

In Girum concerns itself with the world after a series of failed revolutions: France 1968, Italy 1969, Portugal 1974, Italy again in 1977. The flaming moment has passed. The camera holds steady on still pictures of everyday life invaded by the commodity. Debordian insolence is replaced by contempt. But if anything the pathos of the power of memory as the half-life of life itself, the distillate of lived time, is all the stronger. The small-mesh interpersonal aspect of such a project has its stand-ins, such as Doctor Omar, Lacenaire and the Devil.

The large-scale historical moment has its stand-ins as well. From the otherwise appalling *Charge of the Light Brigade* (1936), Debord selects the famous scenes director Michael Curtiz made of the charge itself. From *They Died with Their Boots On* (1941), Raoul Walsh's truly fantastic version of the life of George Custer — another film much used in *Spectacle* — Debord takes the scene of Custer's last stand at Little Big Horn. The cavalry charge is a particle of the combustible moment of historical action. The charge is to coarse-grained events what Omar, the Devil and Lacenaire are to finer ones.

"History advances with its bad side first," as Debord détourns Marx and Engels from the *Holy Family*.[8] Representations — whether art or literature, cinema or song — are where the situation of lived time goes to die. They are the backwash of exhausted forces, which, in exhausting themselves, make the times otherwise. The seventies are a time in which all such forces appear spent. The charge is over, and it is not so much that the good guys lost, as that the fulcrum of conflict, the principle of division, disappears.

The eighties will be a time when the ruling class goes on the offensive again. But its victory is its undoing. Pursued to its limit, the spectacle undoes itself, and in so doing will create the conditions under which the party of fire might appear again, and the critique of the society of the spectacle in acts will reappear, dragging its theoretical understanding along, belatedly, behind it. It is as memory that failed moments of historical action have their other power. Cinema, and the spectacle in general, does a good job of subsuming and defusing the qualitative. It cannot abolish it. The spectacle is haunted by what negates it. Or so Debord seemed to think at the time. In the nineties his mood grew darker.

The police found his friend dead at the wheel of his car in an underground parking lot, with four bullet wounds in the back of his head. No money was taken, only his identification papers. In his pocket was a scrap of paper with the name 'François.' Gérard Lebovici was an agent and producer in the French movie business. The Nazis killed his mother in the camps. When his father died, he had to give up his ambition to be an actor. In 1960 he founded his own management agency. He was radicalized by 1968 and by his wife Floriana, née Valentin. In 1969 he founded the publishing house Champ Libre, which republished Debord's *Society of the Spectacle* in 1971.

Debord denied having any editorial role at Champ Libre, but as his relationship to Lebovici became close, it did start to produce something like a Debordian canon, which grew to include editions of Carl von Clausewitz, Baltasar Gracián, George Orwell, Karl Korsch, and Debord's own translations of the poetry of Jorge Manrique. The filmmaker Olivier Assayas, for whom Champ Libre was something of an education, best captures its qualities: "I remember, I was twenty when the Champ Libre reissue of the *Internationale Situationiste* bulletins came out in 1975. I was discovering Paris ... In Champ Libre's catalogue, even if Debord denies it — there resides something that emanates from his thought ... The unique feature of Champ Libre's editorial project was to have provided an extension of Debord's ongoing dialogue with the works of the past, with the nebulous mass of intellectual and poetic affinities that he increasingly expanded, conjuring in his texts and in his films the shades of writers who, from across the centuries, were his intimates, on the same level as his brawling and drinking companions ... At a time of fearsome ideological puritanism, Champ Libre published classics of political science, but also works that nobody had read for ages ... I have never managed to consider Champ Libre as anything but an extension of Debord's work, publishing as discourse, not only because of what was published there, but also for the juxtaposition of texts that produced another meaning, legible to those who could and wanted to read it."[9]

Lebovici's assassination — there is no other word for it — in March 1984 set off an extraordinary wave of speculation in the French media. Debord documented this with a small book, in which he writes: "We know now what a modern society can do with a parking lot." *Considerations on the Assassination of Gérard Lebovici* (1985) was in part a tribute to his friend: "This century does not like truth, generosity or greatness. Therefore it did not like Gérard Lebovici…"[10] But it had more to say about Debord himself and his curious relation to the spectacle. The occasion was the insinuation by more than one media mouthpiece that he was in some way connected to Lebovici's death. Journalists identified themselves with the assassin, not the victim, and sought with considerable ingenuity to justify the killing. A recurring accusation, which Debord documents in his book, was that it was his friendship with Debord that somehow got Lebovici killed.

"Each epoch uses a particular vocabulary to exorcise the demons that plague it."[11] The eighties were perhaps transitional in this regard. Where one paper accused Debord of accepting "Moscow Gold," another connected him to his mother-in-law's Chinese restaurant, an alleged haven for Moscow's nemesis, the Chinese Communists. These were the old figures of the traitor, from a time when the diffuse and concentrated spectacles confronted each other, across the cold war divide, each internalizing the image of the other as its official enemy. Debord was also attacked variously as a guru, a mentor, a loner, a fanatic, an eccentric, an ideologue, a nihilist, an idealist, a demon, a pope and a terrorist.

Here a more recognizably contemporary figure of the traitor emerges. In the time of the disintegrating spectacle, the global commodity economy relies on Russian energy. The flow of cheap commodities is in the hands of the Chinese Communist Party. New enemies of the people are required. Enemies like Julian Assange, the hacker-journalist-cypherpunk, publishing secret documents on the internet which reveal what those in the know already knew anyway. This was enough to get him labeled a terrorist and—worse—for the *New York Times* to question his personal hygiene.[12]

In the news stories he fulsomely quotes, Debord appears as a shadowy and clandestine figure. He points out that it has become a crime to withdraw from the spectacle when it seeks one out. To remain indeterminate, unnamable, this would be the essential move of those who belong, knowingly or not, to the devil's party. The rumor that Debord *disappeared* after May '68 is based on the illusion that he had previously *appeared*. As Debord insists, "I have never appeared anywhere."[13] The spectacle equates the refusal of celebrity with terrorism. "The mere fact that I have not at all wanted to be around the dreary celebrities of the day would give me, if there were such a need, a sufficient prestige around those who have the unfortunate obligation of having to be around them."[14] Not the least of Debord's achievements was to appear in the spectacle only as its negation.

Two things in particular make Debord's relation to Lebovici appear unacceptable. The first is the gift. Lebovici gave Debord the means to live well, to write, to make his films. In 1983 Lebovici even purchased the Studio Cujas cinema, where Debord's films were the only ones screened, whether anyone showed up to watch them or not. As Martine Barraqué puts it, "people used to say that Guy Debord was Gérard Lebovici's *ballerina.*"

One of the more extraordinary documents of Debordiana is the *Contracts*, which codify the agreements between Debord and Lebovici's film company for *Society of the Spectacle, In Girum* and a film on Spain that was never made. While the first reads indeed like a contract, they become increasingly like a détournement of legal documents. In the last contract, for the Spain film, Lebovici gives and Debord agrees to nothing in return. It is if anything the negation of the contract. No consideration is offered in return for the gift.[15] Or rather, it is the very offering of nothing in return, except the explicit statement that nothing is owed, which permits Lebovici's gift to approximate to the state of being a pure donation.[16]

Debord once claimed the virtue of having "invented some crimes of a new type."[17] Principal among which was the refusal to appear within the spectacle on command. Where this tactic confers on most who try it nothing but obscurity, Debord succeeded in pulling off a uniquely anti-spectacular fame. This strategy was not without its dangers. To the state of a disintegrating spectacle, those who will neither stay in obscurity nor affirm the spectacle with their presence can only be categorized as traitors to the state. As the spectacle disintegrates, it grows far less tolerant of those who refuse it. As Gracián says, the state can counter almost any challenge to itself, but not mockery.

In November 2008 French anti-terrorist police arrested Julien Coupat (b. 1975) and held him for several months without trial. As a condition of his release Coupat had to surrender his passport and identity papers. He was the last to be released of a group that Interior Minister Michèle Alliot-Marie called *anarcho-autonomous*. The government failed to secure any convictions on terrorist charges. The arrests were triggered by the attempted sabotage of a high-speed train. A group protesting the transporting of radioactive waste in Germany had already claimed responsibility for the sabotage. Coupat described his imprisonment as "petty revenge" in the face of the complete failure of the police action that rounded up him and his friends. Giorgio Agamben: "The only possible conclusion to this shadowy affair is that those engaged in activism against the (in this case debatable) way social and economic problems are managed today are considered ipso facto as potential terrorists, even when not one act can justify this accusation."[18]

Just as the spectacle took Debord's refusal of its charms for a threat to its existence, so too with Coupat. "Anti-terrorism," Coupat writes, "contrary to what the term insinuates, is not a means of fighting against terrorism, it is the means by which it positively produces the political enemy as terrorist." This is not the least aspect that connects the Coupat affair to the Situationist legacy. Coupat wrote a paper on the Situationists while at university. He may have been a member of the *Tiqqun* group, which was not unfamiliar with certain figures who once moved in Debordian circles. He may or may not be one of the authors of a text called *The Coming Insurrection*, and which may be the real reason for his arrest. Coupat declares that "unfortunately, I am not the author of *The Coming Insurrection*, and the whole affair will end up convincing us of the essentially policing role of the author-function." He also notes that "In France one can't remember power becoming so fearful of a book in a long time."

Whatever its provenance, *The Coming Insurrection* is surely the first notable political text to pick up where the Situationists left off.[19] Published in the name of the Invisible Committee, it revives the glamour of the spectral party, the devil's party. It takes the refusal of existing power, and its attendant everyday life, as far as the rejection even of the so-called leftist versions within it. It takes it as given that even the ruling class has lost its way. It shows a keen interest in urban affairs, but sees this as a time in which the metropolis has all but engulfed its rural peripheries. The creation of a life in the cracks of the commodity form has to remove itself from its major achievement—the modern city. Hence the group that was arrested with Coupat were known as the Tarnac 9, after the small town of some three-hundred-odd inhabitants in the Limousin region where they ran a cooperative store. Like Debord, late in life, they had withdrawn from the space of the city, to contemplate it from without, to act upon it from without.

15 Guy Debord, His Art and Times

Reputation is more about stealth than deeds.

Baltasar Gracián

It was in the Auvergne region, just east of Limousin, where in 1992 Brigitte Cornand met Guy Debord. He was living in a house there, near the village of Champot, that Lebovici had bought for him. "At that time he was totally broke. He had no money," Cornand says. "Lebovici was shot in the parking lot. Then the wife said 'I keep going, giving you money,' then she died. She passed away two or three years later. Then immediately, no more money. They had the Champot place. So they went there and abandoned Paris because it was too expensive. Hard times, really."[1]

Cornand had been making video works about artists for the Canal+ television station. These were not documentaries, they were "artist films, like a story, like a poem."[2] She made one that détourned the text of *In Girum*, that "gave a perfume, a flavor of it." Via her friend Gil Wolman she wrote to Debord about it, and after it screened, Debord wrote back. When a book collector who knew Debord planned a trip to the Auvergne to see him, he took Cornand along, and at their initial meeting a possible collaboration was floated for the first time.

Cornand: "The idea was to describe a no-future situation. Something like that. He had the idea to show a very dark and very impossible situation for humankind, so he asked me [to find] a list of different extracts from news, and with specific dates, and after that the duration depends on the intensity of each segment. The idea was to make a film only with documents from the television networks." Not that Debord was much of a television watcher himself. "Through conversations he heard about things. He heard something." He would give Cornand lists with dates and subjects, and she would locate the television footage at the archives of the Audio-Visual Institute.

What distinguishes the Cornand video collaboration from Debord's film work is that it takes the freshly sprouting world of multichannel television as its theater of operation. Henri Lefebvre: "The reign of the global would also be the reign of a gigantic tautology, which would kill all dramas after having exploited them shamelessly." Writing in the sixties, Lefebvre thought this final stage of what he alternately called the Spectacle, the Great Pleonasm, and the Thing of Things, was a long way off. Yet it was a tendency to be feared: "It would be a closed circuit from hell, a perfect circle in which the absence of communication and communication pushed to the point of paroxysm would meet and their identities would merge."[3] Debord's last work, made specifically for television, indulged the possibility that this Thing of Things had finally come to pass.

There is no voice-over in *Guy Debord, His Art and His Times* (1995). The spectacle speaks for itself. Debord intervenes through title cards, over which plays the accordion music of Debord's contemporary, Lino Léonardi (b. 1928), from his settings for poems by François Villon. "The accordion means Saint Germain, the fifties," says Cornand. It is the sound of the provincial hoodlum descended upon Paris, among whom Debord counted himself.[4]

The first section, which is very brief, is about his art. Cornand: "For me he is not a filmmaker but an artist. We can see that in the film. People said *filmmaker* because he was using films, but in fact the films are very poetic, very rhythmic, totally personal, not at all a film like Hollywood or a documentary, it is not that. But at the time people were unable to say he was an artist, because he was in a circle of literature. You have different drawers for culture in France. You are put in one box." *Guy Debord* is now included in the boxed set of Debord's films.[5]

A bunch of French literary men discuss Debord's *Comments on the Society of the Spectacle* on a France 2 TV talk show. The most obviously odious of these, Franz-Olivier Giesbert, remarks that "it legitimizes violence," and that Debord "tells us democracy is breaking down … and yet one feels democracy is advancing all over. All you have to do is read the papers!" If this is the taste and judgment of public opinion, all the better to maintain one's distance from it.[6] What Debord avoided is precisely having to live amid such company. Whether it is a work of art or not, it is certainly not cinema, or anti-cinema. It is perhaps television, or rather anti-television.

The accordion plays. Blocky letters scroll: "Guy Debord has made very little art, but the little he has made is extreme." The graffiti "Never work!" is the first of these few art works. Also mentioned is *Howls for Sade* (1952). After Stéphane Mallarmé and the blank white page, after Kazimir Malevich and the white on white canvas, Debord's silent white screen is a fitting extension of extremity into a new form.[7] "Debord has since maintained the same indifference toward the tastes and judgments of public opinion. And he has been reproached for many other immoralities. In particular, for almost always having been rather interested when easy money was involved. Having regularly obeyed the principle, 'never look a gift horse in the mouth.'" It's a perfect statement of indifference to conventional taste and opinion.

Guy Debord contains the now standard Debordian panegyric to the comrades of his youth, in block-lettered inter-titles: "This fine band of hoodlums, his constant entourage, have also been a great influence on his excesses." Only this last tribute is briefer than any others, as if the memory of them was already slipping away. In between Ivan Chtcheglov (1933–98) and Asger Jorn (1914–73), Gil Wolman (1929–95) appears. Of all the comrades from Debord's early days, he was one of the most talented, one of the first to be excommunicated, and one of the last to be rehabilitated.[8] The efforts of this motley crew at not working compare favorably to a promotional film détourned later in *Guy Debord*, which extols the virtues of French prison labor—no absenteeism! Debord pays tribute to those who absented themselves, as much as it is possible, from the prison house of the spectacle.

"And now I will attempt to be as anti-televisual in form as I have been in content." The rapid edits of *Society of the Spectacle* give way to painfully long excerpts from television current affairs and news shows. Yet there is still a strategy to the relation between the détourned videos. A title card quotes Lautréamont: "I will write down my thoughts in orderly fashion, in a pattern devoid of confusion. If they are right, the first to come will be the consequence of the others. That is the true order."[9] The true order cuts video about the artists Christo and Jean-Claude, who wrapped the Pont Neuf in plastic sheets, with another on the disappearance of the Aral Sea, already two-thirds gone thanks to Soviet-era hydrological engineering. The failure of art and the failure of science are for Debord two sides of the same spectacular coin.

Guy Debord contains some truly disturbing images, of a kind rarely seen anymore, at least on American television. They are perhaps from a very particular moment in the unraveling of the spectacle, a moment when those who produced it as much as those who consumed it could watch agog at the spectacle of its own disintegration.

Before showing us lynchings, dead and dying children, nuclear disaster, or the no less terrifying remnants of contemporary art, Debord remarks that for journalists and media producers, such images are "an occasion to discuss in ethical terms about a deontology they might perhaps choose to impose on themselves in certain extreme cases: should such images be shown? Or why should one deprive oneself from showing them?" The Kantian duty of the journalist can only be one of exposure. No image can remain secret, only its reasons for coming into being in the first place remain outside the realm of appearances. The spectacle's categorical imperative is that the showing of something is always the highest good, and good without qualification. But this showing of the particular is the not-showing of the totality to which it belongs, a totality accessible only to historical thought and action.

Debord: "The professionals have all firmly concluded that nothing of the world's sorrows should be hidden. No bogus oversensitivity on the public's part should prevent one from broadcasting what one has the merit and opportunity to record; and even more so when, for once, it is something true. The *media* thus want to prove that they are, in every respect, intent to the extreme on showing the truth, and quite convinced that any detail, put under close enough scrutiny, is usually a perfect and unequivocal model of truth." Only the relations between such details remains a mystery. *Guy Debord* draw attention to the absence of such relations.

Here is a Japanese wrestler in her tiny apartment. She is a premonition of what labor will be like when everyone is the performance artist of their own ritual humiliation, not so much reality television as televisual reality. Here is an oil derrick drilling under the Arboretum of Versailles. No monument of history can withstand the production of value from the destruction of nature and culture. Here is the dynamiting of sub-Corbusian tower blocks, as if to vindicate at last the Situationist critique of them. "What has been built so badly must be demolished even faster." Here is acid rain in Bavaria. "We thought economy was a science; we were obviously wrong. We now know it would be neither the first, nor the last, of the *enemy's sciences* to prove itself deceptive."

Acid rain seems such a period pollutant, now, not the fashionable new pollution. A 2006 study by UCLA scientists found that Hollywood was responsible for sending 140,000 tons of pollutants into the air each year. Most of it came from the diesel emissions of trucks and generators, but the pyrotechnic explosions from special effects scenes were also a cause. An economist for the city advised against regulating Hollywood effluent: "There would be a risk because you have other states out there quite anxious to get a piece of the film industry."[10] In any case, movie-made smog is not a *cause célèbre* among movie-made celebrities at this time.

A brief historical recap on the spectacle of power from Hitler to JFK: "The *democratic* state has become stranger." The opening minute of French 24-hour television news channel, on the model of CNN. The spectacle has become baroque enough to produce its own in-curling commentary on itself, in *real time*. A man stands in front of a line of tanks near Tiananmen Square.[11] The old Soviet guard attempts a coup against Russian president Boris Yeltsin. Riots in Haiti, Algeria, a woman attacked as she flees through a street market in Somalia: "The unverifiable world." An astonishingly long extract from a documentary about the crisis in the schools in the immigrant suburbs around Paris. "The most modern developments of historical reality have illustrated very precisely how Thomas Hobbes thought man's life must have been before he knew civilization and the state: lonely, dirty, devoid of pleasure, dimwitted, brief." The same neighborhoods would erupt in riot and fire in 2005.

Some light relief: Arthur Cravan, Dada poet, boxer, deserter of several nations, nephew of Oscar Wilde, here in some rare footage being pummeled by a much smaller opponent. He fought the great Jack Johnson, the first black man to be world heavyweight champion, even if the Cravan-Johnson bout was something of a scam. Cravan is one of the enduring sources of the Debordian way of life: "The people I respected more than anyone alive were Arthur Cravan and Lautréamont."[12] Debord, who lived his whole life as if answerable to nobody, holds himself answerable to the friends of Cravan and Lautréamont, friends he would lose with any slippage into mere official art or scholarship. And were he to lose such friends, how could he console himself with any others?

If there is a false friend to Arthur Cravan, to what matters about Dada, it is Daniel Buren, who became something of an official artist in the years of the Mitterrand presidency. In *Les Deux Plateaux* (1986), Buren replaced a parking lot at the Palais-Royal with two levels of striped columns, of varying height. Debord has the cheek to compare them to a barcode. The art historian Benjamin Buchloh, after a quasi-Debordian take-down of what became of the avant-garde, offers this apologia for a related Buren work: "Quite unlike recent examples of public monumental sculpture, which pretend to have solved the contradictions between individual aesthetic producer and collective labor conditions, reflected in the transgression of their work from individual sculptural unit to the monumental structures bordering on architecture, Buren's work maintains these contradictions precisely because of its painterly decorative dimensions that dialectically negate the successful achievement of an architectural dimension of public space."[13] Or, in short, even a distinguished spokesman for the neo-avant-garde cannot do much more with it than champion its own acknowledgement of its failure.

But there is a more sinister side to contemporary art as the decoration of power. Shots of sculptures of sheep near the Cattenom power plant, which in 2005 exposed eight workers to radiation. "Nuclear power likes to be surrounded by its favorite animal. Magritte might have written: this is not a sheep." If this is the art that decorates French state power, what does it say for that power?

"Every time Bernard Tapie speaks of himself, one wonders what dishonesty he could ever have been reproached for." Tapie is one of a series of political figures who appear, mostly without much comment, but who are emblematic of a kind of secret history of the disintegrating spectacle. Bernard Tapie was a French businessman, politician and occasional actor, singer and TV host. From 1986 to 1994, he was president of the Marseille Olympic soccer club. He was minister of city affairs in the Bérégovoy government until his indictment for complicity in corruption and the subornation of witnesses. After a high-profile case he was convicted and spent about six months in prison. French politics is a curious affair.

News footage of the full state funeral for Socialist Prime Minister Pierre Bérégovoy. He died after being found in a coma with two bullets in the head. A coronial inquiry ruled his death a suicide. The second bullet was attributed to a *nervous reflex*. Bérégovoy was under investigation over a one-million-Franc interest-free loan by businessman and friend Roger-Patrice Pelat, who had died of a heart attack on March 7, 1989, less than one month after being found guilty in the Pechiney-Triangle affair. Bérégovoy's suicide came on the eve of the opening of a new trial concerning the acquisition of Triangle by Pechiney.

Was Bérégovoy assassinated? Curious similarities exist between his death and that of other figures close to Mitterrand, including: René Lucet, the head of the Social Security public health system, shot twice through the head on March 4, 1982; François de Grossouvre, Mitterrand's adviser, shot in the head twice at the Élysée Palace on April 7, 1994; and Pierre-Yves Guézou, responsible for a phone tapping scandal at the Élysée, found hanged in his home on December 12, 1994. The curious death of Gérard Lebovici seems less curious in such company.

ACT UP protests the indifference of the French state to the AIDS crisis. AIDS had a special resonance for Debord: "Immune defense is a thing of the past on earth." He offers instead his own philosophy of personal health. For those on the AIDS cocktail of drugs: "no drinking, no smoking. Are you kidding?" By early 1985, an American process to heat blood supplies to neutralize the AIDS virus was available to the French authorities, who instead decided to wait until a French product was ready. They continued to distribute blood knowing that the odds were that some was contaminated. A judicial inquiry acquitted Socialist Ministers Georgina

Dufoix and Laurent Fabius of all personal moral responsibility in the matter.

In Girum featured lovingly photographed images of the waters of Venice. But in *Guy Debord*, the river has become a raging torrent. A TV news video shows a caravan floating in flood waters and crashing through a bridge. Some holiday! Cut to a computer-generated image of an estuary landscape, where gleaming glass towers sprout. Having demolished the worst of the tower blocks that once housed the working class in the seventies, in the nineties a new vertical landscape will flourish. It's the same old sub-Corbusian blocks of raw concrete, only this time with a *high-end* kitchen and a veneer of marble in the bathroom. The landscape that disorganized labor refused is now the chosen habitus of the spectacle's young favorites—bankers, lawyers, media execs.

Near the very end, images of François Mitterrand, clutching the red rose of socialism, as he commences his inauguration. *Guy Debord* has already shown the murky venality into which the Socialist government descended, vindicating Debord's refusal to join the more ambitious '68-ers in playing bit parts in that regime. And at last, bringing up the rear, Bill Clinton jogging in the streets of Naples, in town for the 1994 G7 summit, some years before anyone had thought of using such summits as sites of confrontation with a now post-national spectacular power.[14]

In January 2006 boatloads of armed Ijaws overran a Shell oil facility in the Niger delta and took several hostages. World oil prices ticked up briefly on the news. In February they seized a barge and took more hostages, blew up an oil pipeline, a gas pipeline and a loading terminal. In June they took over a rig forty miles out to sea and took yet more hostages. They called themselves the Movement for the Emancipation of the Niger Delta (MEND). An American journalist describes meeting some of them: "One was naked except for his ammunition and a pair of dirty white briefs. They had painted their faces with white chalk to signify purity, and they had tied amulets around their arms and necks and foreheads for protection from bullets." MEND runs its network on cheap cellphones, plastic speedboats and guns bought at floating arms bazaars with ransom money that the oil companies vigorously deny paying them.

The people of the Niger delta scratch out a living from fish caught in its polluted streams. They have no clean drinking water. A MEND member who goes by the name of Brutus: "This is modern day slavery." Sometimes there's no electricity for days. A Shell employee and former MEND hostage observes from the safety of an oil industry compound: "This is obscene. They are looking through the fence at golf courses and tennis courts where the floodlights are on at midnight." Says MEND spokesperson Jomo Ghomo: "We are not communists, or even revolutionaries. We're just extremely bitter men."[15]

São Paulo is one of the favored capitals of the disintegrating spectacle, where money goes to frolic, managed from the computer terminals of shiny high-rise towers, unfettered by regulation or taxation. One weekend in May 2006, a wave of bombings, burnings and shootings hit the city. It wasn't a riot, a revolt or a revolution, but something else. Anonymous people came out of the crowd and set fire to buses and banks. They didn't loot, but they did kill around forty police officers.

The May attack was the work of the PCC, or First Command of the Capital, a network of autonomous cells funded by the drug trade, which controls the inmates of most of Brazil's prisons and extends into the favelas as well. It made no demands. "It denied the government the power to even concede." The attacks just stopped. Nobody knows why, although one rumor has it that the state eventually agreed to provide PCC inmates with flat screen TVs on which to watch the World Cup football matches. The police retaliated with death squads in the favelas and killed over four hundred.

The PCC started out as a prison football team. After killing a rival team, it morphed into a prison gang. Then it became adept at using cellphones to manage itself and became more like a swarm. Its members swear allegiance to a sixteen-point manifesto, the last of which declares "we will revolutionize the country from inside the prisons, and our strong arm will be the Terror of the powerful." Like MEND, the PCC became, for millions of slum dwellers, the law, a substitute for the state in the state's absence.[16] *Guy Debord* is an intimation of this world, a world no longer all that novel or interesting, and so mostly unremarked, where the criminal, the political and the entrepreneurial become identical within the spectacle.

Near the start of *Guy Debord* is a shot of a page from Debord's early work *Mémoire*, a work composed entirely of détourned phrases, including this one: "The organization of the words that produces a discourse transforms things within the world order by way of an action on the consciences: both the one that frames it as well as those who receive it. It is the breach through which a moment of eternity is consumed in a world that darkly rolls to its loss." Debord follows this text with the fragment "How far are we." It's a neat summation of what remains of the Letterist method of his youth, even in late Debord. The moment of eternity, the moment of fire, which sparks amid all that is borne away on the current of time.

The execrable language of his century is that language of the edit, of the organization of pre-existing units, be it of images, sounds or words. In *Guy Debord*, Guy Debord and Brigitte Cornand show the power of the method, one last time. *Guy Debord* screened on Canal+, together with *Society of the Spectacle*, *Refutation of All Judgments* and *Latcho Drom* (1993) by the Algerian-born Romany filmmaker Tony Gatlif (b. 1948), who like Debord enjoyed the patronage of Lebovici. Debord put his affairs in order, then shot himself in the heart.

16 A Romany Detour

When your opponent sees into your reasoning like a lynx, conceal your thoughts like an inky squid.

Baltasar Gracián

When François Mitterrand became president of France in 1981, it appeared for many on the left as if the seeds of May '68 had finally flowered. Debord was not convinced. This was not the longed-for entry of socialists into the state, but the final entry of the state into the Socialist Party. In other words, it was a faded repeat of the final colonization of the Italian Communist Party by the Italian state in the late seventies that Sanguinetti so elegantly exposed. The spectacle was changing form. The diffuse and concentrated spectacles gave way to the integrated spectacle, which combined some attributes of both. The definitive response to May '68 would be the spectacular incorporation of the signs of leftism into the state as a tactical measure. While leftish intellectuals enjoyed a brief honeymoon with the new government, Debord chose to absent himself from the scene even more.

He spent more time out of Paris. From 1981 to 1987 Debord summered in Arles. Perhaps it was at Arles that he became acquainted — or re-acquainted — with Gypsies. The region around Arles has many connections to Gypsies. The nearby town of Saintes Maries de la Mer is home to Sara, patron saint of the Gypsies, around whom there is a famous celebration every May. The popular band the Gypsy Kings formed in the early eighties out of musicians whose families fled civil war in Spain and settled around Arles. While this would hardly be the kind of Gypsy culture that would appeal to Debord, it is a spectacular residue of the significance of Arles in Gypsy life.

Born in Shanghai in 1941, Alice Becker-Ho met Debord in 1963. Her father was in the German Navy, but he deserted. He was from the border province of Alsace-Lorraine and considered himself French. He became a banker in Shanghai but was obliged to move his family to France when the Maoists arrived. Alice came in contact with Debord through hanging around the Socialism or Barbarism group, with which the Situationists were in dialogue at the time. They were married in 1972.

"Guy married me so that I could have the benefit of his work if ever he died or went to jail," she told Debord biographer Andrew Hussey. "We loved each other and sometimes we loved other people, but we had no respect for the institution of marriage."[1] And sometimes they loved the same things. Such as the Gypsies, avatars of everyday life outside of property and the bourgeois family. The Gypsies would be the subject of the first of a remarkable series of books Becker-Ho would later publish. The Gypsies are an evocative figure in many ways for a way of life outside the spectacle.

The Gypsies call themselves Rom and call everyone else Gaje. Here they will be called by the name Gaje give them—and not always kindly—Gypsies. Debord writes in *Panegyric*: "The Gypsies rightly contend that one is never obliged to speak the truth except in one's own language; in the enemy's language the lie must reign."[2] This reads like a détournement of a passage from a famous book about them, by an even more famous author. Jan Yoors (1922–77) writes in *Gypsies*: "In Romani they said, 'Tshatshimo Romano' (The truth is expressed in Romani). It was the Gaje who, by forcing the Rom to speak a foreign language, made the Gypsy lie. The Rom said, 'Mashkar le gajende leski shib si le Romeski zor' (Surrounded by the Gaje the Rom tongue is his only defense)."[3]

Yoors should know: by his own admission, he ran away from home at the age of twelve to live with Gypsies, and did so on and off for many years. The British made him an agent during the war with a special mission to liaise between Gypsies and the Resistance in occupied France. Later he moved to New York, established himself as an artist working in tapestry, and wrote books about his adventures.

On Yoor's account, the Rom are active perpetuators of the myth of the Gypsy. "They created an aura of fearful superstition around

their race, convincingly pretending to possess mysterious powers
… Gypsy men and women were conscious of the image they projected, and amongst themselves they joked about the fear they
inspired in the Gaje." Their gift to the Gaje would be exoticism,
romance, nostalgia, dreams, longings, mystery. But all this would
be carefully managed appearances.

Yoors sums it up in this story, which he presents as told to him by
a Rom elder: "whenever the representatives of authority wanted to
interfere with Gypsy affairs, the first step was to capture and incar-
cerate their King, in the belief that this would destroy the Gypsies'
social organization, being convinced that the King was the fierce
autocrat they were led to believe him to be—whereas in fact life
went on much as before with the exception of the foolish and fooled
King." The Rom have no kings, but the appearance of having kings
could have its uses: "there are lies more believable than truth."[4] One
could say much the same about Debord, *King of Situationism.*

It isn't hard to see what might attract Debord's attention in
Yoors' story. There is a certain unspoken subtlety about it. Perhaps
the Rom deceived Yoors as they deceived other Gaje, merely giving
him the impression of unfettered access to their culture. Perhaps
Yoors did really belong to the Rom community, but was really not
so able to free himself from the Gypsy image of themselves that the
Rom project upon the Gaje for their own benefit. Perhaps Yoors
belonged to the Rom, but in writing for Gaje, adopted their prudent
policy of mystification.

Yoors' account is premised on a certain strategy in which the
playfulness of language directed at power shields something quite
different: a language that is not playful at all, but discreet, even
clandestine. This presents something of a double bind: Is his book
a truthful account of deception or a deceptive version of the facts?
Interestingly, where Yoors writes of the Rom, Debord writes of
Gypsies. Yoors apparently reveals secrets; Debord frankly has
something to hide.

The Rom approach to everyday life might have much to recommend it to Situationists, or Post-Situationists, if there is such
a thing. Yoors presents them as a federation of autonomous *kumpania.* Relations between kumpania were renewed from time to
time with ritual celebrations, gifts and by inter-marriage. Each

kumpania is a fluid association, always gathering and scattering as new alliances form and old relationships expire. They may dissolve at any time by mutual consent. There is no political superstructure. Rom justice is decided by the *Kris*, which may meet when necessary to settle contractual disputes or breaches of the conventions of purity.[5] It is a striking account of the conditions of possibility of life outside the state.

The law of the land is not to be transgressed so much as finessed. Yoors does not deny that the Lowara kumpania, among whom he lived and traveled, had their own distinctive approach to private property. "Stealing from the Gaje was not really a misdeed as long as it was limited to taking basic necessities, and not in larger quantities than was needed at that moment."[6] Many a chicken that crossed their path ended up in a Romani pot. Wealth is for spending, not accumulating. "Communism and capitalism alike were merely reflections of the foolish Gaje's fixation on the accumulation of things, which in time enslaved men."[7]

For the Lowara, Gaje were to be outwitted, but not needlessly provoked. As the Romani proverb has it: "it is easier to milk a cow that stands still."[8] Yoors contrasts them to another kumpania who were caught up in a vicious cycle of hostility from Gaje which prompts the Rom to aggressive thieving, which in turn provokes more Gaje hostility. This allows Yoors' to contrast his *good* version of the culture with a *bad* one, which impeded the Gypsies' ability to live off the land and move freely. "Above all it was their mobility which spared them. They did not fight back; they simply moved away."[9]

Slovenia seems, in the early twenty-first century, to have escaped its past and become a suburb of Europe. Even in the little town of Ambrus there are new cars in the driveways, kitchen renovations. Yet this is where townspeople allegedly surrounded the house of the Strojans, a Gypsy family, shouting, "Kill the Gypsies!" The Strojans hid out in nearby woods for five days. The locals claim their house was built without permits, even though the Strojans have lived there since the sixties.

The interior minister said that the Strojans would not be allowed to return to their house, but that the government would find them a new one elsewhere. When Slovenia's human rights ombudsman raised the matter with the Council of Europe's human right's commissioner, the Slovenian prime minister accused him of "denigrating Slovenia's name."[10] Borderless Europe may if anything be a harder world for the Gypsies today than the bordered one of the thirties about which Yoors writes. Debord: "One cannot go into exile in a unified world."[11]

Yoors' Lowara are indifferent to the ownership of property that does not have immediate use, but they do love a lavish party. The *patshiv* can occur whenever different kumpania meet and are occasions for grand displays of generosity that bring respect to the host. "A patshiv must convey good will to one and all, without exception: the most humble on such occasions must be treated as kings."[12] Yet the Rom are not the libertines of Gaje legend.[13] Yoors describes a rigorous set of ritual obligations, an elaborate concern with separating the pure from the impure, and a distinctive mode of justice. They only appear to the Gaje as disorderly, as the Gaje cannot comprehend that they have a different rigor.

The Gypsies may outwardly acknowledge the God of Islam or Christianity to appease the Gaje. More recently, Saint Sara, the patron saint of the Gypsies, seems to fascinate the Gaje more because some see in her worship traces of ancient rituals the Gypsies have brought with them from India.[14] But for Yoors, the Gypsies only really honor the *Mule*, or ancestors. Interestingly, the Mule are not eternal. The Gods of the ancestors live on only as long as they are remembered. Yoors' Gypsies are an oral culture, passing on strategies for negotiating life through elaborate forms of storytelling and everyday proverbs, not a few of which deal with ways of outwitting Gaje.

The procedures of the state are likewise both accepted and flaunted. For instance, the surnames invented for official documents were often ribald jokes, unintelligible to Gaje in any country but good for a laugh among the Rom. A Romani riddle runs: "A white meadow, some black ewes—they talk continually as they go by, but they don't recognize us." The answer: a document.[15] The Rom appear in written records as Gypsies, but that appearance is a strategy for maintaining as much scope as possible for autonomous action.

Yoors experiences Rom autonomy through the quality of time in everyday life. While bound by rigorous codes and enduring hardship and danger, Yoors finds with the Rom a certain quality and intensity, which collapses, when he writes of it, into banalities. "To the Rom life was an endless flow, like a torrent without form or goal, beyond good or evil, and man's place in it was like a process of self-definition, forbidding the all too human cowardice of weariness and doubt. With a driving urge to seek out what was elemental in life, man was free to react in his own way to its challenges, be what he could make of himself. This was his freedom."[16]

This sounds more like warmed-over Jean-Paul Sartre than the Rom speaking, as if they lived without the *bad faith* of doing things because they are supposed to, were happily *condemned to freedom*, and other existentialist commonplaces. Nevertheless there is something here that points to a reading of Yoor's Gypsies as constructors of situations out of whatever they can borrow as they detour through a world which, in Yoors' time, is already passing into the spectacle.

THE PRINCES DO NOT GIVE UP. This was the graffiti, quite possibly written by René Viénet, that during May '68 earned the Situationists the respect of Tony Gatlif. The Rom might be without a king but the men at least think of themselves as princes. Gatlif came into the same patronage orbit as Debord when he sought Lebovici's help in finishing his first feature film, *The Princes* (1983). Its setting is the same extra-urban transitional zones that so fascinated the Impressionists, only now it is a post-industrial landscape in decline. The factories are closing. Nara, a Rom who no longer wanders, makes a living of sorts stripping valuable scrap from abandoned workhouses.

Nara is harassed not only by the police and by Gaje but also by his daughter, mother and estranged wife. Gatlif's narrative is male-centered but hardly flattering. His women characters all comment on and delimit Nara's aggressive sense of self. A red Mercedes appears bearing three princes in gangster-sharp suits, who turn out to be his wife's three brothers. Nara spurned their sister, and they would kill him for this, only she confirms what is in Nara's eyes her offense: she let some social worker persuade her to go on the pill. Romany women exist in Nara's world to bear children. "You live like our grandparents. You haven't changed," as one of the princes says to him. His own mother claims she lost fourteen to the Nazi camps.

Only the world has changed. Nara has only one sickly white horse, which at the start of the film stands tied up outside a crumbling housing estate. He doesn't get much of a price for it, and returns home shortly after with a TV set. The spectacle is beyond the range of things he can turn to his advantage. Throughout the film he finds odd-jobs, gets out of scrapes: "We don't beg, we *take*," as he says. But he can't finesse the journalist who comes to take down his story.

There's a certain satisfaction in the scene where a tourist takes his picture and Nara responds by beating the crap out of him. The viewer feels the guilty pleasure of taking Nara's side in the attack while knowing at the same time that to view the film at all is to take part in the spectacularization of Rom life that the film both admits and yet tries to finesse. Like Yoors, Gatlif plays at revealing and concealing, seducing and refusing. It's a translation into cinema of what Alice Becker-Ho calls the *language of discretion*. For while not much may remain in the lees of the disintegrating spectacle, there may still be codes of conduct for those in the know.

17   The Language of Discretion

The consummate person—wise in speech, prudent in deeds—is
admitted to, and even desired by, the singular society of the discreet.

Baltasar Gracián

At a Nicaraguan school for the deaf, founded in 1977 under the
Somoza dictatorship and expanded by the Sandinistas, teachers
noticed that students were ignoring their Spanish lessons and were
instead developing their own system of signs for talking with each
other. This discreet language has been developed further as older
children pass it on to younger ones.[1] While this is a remarkable
achievement, the Gypsies kept their clandestine language alive
across and beyond Europe, and for more than half a millennia.
In *The Princes of Jargon*, Alice Becker-Ho quotes the great Dutch
historian and Situationist favorite Johan Huizinga: "It is not surprising that the people of Paris should have believed in the tale of
the Gypsies, who presented themselves in 1427 … They came from
Egypt, they said; the pope had ordered them, by way of penance for
their apostasy, to wander about for seven years."[2]

The story about the pope is a fabrication, a manipulating of what
Yoors would call Gaje appearances. Yoors is cited more than once
in Alice Becker-Ho's *The Princes of Jargon*, but her book has a different purpose. She argues there that Romani language is one of
the sources of the linguistic tactics of the dangerous classes—their
jargon, argot, slang or cant. This in turn she claims accounts for the
origins of far more words in French and other European languages
than conventional linguists credit. She follows in the footsteps of
Marcel Schwob, the symbolist writer, friend to Oscar Wilde, uncle
to Claude Cahun, and Schwob's pioneering Gypsy etymologies.[3]

Where it is respectable to look for the imprint left in language by the great cities of Greece or Rome's powerful empire, Becker-Ho embarks upon a counter-etymology, looking for the traces of those who resisted the state with their own kinds of clandestine organization. Gypsies have "elected to confront the world with ancient weapons (slang, word magic, tribal spirit). To put it succinctly, their history, their memory and their 'writing' are wholly contained in their language which is a language of struggle."[4] They set the standard for discreet uses of language, even of the common tongue.

This might apply also, for example, to the slang of late-nineteenth-century homosexual subculture that Wilde embedded even in his most popular plays. *The Importance of Being Earnest* means one thing to the bourgeois theater audience and quite another to men who earnestly seek unmentionables with other men.[5] Whether it is a question of hiding in a distinct language, such as Romani, or hiding in a jargon made out of the common language, such as cant, it is a tactic for creating a unity of thought and life within and against the language and the power of the state.

Becker-Ho: "The gypsies are our middle ages preserved: dangerous classes from another age."[6] As they traveled across hundreds of miles and hundreds of years, the Gypsies fell in and fell out with other marginal groups, few of which lasted as long or ranged as far as they did. They are the continuous thread through the counter-history of living outside states, faiths and territories. In modern times they become the most persistent of those dangerous classes who constitute themselves through an act of refusal: "You are not born dangerous class. You become so the moment you cease to acknowledge the values and constraints of a world from which you have broken free: we are basically referring here to the necessity of wage-labor."[7]

The Coquillards are one example of organization among the dangerous classes which Becker-Ho thinks borrowed linguistic tactics from the Gypsies. While lacking their elaborate oral culture, the Coquillards included among them the literate. While not above highway robbery, the Coquillards included tavern clerks, capable of forging charters and decrees or passing as pilgrims, and not without some success, at a time when, as Huizinga says, "doubt and rationalistic interpretation alternate with the blindest credulity."[8]

The Coquillards are the dangerous classes' version of the kinds of guild organization that in the late middle ages came up against the rise of individualism and the commodity form.

The legend of the Coquillards remains because they numbered among them the poet François Villon. He made them famous, not least with his *ballades* in the Coquillard jargon. While there is no lack of learned commentary on them, some details remain obscure. Villon's English translator writes: "These poems are notoriously resistant to decipherment (and, some readers may think, scarcely worth the effort required)."[9]

One ballade in jargon includes the lines: "Companions in living it up / keep on taking white for black."[10] Does this refer to counterfeit coins, or does it refer to which road to take to avoid the law? The Coquillard Colin de Cayeux and his associates get their due in Villon's more respectable "Testament." "You handsome lads, you stand to lose / The loveliest rose that's in your crown."[11] Unable to talk his way out of a jam, de Cayeux hung for his crimes.

In *Panegyric* Debord will use Villon's tribute to de Cayeux and other lost children as a *memento mori* for Ghislain de Marbaix, a somewhat shady character whom he knew in his youth.[12] But with the passing of the Situationists, Debord and Becker-Ho sought a discreet way of passing on a certain knowledge of how to use language to organize an inside and an outside to being within the spectacle, which is perhaps of even more interest as this spectacle disintegrates.

True slang, like that of the Coquillards, is minoritarian and centripetal; it is coined for particular use, and uses whatever swims into its orbit. Fake slang is spectacular and centrifugal; it issues from the media and ripples outwards. Becker-Ho: "The slang of times past and its usage signaled one's membership of a particular world. Nowadays people harbor illusions that they are in touch with a host of different worlds."[13] The spectacular circulation of slang allows respectable people to drop into conversation jargon from prison, drug dealing and so on. Becker-Ho: "A language wrought of ingenious tricks, devised for its own use, is today being co-opted by the world which is diametrically opposed to it."[14] True that.

Slang was once an elusive language, of value to a quite select company. Lacenaire: "a thief who doesn't know the slang is nobody."[15] The opposite of fashionable coinage, slang had a quite different purpose. "Nowadays, due to the fact that poetry is no longer practiced, some people think that they can detect it anew in slang, where the share of poetry remains small. Metaphors are to slang what the image of the Gypsy is to the Gypsy."[16] The second term in this parallel, Gypsy/slang, is not the truth of the first, metaphor/image-of-Gypsy. It is rather its secret. The problem with contemporary slang—and poetry, and theory—is that it no longer has anything to hide.

Giorgio Agamben: "Gypsies are to a people what argot is to language."[17] From Becker-Ho's research he derives a larger principle: "We do not have, in fact, the slightest idea what a people or a language is." One of romanticism's least helpful notions was that of the identity of a language and a people. This alleged identity becomes the legitimating ruse of the modern state. The state claims to be founded on language that it has imposed upon its peoples by force. Only by breaking the nexus of people and language can praxis and thought undo the seamless appearance of the state.

Even at the elementary level of the word, sometimes even of the particles of sound, language is détournement, a borrowing of borrowings. Becker-Ho: "Who does the borrowing from whom of a word itself on loan?"[18] The very concept of a loan-word presupposed that language is somebody's property. Argot is then not a language but rather a particular series of techniques that can be used on any linguistic material. Agamben: "All peoples are gangs and coquilles, all languages are jargons and argot." This is where his otherwise pertinent essay over-reaches. While there is no people in perfect identity with a language that is its special property, it is not then the case that we are all Coquillards. It is only the case that we are potentially so.

Agamben misses the far-reaching implications of Becker-Ho's apparently modest study. Jargon, like any kind of language, is nobody's property, but the practice of jargon is part of a practice of life. Becker-Ho: "What comprises dangerous-class *nous* is the continual ability to detect who is on one side of the line or the other."[19] The Coquillards acquire it from the Rom; Villon acquires it from the Coquillards; Becker-Ho acquires it from the practices of all of the above. To practice language as argot, and thus to undo the apparent identity of language and people, takes a certain discretion.

Creating and sustaining a secret language is an acquired art. It is not a quality that can be claimed to dignify, say, the treatises of professors of philology. The jargon of academics is a quite different practice to that of the Coquillards. Academic jargon does not produce a different relation to the world. Becker-Ho: "On the contrary, it defends and reinforces a world based on the division of labor by protecting the privileges of a caste, extending their protection even to the words the latter uses."[20]

In the disintegrating spectacle, argot is likely to proliferate, but in the favelas and refugee camps rather than the lecture halls. "Slang is making a comeback with the creation of as many ghettos as there are cities still standing."[21] This is where Becker-Ho locates the possibility of that language which Debord characterized as "the language of contradiction, which has to be dialectical in form as well as in content."[22] Argot is the language of negation, where words can be turned to show an opposite or complimentary meaning.

Becker-Ho proposes an approach to language that is at odds with both the objectively scientific and the subjectively poetic. Language is conflict, ruse, strategy. Linguistic discovery is not innocent of power. Michel Foucault is drawn to the study of language as power, identifying, classifying, ordering and authorizing; Becker-Ho sides with those for whom language can only be a ruse or a trick. She insists that these marginal and excluded language practices have their own coherence. "It is essential to be able to distance oneself from ordinary social values as well as from the vocabulary that their expression requires."[23] From the point of view of power they can only be defined negatively, as *resistance*, whereas to Becker-Ho they have their own secretive forms and practices.

In 2003 Swiss courts agreed to hear a case brought by a coalition of groups representing the Gypsies against IBM, subsidiaries of which they allege "helped the Nazis automate the Holocaust."[24] Whether the company is responsible or not, it is certainly true that the Nazis used Hollerith machines sold by an IBM subsidiary to tabulate census data and manage the logistics of transporting people to the camps. A similar claim by Jewish survivors was dropped amid negotiations with Germany and Switzerland over compensation.

Gypsy groups say that Gypsy survivors and their descendants, who number about 1.2 million, have been left out of these compensation agreements. Already in the thirties, when Yoors traveled with his beloved Lowara, the document was getting harder to dodge. The "ancient weapons" of the Gypsies may be no match for computerized logistics, but a new breed of cypherpunks may carry on the language of discretion into the new world of code.

Writing in the nineties, Becker-Ho was prescient about the influence of computerization on language, a *big data* project receiving considerable investment at the time. She is particularly scathing about linguists who imagine that having access to a vast digitized corpus of a language will answer all their questions about linguistic origins and use. She does not see the incorporation of language into the archive on this granular level as a neutral fact of merely scientific interest, but nor does she reduce its possible effects to a question of control. Becker-Ho: "All this will bear mainly on the definition of new property rights, whence those 'considerable' economic interests since realized by Google."[25]

If the problem was once the illusion that a language was the property of a people, the problem may soon become that language is the very real property of particular private interests. Take the example of the activists who convened a conference on *radical media*, only to receive a cease and desist order from a media company that has trademarked the name @radicalmedia and thus claims a rather exorbitant proprietary right over the very concept.

By stepping outside the *panoptic* of power, Becker-Ho also steps outside its forensic approach to the marginal. The language of the dangerous classes is not to be freely exposed to just anyone. "If there is a game with words, and to an even greater extent a game going on with their meaning, the real truth lies elsewhere, for the use of the initiated, of those who have already chosen sincerity."[26] What might outwardly appear as a playful approach to language is a ruse designed to shield a relative stabilization of meaning for other purposes. Becker-Ho: "In slang, the indisputably poetic element within it must be situated after, not before its formation … Poetry's route is through culture, slang's is through deception."[27]

Which is why "the playful content increases the further away one gets from serious matters."[28] By the time it becomes modern poetry, playfulness has forgotten its original purpose. "This form of playful diversion (or *détournement*) gives that popular and good natured character to slang, thus helping to mask the latter's primitive technical aspects and at the same time toning down its savagery. The weapon that others have used turns up here with the primer removed; we are left with the game, the contest of words, the release of pent up energy."[29]

Considered as an interiority, as a caché for discreet significance, slang has no author, and no authority. It is not creative or spontaneous. It is not playful for its own sake. It is poor in ideas but abounds in synonyms, as these are a useful way of stabilizing a pattern of terms which can be understood by those in the know. For example, when the Coquillards speak of *marriage*, they have in mind not nuptials, but the noose. Slang is an artificial language meant to be unintelligible to certain people. It doesn't change much or too quickly until it loses its underpinnings in clandestine use. "Slang is language disguised."[30] The more a clandestine group needs to fight and to hide, the more elaborate becomes its slang.

Here is where Becker-Ho also takes her distance from those like Julia Kristeva who focus on the exterior qualities of the poetic and playful attributes of language, and make this exteriority a radical resource in itself.[31] It is the case that in its early days the Situationist International valued poetry as the *anti-matter* of the spectacle, but by this they always mean not just Lautréamont and Fourier but also the wildcat strike.[32] They did not imagine avant-garde poetics, which draws attention to the perverse productivity of language, as an analogy for labor in general. In any case, what is distinctive about the whole Situationist and Post-Situationist project is that it is a certain poetics that it wants to make instrumental. They make use of modern poetry as a resource in the same way the Coquillards used what they could glean from Romani language practices.

As Becker-Ho writes, "the closed realm of slang, encompassing a discreet language and the community that speaks it, has been a continual source of inspiration for many writers past and present."[33] Debord, for instance, uses the words *cave* (sucker) and *baron* (stooge) in *Comments on the Society of the Spectacle*, and in *Panegyric* writes a whole paragraph in the jargon of the Coquillards as a way of gesturing toward his own use of a language that both perpetuates his own appearances and yet has something to hide. Debord chooses to write in a language "generally accessible to those in the know."[34]

Becker-Ho may as well be speaking of Debord's own use of language with her elusive remark that "Historical knowledge allows those things that ought not to be explained in too much detail to be nonetheless presented in the light most appropriate to them."[35] A historical knowledge, in turn, of the language of the Gypsies and the slang of the Coquillards might be a discreet way of describing certain silences in Debordian languages.

Debord's paragraph in Coquillard jargon might these days be his most easily understood. Becker-Ho quotes the writer Pierre Mac Orlan, a longtime Debord favorite: "The last few years have seen argot become an academic jargon destined for little use outside the Sorbonne where candidates in cant studies will thereby be adding a new jewel to their crown. The crown in question here though is no longer the one made of roses that Master François [Villon] referred to whenever a housebreaking would prompt celebration in verse of the chaplets of roses sported by 'his fine lads' from Montpipeau ... Language, whether in the form of argot or of the pure, time honored classical variety, cannot hold out against changes in social conditions, above all when changes are of the type we are presently experiencing."[36] Now that there are scholars of Coquillard, not to mention of *Situationism*, it may be time for another tactic. Debord makes use of what one might call the irony of the spectacle: that a classical written language becomes something like a secret language, outside of the spectacular language both high and low, of left and right.

Debord and Becker-Ho's strategy with language is in the end one of participating in a broad front of practices that make language discreet, which allow it to separate out an internal from an external sense. In a world so devoted to useless exposure, this might be something of an achievement in its own right. "There is in the very use of slang a sense of unadulterated pleasure that already comprises a first result: in the act of poking fun at the uninitiated, it is already in itself a deception, fully the first step on the road to deceit and the initial satisfaction thus engendered. Moreover, there is nothing peculiar to the dangerous classes about this, since it is a feature of any jargon that goes hand in hand with a class consciousness."[37]

In a world that so values the *public intellectual*, who has conceded in advance to be part of the spectacle, there might be something to be said for the *private intellectual*, whose interests remain separate from it. Private here would not be in the sense of the domestic, the familial, the home or bourgeois private property, but rather a discreet kind of sociability, a different and undisclosed code. "I must take care not to give too much information to just anybody," as Debord says. Certain pages will need to be interpolated into his writing, like the secret codicils of certain treaties.[38] The private intellectual is at the same time the *public idiot*, speaking an idiolect known to some but not all.

It may seem strange that Debord and Becker-Ho would celebrate both François Villon and Niccolò Machiavelli, given that one was a thief and the other a secretary of state. They at least had in common that they were both tortured, even if for rather different crimes. In the end, the writers that matter embody strategies, either in the service of the state or against it, and there is something to learn from both. While Machiavelli has his followers, Debord and Becker-Ho's project is a rare one in so thoroughly refusing to identify itself either with the existing state or with the ideal state so beloved of reforming intellectuals. Clément Marot wrote in 1533: "As for the jargon, I leave its correction and exegesis to Villon's successors in the art of the crowbar and the hook."[39] Debord and Becker-Ho's exegesis hewed to different but no less ancient tools.

18   Game of War

> The trick is to know what cards to discard.
> Baltasar Gracián

"We play an effigy of war, and battles made like / real ones, armies formed from boxwood, and play realms, / As twin kings, white and black, opposed against each other, / Struggle for praise with bicolored weapons."[1] These are the opening lines of the 1527 poem "Scacchia Ludus" by Marcus Hieronymus Vida. That strategic genius, in any field, is the only thing worth commemorating is a characteristically Debordian note. The word *effigy* might appeal to Debord in its modern sense, given how careful he was to preserve his bad reputation.[2] But here it might mean something else: that the game is a form, a mold — an allegory, perhaps — for a certain kind of strategic experience.

One of the strangest entries in Guy Debord's bibliography is the 1987 book in which he and Alice Becker-Ho record the rules of the board game Debord designed, variously known as the *Jeu de la Guerre*, *Kriegsspiel* and *Game of War*. The bulk of the book is a move-by-move account of a game between the two of them. *Game of War* is first mentioned in Debord's writings in 1956. In 1977 Debord entered into a partnership with his then-publisher Gérard Lebovici in a company to make board games, of which it was to be the first. A craftsman was commissioned to make four or five sets in copper and silver.[3] On this account, the game was a part of Debord's life for more than thirty years.

Debord was not a casual gamer. As he writes: "And so I have studied the logic of war. Moreover, I succeeded, a long time ago, in presenting the basics of its movement on a rather simple board game: the forces in contention as well as the contradictory necessities imposed on the operations of each of the parties. I have played this game and, in the often difficult conduct of my life, I have drawn a few lessons from it — I also set myself rules and I have followed them. The surprises of this kriegsspiel seem inexhaustible; and I fear that this may well be the only one of my works that anyone will dare acknowledge as having some value."[4]

The record of the playing of the game is both a tribute to his enduring interest in strategy and a remarkable testament to Debord and Becker-Ho's relationship. As Debord writes: "the nature of our collaboration resides in the 'game of war' that we played."[5] Are not all relationships games? Played by more or less adequate rules, and with more or less cheating? As for who won this game, and whether there was cheating, some facts and conjectures will follow in due course.

Game of War is a strategy game, and to see this as a major rather than minor part of his legacy is to insist that above all else Debord was a strategist. Jacqueline De Jong: "He was a great strategist." Giorgio Agamben: "Once, when I was tempted (as I still am) to consider Guy Debord a philosopher, he told me: 'I'm not a philosopher, I'm a strategist.' Debord saw his time as an incessant war, which engaged his entire life in a strategy."[6]

Unlike the scholar, the strategist is not the proprietor of a field of knowledge, but rather assesses the value of the forces aligned on any available territory. The strategist occupies, evacuates or contests any territory at hand in pursuit of advantage. Where philosophers came of late to concern themselves with endless green fields of ineffable traces and immanent virtualities, strategists take their chances against mundane necessity. Debord: "The world of war at least presents the advantage of leaving no room for the silly chatter of optimism."[7] In this regard he is remote from Fourier, and perhaps even from Marx.

The avant-gardes have a long-standing connection to games. The Surrealists invented several. Marcel Duchamp famously gave up art for chess. He even coauthored a book about it. François Le Lionnais: "What [Vitaly] Halberstadt and Duchamp perfected was the theory of the relationship between squares which have no apparent connection, *Les Cases Conjugées*, which was a sort of theory of the structure of the board. That is to say, because the pawns are in a certain relationship one can perceive invisible connections between empty squares on the board which are apparently unrelated."[8] Like the Surrealists, Debord invented his own game, and like Duchamp, it took the form of a sustained effort to create via the game a conception of how events unfold in space, a "schematic representation of the overall agonistic process." Its ambition is nothing less than "the dialectics of all conflict."[9]

Game of War includes more or less plausible parameters of movement and engagement for infantry, cavalry and artillery. Besides the arsenals, two per side, *Game of War* also includes units for communication. With the possible exception of the communication units, it works in much the same way as classic nineteenth-century kriegsspiel, of the kind popularized in the training of the Prussian officer class. Debord claims his is modeled on classic war games and is consistent with the famous treatise *On War* (1832) of Carl von Clausewitz.[10] Its rules capture the essential movements of warfare from the time of Napoleon to the Paris Commune. *Game of War* is a détournement, then, but since what it plagiarizes is essentially an algorithm, a set of rules for a game, then the result is a little different from other instances of détournement. The distinctive correction Debord offers to an understanding of strategy comes out in the specifics of game play.

Debord's ambition seems to be to create a game which has possibilities for play that are as great as chess but which conceives of play in a different manner. As Alex Galloway writes, it is something like "chess with networks."[11] *Game of War* does not enclose space within strategy as chess does. Space is only ever partially included within the range of movement of the pieces. Some space remains smooth and open. The game is also subject to sudden reversals of fortune less common in chess. Debord: "In fact, I wanted to imitate poker—not the chance factor in poker, but the combat that is characteristic of it."[12] Each side makes its initial deployments in ignorance of those of the enemy, introducing at least an element of the unknown characteristic of poker.

The game requires attention to the tactical level of defending each of one's units, since once one starts losing them more pieces can quickly fall. However, units cannot move or engage unless they remain in communication with their arsenals, directly or via relays, making lines of communication particularly vital. Players are usually more concerned with breaking the adversary's lines of communication than with offensive action directed against either the adversary's arsenal or fighting units. Outside of the quantitative struggle between blocks of fighting units is a qualitative struggle, in which a force suddenly loses all its power when the enemy cuts off its communications; "thus the outcome of a tactical engagement over just one square may have major strategic consequences."[13]

Each player has to keep three quite different aspects of the game in mind: fighting units, arsenals, lines of communication. While attempting to maintain freedom of action, each side is also obliged to make difficult choices between qualitatively different kinds of operations, the means for the realization of which are always in short supply. One may have the means but not the time, or the time but not the means. "Each army must strive to keep the initiative, compensating for shortfalls in troop strength by the speed with which it can concentrate its forces at a decisive point where it must be the stronger: strategic maneuvers succeed only when victory yields an immediate return, so to speak, in terms of tactical confrontation."[14]

Among the particular qualities of *Game of War* is that it is not a territorial game. It does not conceive of space as property, to be conquered and held. Antonio Gramsci famously juxtaposed the concepts of the *war of position* and the *war of maneuver*. For Gramsci the war of maneuver is associated with syndicalist approaches to political conflict, with Rosa Luxemburg, and with the events of the October Revolution in Russia. He associates the war of position with mature Leninism and the lessons of the defeats suffered across Europe by the revolutionary movement that the October Revolution was supposed to spark. Gramsci: "In the East, the state was everything, civil society was primordial and gelatinous; in the West, there was a proper relation between state and civil society, and when the state trembled a sturdy structure of civil society was at once revealed. The state was only an outer ditch, behind which there stood a powerful system of fortresses and earthworks."[15]

For Debord this line of thinking can only justify the bureaucratic apparatus of the Communist parties and their obsession with creating one institutional bunker after another, from the trade unions to the official Communist art perpetuated by former Dadaists and Surrealists such as Tristan Tzara and Louis Aragon in their waning years. The Italian Communist Party pursued this war of position with particular vigor after the Liberation. Sanguinetti shows that all that resulted was the co-option of the party by the state. *Game of War* is a refutation of this whole conception of strategy. Debord: "This is a war of movement ... a war in which territory per se is of no interest."[16]

In their film disquisition on *Game of War*, the London-based Class Wargames group goes so far as to claim that "*Game of War* is Debord's answer to the political enigma of Bolshevism."[17] They read, or rather they play, *Game of War* as Debord's meditation on the 1917 Russian revolution, the signal event that shaped the times into which he was born, and which for Debord is a historic defeat of the revolutionary movement. It was through the militarization of daily life that the Soviet experiment degenerated into the concentrated spectacle. "Then as now, radical intellectuals had to ask themselves the key question: do they have the moral strength to resist the temptations of Bolshevism?" Class Wargames sees the four cavalry units as effigies of the Leninist vanguard party, "the new class of warrior intellectual." The cavalry pieces move the fastest, so they can quite literally function as the avant-garde, but this avant-garde is there to be thrown into the maw of time. "In this game, the players must learn how to make the best use of these elite troops on the social battlefield without becoming Bolsheviks themselves."

In the war of position, tactics are dictated from above by strategic concerns with taking and holding institutions across the landscape of state and civil society. *Game of War* refutes this territorial conception of space and this hierarchical relation between strategy and tactics. Space is always partially unmarked; tactics can sometimes call a strategy into being. Some space need not be occupied or contested at all; every tactic involves a risk to one's positions. "It makes sense to move against the enemy's communications, but one's own will be stretched in the process."[18]

Debord moves the conception of conflict away from the privileging of space that persists in Gramsci's war of position. Key to *Game of War* is the question of judging the moment to move from the tactical advantage to the strategic exploit. Tactics and strategy do not have a hierarchical and spatial relation, but a mobile and temporal one. Plans have to be changed or abandoned in the light of events. Debord: "The interaction between tactics and strategy is a continuing source of surprises and reverses—and this often right up to the last moment."[19]

Prussian *kriegsspiel* were often fought using actual maps of contested borders. *Game of War* offers a rather more abstract terrain. Each side has an L-shaped mountain range and a pair of arsenals, but in different positions. The asymmetrical board offers different strategic opportunities to the two sides, which are labeled simply North and South. Class Wargames: "Players who lack a profound knowledge of psychogeography will find themselves at a loss, while their opponents weave the disruption of the mountains and the bulwark of the forts into a more proficient command of the terrain as a whole." This asymmetry is perhaps Debord's way of encoding something key to Clausewitz's understanding of war, namely that the two sides in conflict always confront each other as something incommensurable. Calculation is clearly a key to Clausewitzian conduct, but he does not treat the world of war as a closed one in which calculation replaces strategic intuition.

Game of War is a rigorous and schematic presentation of conflict, if missing certain qualities. The spatial field is asymmetrical but unchanging. The moment of surprise comes only once, when each side reveals to the other the initial disposition of its forces. In documenting the playing of a single game for their book, Debord and Becker-Ho present each move on a diagram that outlines as a static figure the changing disposition of forces, but this gives no real sense of the ebb and tension in time of game play. Still, the ambition of documenting the play-by-play with these diagrams of *Game of War* is clear: "Before they went to the printers, the figures looked like a truly dazzling puzzle awaiting solution, just like the times in which we live."[20]

19   The Strategist

> Never reveal the final stratagems of your art.
> Baltasar Gracián

Debord is a strategist, not a philosopher. History is a matter of will, luck and calculation, of "the simultaneous consideration of contradictory requirements."[1] There is nothing ineffable or sublime about it. Here he differs from a great deal of modern leftist thought. Writing of the Iranian revolution, Michel Foucault declared: "The man in revolt is ultimately inexplicable."[2] Alain Badiou persists in an irrational fidelity to the event of Mao's Cultural Revolution.[3] When not admiring Robespierre, Slavoj Žižek dreams of repeating Lenin, who seems to cause him indigestion. While Foucault, like his friend Gilles Deleuze, prefers the ineffable revolt to revolution, Badiou and Žižek put their faith in the memory of great leaders, whose proper names seem strangely to occlude, not to say occult, thinking about historical time itself. In either case, leftist philosophers react against what Žižek calls "the reinscription of a revolt into the process of strategic-political calculation."[4]

But from whose point of view is revolt itself a lawless event, or a dissolute moment where the Real and the Symbolic have illicit congress? From the point of view of the priest—and the police. The movement of revolt is no exception to the fluid dynamics of historical time. Debord is quite clear on this: *Game of War* is a practice he found useful for the difficult conduct of the whole of his life. There is nothing ecstatic about *Game of War*, and that perhaps makes it the better legacy of the late twentieth century's lessons in action.

Strategic thought confronts the gap between the possible and the actual, without the silly chatter of the impossible intruding. Boris

Groys: "The irreducible, unhomogenizable, infinite, virtual empire of heterogeneities and differences is actually nothing but bourgeois pluralism without market losers, capitalism as utopia … a neo-theological opiate of the people."[5] Or more succinctly — Clausewitz: "there is a great difference between possibility and fact."[6]

Above all, Debord is not someone who ever went looking for this theological utopia in the moment of revolt. Such times are in a certain sense playful, but they aren't festivals, and still less sacred rites. The strategist's world is necessarily secular. The strategist enacts the gap between the known and the unknown in tactics. Debord: "Though the basic principles are certain, their application is always a matter of doubt."[7] To the strategist, unlike the philosopher, the event comes as no surprise.

While *Game of War* distances itself from the incalculable time of the romantic left, it also differs from the closed world of cold war strategy. This brought together advances in mathematics such as game theory, the modern programmable computer, and global surveillance and intelligence gathering, all in an attempt to rationalize strategic thinking. The fog of war would dissipate under the combined attack of a vast expansion in information gathering, computing power capable of analyzing this data with cool efficiency, and, above all, centralized command. The defense intellectuals who embarked on this path brought the specialized tools of social science to bear on problems of fighting the strictly spectacular war of nuclear deterrence.[8]

The ancestor of what becomes the dominant model of the defense intellectual was not so much Carl von Clausewitz (1780–1831) as his contemporary Antoine-Henri Jomini (1779–1869).[9] Where the former stressed the continuity between war and politics, and between calculation and intuition, Jomini treated war as a thing apart, a thing governed by ratios of *mass x velocity.*

Unlike Jomini, von Clausewitz has a supple sense of the array of facts that compose a situation and the difficulties they put in the way of action. Clausewitz: "In war, action is like swimming against the tide, where normal attributes are insufficient to achieve even mediocre results."[10] One difficulty is what we might now think of as the network of information relayed both to and from the front lines. In *Game of War*, Debord tries to capture the effect of tidal friction by allowing a limited number of pieces to be moved in each turn. No grand strategy can unfold all at once. While the pieces have different values, all must remain in line of sight contact.

Clausewitz writes of war as "a wonderful trinity, composed of the original violence of its elements, hatred and animosity, which may be looked upon as blind instinct; the play of probabilities and chance, which make it a free activity of the soul; and of the subordinate nature of a political instrument, by which it belongs purely to the reason."[11] For Clausewitz, the first element (instinct) is the people, the second (probability) is the General and the last (reason) is the calculus of state power. In cold war decision science, everything collapses into calculation. Where leftist philosophers take refuge in the incalculable event like the good humanists they somehow remain, the cold war scholars of the *inhumanities* delight in making history disappear completely into the algorithms of the rationalization of choice.

Clausewitz is famous for *On War*, which appears at times to distill military experience into axioms. But when he writes about actual campaigns, particularly those he witnessed, there is more subtlety to how he presents the situations of war. Here he is, for instance, on Napoleon's main strategic innovation: "Bonaparte was the first to risk everything on a single great battle. This use of the word *risk* does not imply that more would be risked than if the forces and actions were divided, for there can be situations in which dividing them could be a thousand times more hazardous than risking them in a single battle. Rather, it is a gamble because, forgetting all rational calculation, the human mind is reluctant to concentrate a decision of enormous consequence in a single moment, as a battle requires. It is as if the mind felt restricted by such a limited amount of time. A vague feeling arises that if only given time, additional strength from within would be found, all of which, if it is not based on objective facts but instead only on feelings, is just natural human weakness."[12] Here the situation is neither objective nor subjective, aleatory nor determined, rational nor irrational. All has to be considered at once, but yet with clarity and precision. By considering the subjective as an objective factor, Napoleon, as Debord observes, was able to "use victories in advance, on credit."[13]

The art of *Game of War* may lie in maintaining the properly

Clausewitzian dimension within which strategy operates, which is not susceptible to capture by the techniques of either poetics or mathematics. Debord's understanding of Clausewitz restores the *aesthetic* dimension, if one can call it that, of assessing situations and determining courses of action. Rather than Jomini meets the computer, Debord offers von Clausewitz crossed with their contemporary Stendhal (1783–1842).

In Stendhal's astonishing account of the Battle of Waterloo, the fog of war becomes a veritable shroud, and despite the fine weather. Our hero Fabrizio wanders about in the train of Marshall Ney, not even sure if what he is experiencing is an event at all, shocking though it is: "What he found horrible was a horse all covered in blood that was struggling on the ploughed soil, its feet caught up in its own entrails. It was trying to follow the others; the blood was flowing into the mud."[14]

Having believed all day in victory, Stendhal's army of Napoleon finally retreats in disarray, with many casualties, and among them obedience. Debord: "There is simply no way of obtaining cast-iron certainty as to what should be done, and this holds true even after crushing numerical superiority has been achieved, for there are circumstances in which a seemingly defeated army may still launch decisive actions against its opponent's communications."[15] Perhaps the strongest lesson Debord encodes in *Game of War* is that even the most powerful adversary has as a weakness the communication of the parts with the whole. The successful counter-attack is on communication, which is to say, on the *totality*.

The plane on which all the particular units move has its own temporality, in which mass and speed are bound in the kind of reciprocal relationship Jomini would have understood. The larger the mass one fields against the enemy, the slower it moves; the faster it moves, the smaller the mass. When a particular unit engages not another particular unit, but the line of communication, it touches instead on another plane. This other plane is the network of communication, where so long as the lines are not broken, communication is instantaneous and direct. As Class Wargames counsels players of *Game of War*: "if the coherence of their networks of communication breaks down, they will experience a kind of vertigo, whereby the stability of their psychogeographic perception is disrupted." Debord's dialectic of conflict steers the gamer toward the conduct of struggle on the plane of communication where cutting the lines can afford a quick victory. The plane of communication is the plane of the totality. Cutting communication disables not a particular unit but the network connecting units. The plane of communication is one of simultaneous and homogeneous time, or of what Debord in *Society of the Spectacle* (1967) conceives of as *spectacular time.*

So while it looks like its nineteenth-century ancestors, *Game of War* is also a diagram of the strategic possibilities of spectacular time. Debord: "The bourgeoisie has thus made irreversible historical time known and has imposed it on society, but it has prevented society from using it. 'Once there was history, but not anymore,' because the class of owners of the economy, which is inextricably tied to economic history, must repress every other irreversible use of time because it is directly threatened by them all. The ruling class, made up of specialists in the possession of things who are themselves therefore possessed by things, is forced to link its fate with the preservation of this reified history, that is, with the preservation of a new immobility within history."[16] This very totality of homogeneous time becomes at once the spectacle's great strength and its fatal weakness — its Achilles' heel.

One could add Debord to that list of modern figures who never quite got over Napoleon Bonaparte. His conquest of Europe is the breech that establishes the nascent form of the bourgeois state. His campaigns absorb the masses into history in their wake. Georg Lukács: "What previously was experienced only by isolated and mostly adventurous-minded individuals ... becomes in this period the mass experience of hundreds of thousands, of millions."[17] For Lukács, the lessons of this time remain in the great historical novels, those of Stendhal included, in which the bourgeoisie narrates to itself the relation between individual experience and historical totality.

Debord, whose *Society of the Spectacle* often reads like détourned Lukács, looks elsewhere here, to Clausewitz, not to Lukács, or Hegel, or Stendhal. Even though he pays tribute to that Stendhal who, as "second lieutenant in the 6th Dragoons Regiment in Italy, captured an Austrian battery."[18] Nor does Debord turn so much to Fourier as Vaneigem does. The form Debord chooses to memorialize the lessons of the great bourgeois epoch is neither philosophy nor the novel nor utopia, but the kriegsspiel. Not the legacy of the bourgeois scholar, artist or prophet, but that of the officer class.

Game of War also contests the popular legacy of the Napoleonic era in the world of games. Keith Sanborn: "Compared to its popular contemporary American formulation of Napoleonic warfare, the game of *Risk*, the Debord and Becker-Ho game is vastly more complex. In *Game of War*, evaluating lines of communication, geographical position, logistics, and the relative speed and strength of different units all factor into the outcome. In *Risk*, the meaning of geographical position is reduced largely to simple topological adjacency; the concentrated quantities of armies and their offensive and defensive coefficients determine the stochastic representation of their force. Dice are thrown and the final outcome of battle is then determined largely by the law of large numbers. Individual player intervention has fairly minimal effect. *Risk* is, thus, an historical reflection of the global outlook of cold war technocracy. The statistically oriented logistical bias of that outlook appears on the horizon of military history as a positivistic misreading of the construct of total war."[19]

This is the context in which to recognize the historical stakes at work in not only Debord's efforts to publish his game, but also the strange interest of the publishing house founded by his friend Gérard Lebovici in reissuing works by Jomini, but particularly by Napoleon and Clausewitz. Napoleon's maxims put alternating stress on the logical and sensory aspects of war. Clausewitz's account of Waterloo has the temerity to vivisect the mistakes of the winning side.[20] If there is a literature to which Debord aspires to append his own modest contributions, it is the strategic thought of those who, whether they had major or minor roles in it, and whether they were on the winning side or the losing, adjoined themselves to their specific historical moment.

Game of War likewise offers an understanding of conflict that, unlike *Risk*, draws on what might be called a certain style of *participant observation*. Curiously, *Risk* (1957) was also invented by a filmmaker, Albert Lamorisse. Whatever the merit of *White Mane* (1953) and *The Red Balloon* (1956), both of these noted children's films offer idealized and magical solutions to conflict, and reintroduce the theological dimension that Debord tries valiantly to exclude.

In a remarkable reading of Debord and Becker-Ho's account of a single game, Galloway makes two striking claims: That the unidentified player who wins the game is Becker-Ho; that the losing player, Debord, broke the rules. Galloway claims that in *Game of War*, optimal troop deployments have crystalline shapes such as lattices, ladders and crosses. "If a gamer is sufficiently experienced with the rules of a game he or she will learn the point of maximal exploitation and, since it is in his or her interest, will enact these techniques of optimal exploitation as often as possible." And that is what the losing side—South—does. South, Galloway asserts, plays as if they had intimate knowledge of the algorithm of the game and of the formations its rules favor. And yet all is for naught, for North out-plays South in the end. An ill and ageing Debord is outplayed by, and will be outlived by, his younger partner. In spite of his best efforts, he cannot outwit his times.

Morale is a constant theme in the writings of both Clausewitz and Napoleon himself. Something no calculation of *mass x velocity* can measure is the morale of the forces themselves. If there is a key to understanding the experience of a *situation*, it is that its openness to setting the course of events one way or another depends to an immeasurable degree on courage. The specific talent of the strategist is in assessing morale as much as in calculating the mechanics of circumstance.

Philosophy detracts from the strategist's art by excesses of both optimism and pessimism. On the one hand, its gay combinations of language make everything seem possible; on the other, its disappointment with the actual world leaves a bleak and metallic aftertaste. It is as if philosophy could do nothing but binge-drink on hope and bemoan its historical hangovers. Vaneigem: "Revolt has less need of metaphysicians than metaphysicians have of revolt."[21] The legacy of the Post-Situationists points toward something quite different, to tactics that might open toward strategies, starting from the most minor moments of the everyday. It is a low theory that moves from the everyday to the totality, rather than a high theory that institutionalizes the mere thought of extremes.

Perhaps the last word should be that of Alice Becker-Ho: "Need we add again, to that which we'd stated in the preamble, that all play is first and foremost free action ... is liberty? It appears the answer to this question is yes. This, at any rate, is what the preceding pages have attempted to emphasize. The finest players having been those who, free until the very end, conducted a game in which they themselves fixed the rules, guided by this virtue so badly perceived nowadays: loyal, before all else, to oneself."[22]

20 The Inhuman Comedy

Know how to forget. It takes more luck than skill.
                                                Baltasar Gracián

The spirit of American capital at its peak in the twentieth century can be summed up in the famous statement: "What's good for General Motors is good for America." In the twenty-first century, one might say, rather: "What's good for Goldman Sachs is none of your fucking business." The spectacle of disintegration no longer bothers much with keeping up appearances. It is as if, having realized that commodified life offers nothing of much value to anyone, that which might be of some use is to be withdrawn so that a few, a miserable few, might at least hoard its paltry splendors in the most extravagant fashion. It can't last, so why worry? Keynes had it almost right: In the long run we're all dead, and the long run itself is running poorly.

Which makes it all the more puzzling why critical thought has not seized upon the moment to at least offer a few glowing embers of clarity. But that would require a mode of thought as total as the inhuman comedy that confronts it. For that mode of thought to exist would require a coalition of practices in which everyday life could be brought to consciousness of itself in a language—whether earthy or rarified it hardly matters—which refuses the separate compartments of the intellectual division of labor and comports itself discreetly.

Perhaps the wrong turn was to pay too much attention to Louis Althusser, whose brilliant and seductive project had the dubious merit of making it possible to assume that one could practice critical thought inside the academy without confronting the intellectual division of labor that is the law of the land there. Althusser sliced the totality into separate instances: economic, political, ideological, each as *relatively autonomous* as the university departments that claimed one of these territories for itself. Each was to have its privileged technical terms and scientific techniques. Thus one could comfortably adopt the language of one's discipline but inflect it with a *marxisant* flavor, which itself becomes increasingly hard to savor.

In Althusser's world, this division of labor was presided over by a master-discipline, which naturally was his own—philosophy— that became a sort of police agent assuring that in each of the other levels the practices that obtained were intellectually lawful. Whether what is ventured is a concept or a practice, the voice that hails from the other side of the street or the back of the hall with a "hey you!" is that of the Althusserian. So much so that we internalize this philosophical cop in advance. It is by Althusser himself that we are interpolated. As T. J. Clark once noted, it is no accident of timing that Debord's *The Society of the Spectacle* came out in 1967, just after the start of the Althusserian boom.[1]

Just as the entry of the worker's parties into the state turned out really to mean the entry of the state into the worker's parties, so too with this entrist project in the realm of knowledge. We became what we beheld. Critical thought did not take over the academy; the academy took over critical theory. It became hypocritical theory, the bad conscience of the scholar who knows too much to take the game all that seriously. Obvious though this is, one is not supposed to admit it; this in itself becomes a barrier to thought.

Having, like Napoleon, crowned itself at the head of this empire of knowledge, what a dismal business philosophy ends up being! The philosophers have only interpreted the world, Marx said. And his would-be inheritors complete the thought thus: the point, however, is to interpret those philosophers. The philosophy of history becomes merely the history of philosophy. The ruthless criticism of all that exists is replaced by the apostolic succession, of great men succeeded by great men, as if this view of history had not been soundly exposed as fairy tales in every other domain in which it once prevailed.[2]

While hardly recognizing the sovereignty of philosophy, those other knowledges which attempt critique more often than not do so only in the language of their discipline, and direct themselves at that level of the totality over which their discipline claims proprietary rights. Thus the disintegrating spectacle finds itself confronted with fragments of specialized knowledge that cannot but think in the fetishizing terms of the disciplines that birth it.

The serious business of the critique of political economy continues, but it is usually a humorless affair, uncomfortable with just how fictional the business of business has become. Meanwhile, the political becomes the precious object at the center of a whole cult of discourse, rendering it impossible to ask the prior question of whether politics can really be said to still exist.

It seems the height of philistinism to quote that notorious fascist phrase: when I hear the word culture I reach for my revolver. These days what remains of the ruling class is quicker on the draw, not to mention trigger-happy. It requires no such pretext. Yet culture continues to be the magic kingdom in which most critical intellectuals spend their days. When we hear revolvers we reach for our culture.

Against all of which, perhaps a different path—or different paths—could be carved through the critical practices of the late twentieth century. But it requires some back-tracking to find the way. What Debord called "the repugnant seventies" appear as a turning point where battles were lost, where what appeared to be strategic advances turned out to be retreats into dead ends.[3]

Hence the backward <->> forward itinerary of this book. As a first step, a return to the bourgeois revolution as precursor, to open up the question of what is living and what is dead in the memory of it. Through the work of T. J. Clark, an aesthetic economy emerges, via the concept of spectacle, as a domain in which the two categories have to be thought together, grounded in a Marxist sense of class struggle, and one not severed from its anarchist double. But Clark himself ends up boxed in to the aesthetic as the domain of mourning for a lost art of critical practices.

And so: Vaneigem, who opens up toward the imbrication of the struggle in and against the spectacle more properly in everyday life. This also is the occasion for broaching the value of the utopian as a practice of the everyday, extending and permutating on its possibilities. Vaneigem rediscovers and revises Fourier's great discovery:

a language of the passions practiced as a totality that excludes the necessity of sacrifice.

In René Viénet, the Fourierist and Marxist critiques come together in comedic interventions in the struggles of his time, where earthy humor mixes with heretical critique. Viénet thought all Situationists should know the basics of film production. He advances a critical embrace of a technics; he thought and practiced outside of specialization and its professional guilds. Nothing could be easier in the twenty-first century, and yet this supposed democratizing of the means of communication usually lacks his historical sense.

Viénet also has the merit of his relentless attack on one of the great mythic recuperations of radical energy, the Maoist dictatorship and the civil wars it spawned. In the disintegrating spectacle, historical thought has declined so far that the fantastic legends about Lenin and Mao, long since exposed as spectacular doubles of genuine popular struggles, have resurfaced among would-be leftists in search of saints to venerate.

A more plausible story is found in the struggles of disorganized labor in Italy through the seventies and after. Sanguinetti provides a counter-history, and one that considers more closely what transpires within the ruling class at this time. The people make history, but the properties of that history are recovered by the more skillful agents of the ruling class and subsumed within the history of property, the closest thing to a history that can be officially acknowledged.

And yet the ruling class appears to have lost the ability to think historically.[4] This distinguishes the disintegrating spectacle from its predecessors. Having gone on the offensive, and had victories aplenty in its advance, the ruling class comes to believe its own legends. At the acme of its power we see the acne in its beauty.

Today's ruling class are such philistines that they collect contemporary art. They seem dimly aware that the joke is on them and gamely laugh along to pulled-punch lines they don't get. One has to admire the gumption of the gallerists who convince them to part with millions for such bric-a-brac. Even Jeffrey Deitch, one of the great carnival barkers of this art world circus, could be amazed to find a Courbet worth less than a Warhol.[5] This is not a great age for patrons.

In the overdeveloped world, the ruling class no longer sees the point of maintaining vast cultural and educational institutions for the edification of the masses, and whether by increments or sudden cuts, their state withdraws from them. There shall be no social practice for the evaluating of the world outside the market. It is quite possible that for those canny enough to search for a modus vivendi in this world, the editorial, curatorial and educational professions might no longer provide it. This leaves, as in previous ages, the art of seducing patrons. One has to admit: Debord had a talent for this; and Lebovici, in turn, had a talent for being talent's patron. Let his name not be forgotten. What a friend to his friends! He made of the profits of the spectacle itself a gift for something of far greater interest than mere art or literature.

Let us not get too carried away with substituting a rogues' gallery for the usual lives of the saints. There is a certain tactical use to be made of naming tavern clerks and vagabonds in the place of the great thinkers of an age. Above all, let's not hoist Guy Debord into the pantheon. That is why in *The Spectacle of Disintegration* he at least appears in the company of some supposedly minor figures. It's a gesture toward the proposition that what's of enduring interest is always collaborations, practices, situations, moments, forms of everyday life, not the great and their singular works. What matters in the end are not the proper names but the improper names, which announce that voice which can denounce this world.[6]

When the holy spectacle subsumes even the signs of its enemies into its nave of all knavery, when all other practices retreat to the margins, it is time for the devil's party. There's nothing that isn't in somebody's database, somewhere. While refusing the vanity of assuming that one is under surveillance by any agency of consequence, one should perhaps be a little discreet about what one says to just anybody. Socrates had a point when he suggested that the written word goes out like an orphan into the world. Some thoughts should be kept within that other family of those who adopt each other for the sole purpose of carving out quiet spaces for the practice of life.

And yet it's a great age for détournement. This is not the same as the remix culture that proliferates so wildly, working and reworking any and every fragment of text, sound or image. Détournement imbues such practices with a strategy that is quite distinct from their usual raison d'être. As Debord's late works in (anti)film and (non)television demonstrate, détournement has no particular style or flavor. It is rather a matter of connecting the fragments of spectacular culture in such a way as to reveal the absence of the historical trajectory which those fragments both embody and refuse. As Courbet realized with *A Burial at Ornans*, the means are present within the tensions of existing signs to construct a proxy for the destiny of which they protest their innocence.

If there are strategies of revealing that détournement proffers, there are also strategies of concealing, of which argot is an exemplar, as Alice Becker-Ho's researches show. A language made for everyone has nothing left of it but the dogmas and doxas that the spectacle leaves like used shopping bags in the corners of the everyday. A language made for anyone is something else, a language which conceals something of its intentions for those not in the know. A language for anyone, but not for everyone, conveys a subtle other sense for those who discreetly accept the principles of historical thought and action.

These days, the devil's party may be impossible to spot. Everything about them, like their language, looks at first glance like everyone else. Yet one knows from certain details just whom one is dealing with, if one knows where to look. The devil's party is not entirely anonymous. It works silently to create a certain seductive aura around a version of what it is in itself that deflects attention from what it is for itself. The key to which is the passions and their expression within everyday life. The knowledge the devil's party values is accorded no prizes, for it can only be valued otherwise.

The problem with politics is that one spends too much time on the phone. And to organize what? Sometimes it seems the intellectuals are the last to know. How else to explain the fascination with The Political just at that time when it has all but ceased to exist? Like a species of endangered owls, the philosophers hoot about The Political as if such a habitat still existed. The Political was always that aspect of the state most encrusted with ideological escutcheons. Better to turn to the discourse of strategy, which while hardly free from decorative effects, nevertheless is obliged from time to time to speak not of the emblem but of the shield behind it.

In the realm of strategy one finds in a more general form principles to be discovered via the practice of applied art and writing. On the one side is the folly of a free poetics, a great tumbling acrobatics in which anything seems possible. On the other side is a pure objective calculation, which relieves its functionaries of the necessity of decision. Professional life in the disintegrating spectacle is built on the separation of the two into distinct orders of discipline: the creative and the technical. Both are relieved of responsibility for action: the first by appeals to romantic authority; the second by resignation to objective functions. Strategy takes as its domain what lies between.

Strategy is part calculation and part inspiration, part objective conditions and part empathetic intuition. Its domain is the situation, which can be only partly known, but is not for all that a mystical event. Strategy is the ordering of actions within a situation that reveals its contours via a form of engagement. The disintegrating spectacle can get by just fine without the High Theories which would either poeticize or rationalize its totality, for the bitter truth is that it is a totality without either poetry or reason. But it cannot get by without strategies.

Perhaps one could, like Censor, apply oneself to the study of what strategy this ruling class ought to pursue if it were still capable of forming one. At the level of the individual firms and their contestations over the future of the commodity form, the disintegrating spectacle is a world of brilliant campaigns and honorable defeats. At the level of the aggregation of interests among the ruling parties via the state that might ensure the long-term survival of the world on which it feeds, this ruling class has failed the ultimate test, that of historical thought in action. What is at work in the world is the punning of history, the invention of ever-new slogans and brands for the inability of competing forces to find the terrain on which their conflicts could be resolved in a more capacious form. Perhaps because the forms for which history calls are finally those beyond the commodity itself.

The Situationist International dissolved itself in 1972. Let's call the various projects attempted after that by various former members Post-Situationist, in the double sense of coming after and yet still marked by and indebted to that which it succeeded. *The Spectacle of*

Disintegration attempts to pick up the threads of these diverse and incommensurable projects, to find what in them might speak to a world they allegorize and foreshadow but do not fully inhabit. Their ideas, it turned out, really were on everybody's minds, and their influence turns up, for good or ill, far and wide.

Let's pick up just two strands to mark where one might advance a critical project in their wake, and along quite different paths to the rut in which hypocritical theory now runs about. Let's conclude with one instance of a renewal of critical theory (which was also a practice) and one instance of a critical practice (which of course also experimented in new concepts). As an instance of the former, the journal *Tiqqun*; as an instance of the latter, Occupy Wall Street.

If there is a place where the Post-Situationist current was revived in an original way, it was in the two issues of the journal *Tiqqun*, which appeared in 1999–2000, and which challenged *Internationale Situationiste* in both style and substance, if not longevity. While in some ways *Tiqqun* was an advance, the Post-Situationists who precede them also provide certain correctives to *Tiqqun*. In the writings of *Tiqqun*, there is a slippage from revulsion against the party of the working class to revulsion at the working class itself. These new narodniks make of the dangerous classes a romantic image only, one no longer subject to the kind of street ethnography of which Debord—let alone Fourier—was once capable. There is a slippage also from the terrain of capital and spectacle to spectacle and police, and finally to an exclusive interest in the police—or in *biopower*.

Like the Situationists and Post-Situationists, *Tiqqun* sees the working-class movement as caught up within the styles and forms of capital. Labor became what it beheld. But their own trajectory is to advance, in negative, a whole mess of petit bourgeois desires. The stylish business, the select company, even the country house— all the trappings of petit bourgeois life—are rejected in *Tiqqun*, and yet leave their mark. Their *imaginary party* repeats the devil's party, with more footnotes and less discretion.

Still: if it is the case, as *Tiqqun* proposes, that the more doctrinaire Autonomists are just the idealists of the managerial class, then it is also the case that the Situationists became the fantasy other life of the so-called creative class.[7] If the Post-Situationists are a corrective to some of *Tiqqun*'s foibles, *Tiqqun* in turn is a corrective gift in return. It is not unlike Clark's anarchist-Marxist dialogue, transposed to another time and conjuncture.

One of *Tiqqun*'s lesser-known works provides a real extension of Post-Situationist thought: the critique of the figure of The Girl. Here they advance onto the terrain of the critique of the overdeveloped world on its own terms, as if taking that sage Situationist advice not to hanker after the garb of situations past. For is it not the case that hypocritical thought is still traumatized by the past, and not even the past of 1968, but the past of the early twentieth century?

Between them, Žižek and Badiou on the one hand, and Hardt and Negri on the other, seem to repeat the debates of the inter-war period: The Leninist party without the popular front; the popular front without the Leninist party. The Great War, the Russian Revolution, the jazz age and the Great Depression seem to constitute the locus of several breaks with bourgeois thought's self-regard. The left-Heideggerians can only manage a melancholy remembrance of the most hideous consequences of this sequence of events.[8] Out of the shards of a fracturing order they claim only the most grisly: the Nazism of the camps and the terrible vision of those philosophers attracted like moths to the flames: Ernst Jünger, Martin Heidegger, Carl Schmitt. Meanwhile, the psychoanalysts seem puzzled by the "decline in symbolic efficiency" that comes after the inevitable eclipse of the father figures who supposedly stood above it all, not least the declining efficiency of the invocation of father Freud himself.

It's true enough that the Situationists had their version of this period, alighting instead upon the Kronstadt rebellion and particularly on the Spanish Civil War. What they attempted to salvage from the wreckage was critique in action. They built their critique on the lessons learned from the defeat of the Spanish Revolution, and on the limits to Surrealism's intuitive and impassioned critique of colonialism. In this age of the Lesser Wars and the Lesser Depression, the early twentieth century might indeed offer up some avatars for a renewal of critical thought. Not perhaps the Surrealism of Breton and friends, but of more marginal figures like Claude Cahun and Mina Loy.[9]

It is time to draw together a thread from this *Spectacle of Disintegration* that has so far eluded a coherent critique. One finds it in the split between Pissarro's peasant women and Manet's shopgirls. It reappears in both Debord and Viénet's films as the split between the image of The Girl that they détourn from popular magazines and pulp movies, and the words they appear on screen to voice, like ventriloquist dummies. Mina Loy and Claude Cahun saw her coming and tried to speak otherwise, from everyday life rather than from this cool abstraction. Vaneigem acknowledged that the whole spectacular order rested on the struggle for which she was a body double.[10]

Little sister is watching you. She stares out at you from billboards, magazines, screens large and small. Behind the production of her image is not some quirky dictator and his nervous minions, but a small army of stylists, hair dressers, photographers and, of course, models.[11] Whole industries exist to find and groom actual bodies who might embody this abstract, ultimately philosophical figure, who is one of the central modes of the contemporary world of images. She has a privileged place within the spectacle. She won't send the secret police to kick down your door in the middle of the night, but she might send you to the mall to get new shoes—and quite possibly in your sleep.

The Girl hasn't much to do with actual women, although women might or might not feel obliged to mark their distance from her. The Girl is not even necessarily female or even all that young. Sometimes men's bodies or older bodies populate the images that constitute her. She isn't always white. She isn't always human. Sometimes she is a robot or a cartoon or a flower. The norms around which she gravitates are geometrical.

The Girl is the marker of the success and the failure of feminism. Like most social movements, its gains come at the price of a certain incorporation into the very order it opposes. The women's liberation movement begat, as an unintended consequence, *girl power*. Tiqqun: "The supposed liberation of women has not consisted in their emancipation from the domestic sphere, but rather the extension of that sphere over the whole of society."[12]

It is not the factory that was extended across the social domain, but the boudoir. Life in the overdeveloped world is not a social factory, but a social boudoir. It even extends itself into the workplace, which now harbors rituals of tact and gestures of politeness that could be worthy of Vienna and the Dancing Kid. In the overdeveloped world, labor became affective labor. Politics became family drama. Art became interior decoration. The struggle over the remaking of the form of social life became kitchen renovation.

It's not that women are to blame for any of this, although a certain misogynistic tendency might have it that way. Rather, it is that the image of The Girl becomes the emblem through which this modification in the world of images is managed and felt. That modification of the world of images corresponds in turn to an extension and modification of the spectacle. The demise of the concentrated spectacle lays the groundwork for the supersession of Big Brother by the little sisters. She first surfaces in the diffuse spectacle, but puts paid to her rivals only after the integrated spectacle starts to disintegrate. She is the figurehead nailed to the prow of its disintegration.

The omnipresence of The Girl only shows that the legend of the intimacy of woman with nature has found a new home, that of second nature, or the spectacular world of finishes and veneers. The Girl's utopia is domestic, but the domicile of the domestic is imagined as the whole world. The Girl makes every scene an interior, as if any place in the world could be made her private domain by her presence.

Her power to create this domain is her beauty. She is sequestered in her own beauty. A certain moralizing tone in contemporary discourse holds somewhat paradoxically that beauty is only skin deep and at the same time what matters is really inner beauty. But, like the Greeks, the world of the contemporary spectacle regards beauty as having both spiritual and philosophical import. Debord: "what is good appears; what appears is good."[13] The good that appears — beauty — is outside of time. Experience, ageing, memory — in short, history — is not to appear. Time is marked out by the structural permutations of the fashion cycle.

The Girl is quite naturally not just about beauty but also about sex. Or rather, she is about sexuality, a sexiness detached from any particular sex act. Sexual liberation did not free people to have sex in all the Fourierist permutations. Rather, sexual liberation liberated sex from people. It even liberated sex from the human. Ever since Manet's *Olympia*, The Girl has had an embarrassing relation to the specifics of sex, not to mention the specifics of money. She is not supposed to be locatable in any particular intercourse of either kind. The Girl is about *seduction* more than sex.[14]

And yet there is a certain nobility about The Girl which is not supposed to be questioned. She stands, as embodiment of beauty, on the one side for venal seduction, but on the other for romantic love. Love is the last unquestionable ideology of the disintegrating spectacle. After the death of God comes the death of the oedipal father-figures who are His stand-ins, including Big Brother. No third term mediates any more between the self and what appears to it. Yet romantic love lives on. Pop songs still speak endlessly of it, declaring their loves to "you, you."

The Girl is only partly there as the object of desire, as stand-in for the commodity. *Tiqqun*: "The Girl is the dominant social relationship, the central form of the desire of desire, within the spectacle."[15] As Kojève parses Hegel: I don't desire the other as a thing. I desire the other's desire. Or to translate that into pop: "I want you to want me / I need you to need me." The Girl is a commodity that appears to desire its acquirer. Or rather, she might desire us. The suspension is key. The universal and eternal seduction projected by The Girl might or might not alight specifically on us. She is available to be available, but she isn't cheap: "Because I'm worth it!"

One could read a lot of hypocritical theory and not find any mention of The Girl, or any of the other handful of figures who populate the disintegrating spectacle and do the work—or something like it—of all the Holy Fathers, Big Brothers and Fraternal Functionaries who used to populate it. Debord and Viénet's films appear transitional in this respect.[16] Which is why, to go forward, the best way is to go back, back at least to the Post-Situationist moment, when everyday life was still the ground of an attempt at the critique of the totality, expressed in acts.

Speaking of acts: On September 17, 2011, a small band descended on Zuccotti Park, a little square of concrete planter boxes in downtown Manhattan, and declared that they had "occupied Wall street." They hung on long enough for it to turn into a situation that, if not on the scale of May '68, at least gave the ruling class something to think about.

Organized labor got involved. Labor has been in retreat for decades in the overdeveloped world, so mobilizing ten thousand people, as they did on October 5, 2011, is something of a rearguard action. Still, it is unusual for New York, if not for Paris, and at least seemed to confuse the police for a while. So I want to end *The Spectacle of Disintegration* with some notes, tentative though they are, recorded from the occupation. I have kept them in the present tense for reasons that will become obvious.

The confrontations with the police usually get the most attention, but they're not the only thing going on at Occupy Wall Street. I went down to Zuccotti Park at about 9 p.m. on Wednesday, October 5, 2011, after putting the kids to bed. I was alarmed by stuff on the Twitter feed that telegraphed incidents of contact with the police but which were not clear about the location. I wanted to make sure our park was still there.

Just off the subway, and heading down Church street, I catch a glimpse of a march going north, up the street parallel to the east. I see a mass of closely ranked bodies and banners and hear some vigorous chants. I'm not sure where they'd be going, as Wall Street is to the south. I decide to keep going down Church to Zuccotti Park and maybe catch up with that group later.

I hear the park before I see it. At the western end, about a hundred people are chanting, singing, dancing, banging on drums. I hang out with them for a while. This crowd is young, fun, and a bit crusty. The financial district is usually so dead after working hours. Even the idea of a party at night here is something.

It is hard to work my way into the park. Piles of stuff are arranged around the planting beds. Mostly disassembled tents. The police are pretty clear that they will not tolerate "structures" without a permit, and apparently a tent is a "structure."

A young man lies flat on his back in a sleeping bag. I narrowly miss kicking him in the head on my way by. He looks exhausted, as do a few others in sleeping bags that I find in the west end of the park, just past the drum circle at its westerly end.

Under the sound of the drumming is the thrum of a generator. A small knot of young men crouch around it, powering up devices. Most of the signs of organized activity are east of the crumpled tents and random sleepers. Knots of people cluster around tables dedicated to one function or other of keeping the park running.

Here was where I find people you might think of as "anarchists," if only in the sartorial sense. People who have some experience at self-organization. Otherwise the crowd is mostly dressed like any other crowd of college or post-college age young people in New York City, although here and there you find older people as well.

A young woman explains what is "problematic" about the occupation to two friends, and allows me to listen in on their conversation for a while. There are a lot of small groups talking amongst themselves. A man in a business suit raises a red and black flag while talking to another man in a track suit and hoodie.

A woman smiles at a man sitting on one of the stone benches. She parts her thighs and plants herself on his lap. He kisses her; she kisses him back. Her hands are in his hair. I thought of that line in Raoul Vaneigem about those who go on and on about class struggle without speaking of love. They speak with a corpse in their mouth, he says.

An older group, earnest, weathered, holds up signs about class struggle so that the TV crew on the southern side can see them. They do not have the curious, expectant, hesitant look of some of the younger people. Not everybody finds all this so surprising. As René Viénet put it: our ideas are on everybody's minds.

At the eastern end of the park is a group, about the same size as the drum circle, who prefer to chant slogans. They are standing tightly packed in an oval, doing call-and-response chants of the popular memes of the occasion.

It strikes me as curious how the park is polarized between these two ambiences: the drum circle at one end and the chanters at the other. The drum circle understands the place as something like a festival. They aren't for or against anything; they just are. Here, in this improbable, unlikely place.

The chanters feel more in need of a binding ritual that would settle at least for the moment who we are and who we aren't. They seemed more interested in making explicit the terms of the cleaving to and the cleaving from.

The northern side is strangely bare. It is supposed to be an area for art and signs, but something about that part of the park doesn't seem appealing, even though people are tightly packed into the middle. Along the northern edge are handmade posters, arranged so they can be seen in a stroll down that side. My favorite is "the medium is the message." Done rather patiently in several colors.

Someone wades in with a stack of pizzas. The food carts that are usually here anyway are still open. I would like to know what they made of it all, but they are doing a fairly brisk business and I don't want to hold anyone up. Both cops and occupiers line up for coffee, and perhaps a few office workers held back late.

A police truck arrives and barriers are slid off and erected down the southern side. Quite a few people get up to watch. A palpating rise in the level of tension. Who knows who ordered the new barriers or why? It could just be to make people a little tense.

The police seem relaxed, however. A policewoman leans against the barriers on the north side and chats on her cellphone. A cluster of maybe ten blue-shirted officers lean against the wall outside the Brooks Brothers store on the other side of the street. A white-shirted officer rests his bullhorn on the barriers for a moment. It isn't always like this, of course. I saw police arrest three people in broad daylight on the morning of September 20. At this moment, all is calm. Nothing is forever in these kinds of situations.

Wandering around the park, I talk briefly to a few people. I steer away from people who looked like old hands. I am interested in those people who seem in a sort of a fugue state. Mostly, they can not quite find words to describe the sensation. There is just something about this moment in space and time that is hard to describe.

It isn't obvious what one should be doing. It isn't work; it isn't leisure. There's nothing to buy. The union-organized marchers are long gone by the time I get there, so there isn't really any protesting to be done. In the park at this moment there are no police to confront. If you want to make the moment intelligible to yourself, you have to find your own way to do it.

The chanters and the drummers are two ways to go about it. Or perhaps it is a good moment just to try and sleep. There's always something to organize. There are always points to debate. Or, you could just *be there*. In some ways that's the hardest part. To just be there, in a moment carved out of the division of daily life between the time of work and the time of leisure. In a space that is supposed to be where office workers go for coffee and a cigarette on their breaks.

There's a division of the space of the park into functions, and usually this does sort of function. At night, with such a big crowd in it, the space starts to redefine itself a bit, and more by ambience than function. People arrange themselves in it more according to how they felt about it. There is an unanswerable question in the air, or so it seems to me, about what forms of life are possible. In different parts of the park people gravitate toward different answers. This is what you might call the *psychogeography* of the place.

When there's nobody really watching, when there's nothing to confront, when there's nothing to debate—this is what's left: How is it possible to create forms of life for ourselves, even if it's in the shadow of tall buildings that cast long shadows?

I sit for a while writing these notes, then I prepare myself to leave the Park and head back to the subway. I have to get up the next morning to get the kids off to school. People drift away, although it is clear that a fairly large group will stay on for most of the night. And others will be back in the morning.

Not many people can inhabit this place outside of work time, but a lot of people come to visit, and to glimpse something of another way in which the city might function. Other lives are possible; sometimes they even actually exist.

No matter what happens here next day or next week, I just want to record the fact that this actually happened.

Zuccotti Park, October 5, 2011

Acknowledgments

> The truths that matter most to us are always half spoken, fully
> understood only by the prudent.
>
> Baltasar Gracián

I learned so much of what I needed to know to write this book not
in school but from certain parties encountered outside of it. Here
I would like to pay a special tribute to the network of artists, theo-
rists and activists whose various projects intersected in the nineties
under the banner of Nettime, and who in various productive ways
continued, détourned, remixed, shredded, critiqued or ignored the
legacy of the Situationist International.

Thanks also to Raoul Vaneigem, René Viénet, Martine Barra-
qué, Brigitte Cornand, Jacqueline de Jong, Arthur Guibert, Simon
Guibert, Aliette Guibert, Hedi el Khoti, Sylvère Lotringer, Dana
Polan, Michael Pettinger, Alex Galloway, Richard Barbrook, *Red
Channels*, Project X, ISSUE Project Room, *Cabinet*, Sam Cooper,
Tom Bunyard, Jen Kennedy and the late Mark Poster. Thanks
to my research assistants Julia P. Carrillo and Pablo Bustinduy
Amador. Thanks to everyone at Verso Books, including Rowan
Wilson, Sarah Shin, Jacob Stevens, Mark Martin, Tim Clark, and
the late Clara Heyworth. Thanks especially to my students at Lang
College and the New School for Social Research.

Earlier versions of bits of this book appeared previously in *Angelaki*, *October*, *Social Research*, *DATA browser*, *Grey Room* and in the
booklet *50 Years of Recuperation of the Situationist International*. My
thanks to my hosts at *Cabinet*, Whitechapel, UC Berkeley, UC
Davis, SVA, Duke University, University of Western Ontario,
University of Sussex, University of Sydney and Iaspis Stockholm,
where chunks of it were first presented.

Notes

1 Widening Gyres

1 cnn.com, May 28, 2003; *Sydney Morning Herald*, December 29, 2007. *New Hawaii*, Bernadette Corporation, *Eine Pinot Grigio, Bitte*, Sternberg Press, New York, 2007, p. 10.

2 Comte de Lautréamont, *Maldoror and the Complete Works*, translated by Alexis Lykiard, Exact Change Press, Cambridge MA, 1994, p. 38.

3 Guy Debord, *Society of the Spectacle*, Zone Books, New York, 1994, s. 12. The displacement of Big Brother by all the little sisters is analogous to what the Lacanians call the decline in symbolic efficiency. See Slavoj Žižek, *The Ticklish Subject*, Verso, London, 1999.

4 Guy Debord, *In Girum Imus Nocte et Consumimur Igni: A Film*, translated by Lucy Forsyth, Pelagian Press, London, 1990, p. 74. This may not be the most accurate translation, but it is the one that best captures the spirit. See *In girum imus nocte et consumimur igni*, Gallimard, Paris, 1999, p. 54, or Guy Debord, *Oeuvres*, Gallimard, Paris, 2006, pp. 1399–1400.

5 Guy Debord, *Comments on the Society of the Spectacle*, Verso, London, 1988, p. 20.

6 T. J. Clark, *The Sight of Death*, Yale University Press, New Haven CT, 2008, p. 184.

7 Mustapha Khayati, "On the Poverty of Student Life," in Ken Knabb (ed.), *Situationist International Anthology*, Bureau of Public Secrets, Berkeley CA, 2006, p. 408. Khayati was one of the most able Situationists of the later period. Regrettably, he will make only one further appearance in this book, as I have little to add to this marvelous text. The best tribute to him is the plethora of anonymous texts—some quite fine—that came out of the occupation movement at the University of California, the New School and elsewhere from 2008 onwards.

8 Guy Debord, *Society of the Spectacle*, s. 9. See also Debord, *Comments*, p. 50. Compare to Theodor Adorno, "The whole is the false," *Minima Moralia*, New Left Books, London, 1973, p. 50.

9 On "content critics," see Todd Gitlin, *Media Unlimited*, Henry Holt, New York, 2007, p. 136.

10 *New York Times*, March 15, 2007. See the video by Isaac Cronin and Terrel Seltzer, *Call It Sleep*, 1982.

11 Raoul Vaneigem, *The Revolution of Everyday Life*, Rebel Press, London, 2001, p. 26.

12 Debord, *Society of the Spectacle*, s. 4.

13 *Des Moines Register*, January 19, 2007. See also the conference proceedings at digitallabor.org and Trebor Scholz (ed.), *Digital Labor: The Internet as Playground and Factory*, Routledge, New York, 2012.

14 Debord, *Society of the Spectacle*, s. 8.

15 *Daily Telegraph*, March 17, 2007. Jean Baudrillard developed this line of thinking in his early work. See Jean Baudrillard, *The System of Objects*, Verso, London, 2006.
16 Debord, *Comments*, pp. 9–10; *Oeuvres*, p. 1598.
17 msnbc.com, June 11, 2006.
18 Debord, *Comments*, p. 60.
19 *Business Week*, February 21, 2008.
20 *New York Times*, August 15, 2005.
21 *New York Times*, February 14, 2000.
22 Guy Debord, *Complete Cinematic Works*, edited by Ken Knabb, AK Press, Oakland CA, 2005, p. 29; *Oeuvres*, p. 531.
23 See "Address to Revolutionaries of Algeria and All Countries," in Knabb, *Anthology*, p. 191; *Internationale Situationiste*, No. 10, March 1966, p. 46: "surdéveloppment irrationel."
24 Guy Debord, *Panegyric*, Verso, London, 2004, p. 67; *Oeuvres*, p. 1685.
25 Henri Lefebvre, *Critique of Everyday Life*, Vol. 2, Verso, London, 2008, p. 3; *Critique de la vie quotidienne II. Fondements d'une sociologie de la quotidienneté*, L'Arche Editeur, Paris, 1961, p. 9.
26 Interview with Alex Galloway, available at lacan.com. Regrettably, in making a break from Alain Badiou, Mehdi ran straight into the arms of Bernard Henri-Lévy. See *Après Badiou*, Éditions Grasset, Paris, 2011. But enough with the provincial gossip that is French letters today.
27 "Address to Revolutionaries of Algeria and All Countries," in Knabb, *Anthology*, p. 189; *Internationale Situationiste*, No. 10, March 1966, p. 43.
28 *Seattle Times*, April 9, 2006.

2 The Critique of Everyday Life

1 Debord, *In Girum Imus Nocte*, p. 54. See also: *In girum imus nocte et consumimur igni*, Gallimard, Paris, 1999, p. 42, or *Oeuvres*, p. 1382.
2 "Now the SI," in Knabb, *Anthology*, p. 177; *Internationale Situationiste*, No. 9, August 1964, p. 5: "pour sortir du vingtième siècle."
3 See Tom McDonough (ed.), *Guy Debord and the Situationist International*, MIT Press, Cambridge MA, 2004; Georgina Bertolino et al., *Pinot Gallizio*, Charta, Milan, 2005.
4 Of the figures from the later, "political" phase of the Situationist International, Raoul Vaneigem has attracted particular attention: Pol Charles, *Vaneigem l'insatiable*, L'Age d'Homme, Laussane, 2002; Grégory Lambrette, *Raoul Vaneigem*, Libertaires, Brussels, 2007; Larent Six, *Raoul Vaneigem*, Éditions Luce Wilquin, Avin, 2005.
5 Some versions of the Debord biography: Literary version: Vincent Kaufmann, *Guy Debord*, University of Minnesota Press, Minneapolis, 2006; Marxist version: Anselm Jappe, *Guy Debord*, University of California Press, Berkeley, 1999; philosophical version: Jean-Marie Apostolides, *Tombeau de Guy Debord*, Exils, Paris, 1999.
6 *Le Monde*, June 14, 2009; *Le Monde*, June 17, 2009; *Libération*, June 17, 2009. The Library eventually succeeded in acquiring these materials.
7 See Simon During, *Exit Capitalism*, Routledge, London, 2009.
8 Guy Debord, *Panegyric*, Verso, London, p. 68; *Oeuvres*, p. 1685.
9 Guy Debord, *Considerations on the Assassination of Gérard Lebovici*, Tam Tam Books, Los Angeles, 2002, p. 37; *Oeuvres*, p. 1557.
10 Debord, *Considerations on the Assassination*, p. 79; *Oeuvres*, p. 1577.
11 *What other success?*, Debord, *Considerations on the Assassination*, p. 79; *Oeuvres*, p. 1577. *At war with the whole world*, In Girum, p. 44; *Oeuvres*, p. 1373.

12 Alice Becker-Ho, *The Princes of Jargon*, Edwin Mellen Press, Lewiston NY, 2004, p. 7.

13 Art history has lately come to undo the category of the originary author, even in its most canonic locus, the art of the Renaissance. The pressure of past forms, seeping into present expressions, comes into play even there. But that signs of this at work in art are instances also of détournement as popular practice has not yet broken into the light of day among historians. See Alexander Nagel and Christopher Wood, *Anachronistic Renaissance*, Zone Books, New York, 2010.

14 "Guy Debord's Widow Threatens NYU Professor with Copyright Violation," *Chronicle of Higher Education*, April 28, 2008; see also *Artforum*, November 1, 2008, pp. 167–8.

15 Some versions: Pomo version: Sadie Plant, *The Most Radical Gesture*, Routledge, London, 1992; punk version: Greil Marcus, *Lipstick Traces*, Harvard University Press, Cambridge MA, 2009; art version: Elizabeth Sussman (ed.), *On the Passage of a Few People Through a Rather Brief Moment in Time*, MIT Press, Cambridge MA, 1989; anarchist version: David Graeber, *Direct Action: An Ethnography*, AK Press, Oakland CA, 2009; new left version: Peter Wollen, *Raiding the Icebox*, Verso, London, 1993; Paris-centric version: Patrick Marcolini, *Le Mouvement Situationiste: Une histoire intellectuelle*, L'Échappée, Paris, 2012.

16 Guy Debord, writing to Constant on April 26, 1959. See Guy Debord, *Correspondence*, Semiotext(e), Los Angeles, 2008, pp. 242–5.

17 Debord, *Considerations on the Assassination*, p. 31; *Oeuvres*, p. 1553.

18 Cardinal de Retz, *Mémoires*, Société des Bibliophiles, Paris, 1903, p. 236; quoted in Debord, *Panegyric*, p. 18; *Oeuvres*, p. 1665.

19 See Alberto Toscano, *Fanaticism: The Uses of An Idea*, Verso, London, 2010, on the rhetorical function of the fanatic in liberal politics.

20 Simon Critchley, *Infinitely Demanding*, Verso, London, 2008; Alain Badiou, *The Century*, Polity, Cambridge, 2007; Jacques Rancière, *The Future of the Image*, Verso, London, 2009.

21 Debord, *Panegyric*, p. 40; *Oeuvres*, p. 1673.

22 Debord, *Panegyric*, p. 29; *Oeuvres*, p. 1668.

23 Louis-Ferdinand Céline, *Journey to the End of the Night*, New Directions, New York, 2006, p. 18.

24 "Le monde dont nous parlons," *Internationale Situationiste*, No. 9, August 1964, p. 6; Sussman, *On the Passage of a Few People*, p. 154.

25 Debord, *In Girum*, p. 24; *Oeuvres*, p. 1354.

3 Liberty Guiding the People

1 Clark, *The Sight of Death*, p. 185.

2 T. J. Clark and Donald Nicholson-Smith, "Why Art Can't Kill the Situationist International," in McDonough (ed.), *Guy Debord and the Situationist International*, p. 485.

3 Kathryn Tuma, "In Conversation: T. J. Clark with Kathryn Tuma," *Brooklyn Rail*, November 2006.

4 Clark, *The Sight of Death*, p. 114; see also p. 239.

5 T. J. Clark, *The Painting of Modern Life: Paris in the Art of Manet and His Followers*, Knopf, New York, 1985, p. 36. A book that seemed untimely in the "postmodern" moment in which it was published, but that context will be ignored here.

6 See Michel Foucault, *Discipline and Punish: The Birth of the Prison*, Vintage, New York,

1995. Foucault takes oblique aim at Debord in the overture to this famous book, which sees the spectacle end with the spectacle of the scaffold, replaced by the new order of visibility of disciplinary institutions like the prison. But perhaps it's more an instance of anxiety of influence: Is not Debord the one who had first asked seemingly Foucauldian questions about regimes of visibility? Is it not Debord who notices first asymmetries of who sees who or what? In breaking with Marxism in the Stalinist mode—still a powerful force in seventies France—Foucault erases the traces of his debt to the non-Stalinist left.

7   T. J. Clark, *Farewell to an Idea*, Yale University Press, New Haven CT, 1999, pp. 7–8. Released the year of renewed activism around the World Trade Organization, Clark was again somewhat untimely.

8   T. J. Clark, *Image of the People: Gustave Courbet and the 1848 Revolution*, Thames & Hudson, London, 1982, p. 10.

9   Clark, *Farewell to an Idea*, p. 28.

10   Ibid., p. 47.

11   Ibid., p. 34.

12   Ibid., p. 48.

13   T. J. Clark, *The Absolute Bourgeois: Artists and Politics in France 1848–1851*, Thames & Hudson, London, 1982, p. 19.

14   Clark, *Image of the People*, p. 19. See also T. J. Clark, "A Bourgeois Dance of Death," *Burlington Magazine*, April 1969.

15   See Jerrold Seigel, *Bohemian Paris: Culture, Politics and the Boundaries of Bourgeois Life, 1830–1930*, Johns Hopkins, Baltimore, 1999.

16   Clark, *Image of the People*, p. 33.

17   Ibid., p. 14.

18   Ibid., p. 34. On over-identification, see Slavoj Žižek, *Metastases of Enjoyment*, Verso, London, 2005, pp. 70–3. Perhaps the best case for it as an avant-garde strategy is Alexei Monroe, *Interrogation Machine: Laibach and NSK*, MIT Press, Cambridge MA, 2005.

19   On total semantic field, see Henri Lefebvre, *Introduction to Modernity*, Verso, London, 1995, p. 239; *Introduction à la modernité. Préludes*, Les éditions de minuit, Paris, 1962, p. 235. On Lefebvre's attempt to redeem romanticism, see McKenzie Wark, *The Beach Beneath the Street*, Verso, London, 2011.

20   Karl Marx, "The June Revolution," in Karl Marx, *The Revolutions of 1848: Political Writings Volume 1*, edited by David Fernbach, Penguin, Harmondsworth, 1978, p. 131. Marx here makes romantic imagery politically productive again.

21   Clark, *Image of the People*, p. 74.

22   All of these Thailand stories are sourced from news.bbc.co.uk.

23   Clark, *Image of the People*, p. 159.

24   Ibid., p. 73. Compare to Debord's classic statement on détournement: *Society of the Spectacle*, paras. 206–11. The practice of détournement is itself détourned. Debord détourns Lautréamont (207), but interestingly chooses to quote from Kierkegaard. Debordian détournement arises from Lautréamont and his contact with Belgian Surrealism. The quote from Kierkegaard (206) is perhaps a nod to his old friend Asger Jorn, who always preferred to source his ideas from his fellow Scandinavians.

25   Clark, *Image of the People*, p. 140.

26   Ibid., p. 149.

27   Ibid., pp. 160–1.

28   Clark, *The Painting of Modern Life*, p. 15.

29   Ibid., p. 44. On moral panic, see the classic work by the late Stanley Cohen, *Folk*

Devils and Moral Panics, Routledge, London, 2003. Of the many books on Paris, see David Harvey, *Paris, Capital of Modernity*, Routledge, New York, 2005, which engages with, and usefully enriches, Clark's account.

30   Clark, *The Painting of Modern Life*, p. 69. See Louis Chevalier, *The Assassination of Paris*, University of Chicago Press, Chicago, 1994. Originally published in 1977, this conservative historian's lament for the city struck a chord with Debord. See *Panegyric*, p. 39.

31   "Theses on the Paris Commune," in Knabb, *Anthology*, p. 400. See also the classic study: Prosper-Olivier Lissagaray, *History of the Paris Commune*, translated by Eleanor Marx Aveling, Verso, London, 2012.

32   Henri Lefebvre, "Excerpt from *The Proclamation of the Commune*," in Tom McDonough (ed.), *The Situationists and the City*, Verso, London, 2009, p. 175.

33   Clark, *Image of the People*, p. 154.

34   Clark, *The Painting of Modern Life*, p. 69.

4   The Spectacle of Modern Life

1   Clark, *The Painting of Modern Life*, p. 49. On modernity and the city, see Marshall Berman, *All That Is Solid Melts Into Air*, Penguin, New York, 1988.

2   The early twenty-first-century Olympia might well be Sasha Grey, porn star and actor. On the question of the black supplicant with flowers in this painting, see the work of artist Mickalene Thomas.

3   *New York Magazine*, July 10, 2005.

4   It would be worth pausing here over the agency of Victorine Meurent, and of models in general. See Wendy Steiner, *The Real, Real Thing: The Model in the Mirror of Art*, University of Chicago Press, Chicago, 2010, and Eunice Lipton, *Alias Olympia*, Cornell University Press, Ithaca NY, 1999.

5   Clark, *The Painting of Modern Life*, p. 108.

6   Ibid., p. 128.

7   One might begin here with: Laura Mulvey, *Visual and Other Pleasures*, Palgrave Macmillan, London, 2009. Clark's distance from other leftist cultural critics of the time, such as Mulvey, can be measured via T. J. Clark, "Preliminaries to a Possible Treatment of Olympia," *Screen*, Vol. 21, No. 1, 1980.

8   Clark, *The Painting of Modern Life*, p. 147.

9   Ibid., p. 165.

10   Ibid., p. 164.

11   Ibid., p. 203.

12   *ABC News*, September 20, 2006.

13   Clark, *The Painting of Modern Life*, p. 229. See also the fine essay by Greil Marcus, "The Dance That Everybody Forgot," *New Formations*, No. 2, Summer 1987.

14   Clark, *The Painting of Modern Life*, p. 236.

15   Ibid., p. 229.

16   Ibid., p. 236.

17   Ibid.

18   Ibid., p. 205.

19   See Mark Andrejevic, *Reality TV: The Work of Being Watched*, Rowman and Littlefield, Lanham MD, 2007; Jodi Dean, *Publicity's Secret*, Cornell University Press, Ithaca NY, 1988.

20   Clark, *The Painting of Modern Life*, p. 253.

21   See for example Kai Fikentscher, *You Better Work! Underground Dance Music in New York City*, Wesleyan, Hanover NH, 2000.

22   *New York Magazine*, April 4, 2010.

5   *Anarchies of Perception*

1   Clark, *Farewell to an Idea*, Yale University Press, New Haven CT, p. 104.

2   *Every act*, and *folding of parts*: Clark, *Farewell to an Idea*, p. 180.

3   Clark, *Farewell to an Idea*, p. 62. See also Félix Fénéon, *Novels in Three Lines*, New York Review of Books Classics, New York, 2007.

4   Kojin Karatani, *Transcritique*, MIT Press, Cambridge MA, 2003, also attempts to rethink the logic of the Marxist-anarchist split and repair it.

5   Clark, *Farewell to an Idea*, p. 103.

6   Clark, *Farewell to an Idea*, p. 121. On the institutionalizing of geography in France and an anarchist social geography, see Kristin Ross, *The Emergence of the Social*, Verso, London, 2008, p. 75ff.

7   See J. M. Bernstein, *Against Voluptuous Bodies*, Stanford University Press, Stanford CA, 2006, and Eric L. Santner, *The Royal Remains*, University of Chicago Press, Chicago, 2011. These two erudite books read Clark in the context of critical theory and psychoanalysis, respectively, and are concerned to place Clarkian aesthetics in readings of modernity based on sovereignty and rationalization, respectively. Yet what is distinctive about Clark, and this connects him to the Situationist current, is the question of aesthetics considered not from above but from below. Or rather: how popular forces pushing from below do so, in part at least, via the struggle over the means of representation, and not just over what is pictured within it. See also Gail Day, *Dialectical Passions: Negation in Postwar Art*, Columbia University Press, New York, 2011, which places Clark more in the history of New Left aesthetics.

8   Debord, *Comments*, p. 3; *Oeuvres*, p. 1595. Clark argues that Debord avoids periodizing the spectacle in *Society of the Spectacle*, but in the light of this later text this might not be strictly the case. See T. J. Clark, "Origins of the Present Crisis," *New Left Review*, No. 2, March–April 2000.

9   Debord, *Society of the Spectacle*, s. 100. Jonathan Crary manages to embellish this simple point nicely; see McDonough (ed.), *Guy Debord and the Situationist International*.

10   T. J. Clark, "Foreword," Anselm Jappe, *Guy Debord*, p. viii.

11   *Brooklyn Rail*, November 2006.

12   Retort, *Afflicted Powers: Capital and Spectacle in a New Age of War*, Verso, London, 2006, pp. 3, 5.

13   Ibid., pp. 28, 37.

14   Ibid., p. 20.

15   Clark, "Foreword," pp. ix–x.

16   Ibid.

6   *The Revolution of Everyday Life*

1   Hans Ulrich Obrist, "In Conversation with Raoul Vaneigem," *e-flux journal*, No. 6, May 2009.

2   Debord to Vaneigem, March 8, 1965, in Guy Debord, *Correspondance*, Vol. 3, Fayard, Paris, 2003.

3   Vaneigem, *The Revolution of Everyday Life*, p. 13. On the Provos, see Richard
    Kempton, *Provo: Amsterdam's Anarchist Revolt*, Autonomedia, New York, 2007.
    Henri Lefebvre goes to some lengths to debunk the popular idea that Herbert Marcuse
    was the prophet of '68, in part to bolster his own claim. See *The Explosion*, Monthly
    Review Press, 1969, surely a candidate for the honor of being his worst book.

4   From the 1991 preface to *The Revolution of Everyday Life*.

5   Laurence Remilla, "In Conversation with Raoul Vaneigem," *The Idler*, No. 35,
    Spring 2005, p. 82.

6   From Vaneigem's resignation letter, in Guy Debord and Gianfranco Sangui-
    netti, *The Real Split in the International*, translated by John McHale, Pluto Press,
    London, 2003, p. 142. Friedrich Hölderlin, *Hyperion*, translated by Ross Benja-
    min, Archipelago Books, Brooklyn NY, 2008, see p. 172. Georg Lukács, in *Goethe
    and His Age*, Merlin Press, 1968, makes the case for Hegel's supersession of the
    political instincts that he shared with Hölderlin in their youth. Vaneigem's writ-
    ings are more in the spirit of Hölderlin than Hegel, and on this point he differs
    from Debord.

7   Regarding Vaneigem on heresies, see Alexander Galloway, Eugene Thacker and
    McKenzie Wark, *Excommunication*, University of Chicago Press, Chicago, 2013.

8   The standard work on Debord's relation to Hegelian Marxism is Anselm Jappe,
    Guy Debord.

9   Lefebvre, *Critique of Everyday Life*, Vol. 2, p. 288; *new life*, Lefebvre, *Introduction to
    Modernity*, p. 69.

10 Raoul Vaneigem, "Some Theoretical Topics That Need To Be Dealt With Without
    Academic Debate or Idle Speculation," Knabb, *Anthology*, p. 221; *Internationale Situ-
    ationiste*, No. 10, 1966, p. 42.

11 André Breton, *Ode to Charles Fourier*, translated by Kenneth White, Cape Goliard
    Press, London, 1970. See Theodor Adorno, *Prisms*, MIT Press, Cambridge MA,
    1988, p. 34. The Fourier of liberated desire was taken up in the United States by
    Norman O. Brown and Herbert Marcuse.

12 Guy Debord, letter to the Italian section, March 12, 1969, in Guy Debord,
    Correspondance Volume 4, 1969–1972, Fayard, Paris, 2005.

13 Roland Barthes, *Sade / Fourier / Loyola*, Farrar, Straus and Giroux, New York, 1976,
    p. 87.

14 See *Topique*, October 1970, with contributions by Maurice Blanchot, Michel Butor
    and Pierre Klossowski; and Emile Lehouck, "La Lecture surréaliste de Charles
    Fourier," *Australian Journal of French Studies*, Vol. 20, No. 1, 1983, pp. 26–36.

15 Raymond Queneau, "Dialectique hégélienne et series de Fourier," *Bords*, Paris,
    1963. Walter Benjamin, *Charles Baudelaire*, Verso, London, 1985, pp. 159–60. Italo
    Calvino, *The Uses of Literature*, Harcourt Brace, New York, 1986.

16 Fredric Jameson, *Archaeologies of the Future*, Verso, London, 2007, p. 251.

17 From an email interview with Vaneigem, conducted in May–June 2011.

18 Charles Fourier, in Jonathan Beecher and Richard Bienvenu, *The Utopian Vision
    of Charles Fourier: Selected Texts*, Beacon Press, Boston MA, p. 268; Francois Bott,
    "Raoul Vaneigem," *Le Monde*, September 12, 2003.

19 Vaneigem, *Revolution of Everyday Life*, p. 84.

20 Vaneigem, *Revolution of Everyday Life*, p. 190.

21 Raoul Vaneigem, *A Cavalier History of Surrealism*, AK Press, Oakland CA, 1999, p. 8.
    Vaneigem's surrealism is a Paris-centric parade of white guys, even if (at least) one
    of them was not so straight. A usefully decentering resource is Franklin Rosemont
    and Robin D. G. Kelley, *Black, Brown and Beige: Surrealist Writings from Africa and the
    Diaspora*, University of Texas Press, Austin TX, 2010.

22 Vaneigem, *A Cavalier History*, p. 5.
23 Ibid., p. 10.
24 Ibid., p. 12.
25 Ibid., p. 74.
26 Ibid., p. 54.
27 René Crevel, *My Body and I*, Archipelago Press, Brookyn NY, 2005, p. 83, written when he was twenty-five and ten years before his suicide.
28 Vaneigem, *A Cavalier History*, p. 73.
29 Ibid., p. 113.
30 Michel Leiris, *Manhood*, University of Chicago Press, Chicago, 1992. See the essay on Leiris by John Conomos in *Flesh*, Intervention Publications No. 22, Sydney 1988.
31 Vaneigem, *A Cavalier History*, p. 100.
32 Jonathan Beecher and Richard Bienvenu (eds), *The Utopian Vision of Charles Fourier: Selected Texts*, Beacon Press, Boston MA, p. 289.
33 Fourier, *The Utopian Vision*, p. 158.
34 Ibid., p. 157.
35 Charles Fourier, *The Theory of the Four Movements*, edited by Gareth Steadman Jones and Ian Patterson, Cambridge University Press, Cambridge, 1996, p. 233. Actually, he thought there were thirty-six kinds of bankruptcy, that being the magic number in his series. See Charles Fourier, *The Hierarchies of Cuckholdry and Bankruptcy*, translated by Geoffrey Longnecker, Wakefield Press, Cambridge MA, 2011.
36 Fourier, *The Utopian Vision*, p. 142.
37 Vaneigem, *The Revolution of Everyday Life*, p. 258.
38 Raoul Vaneigem, "Basic Banalities Part 1," in Knabb, *Anthology*, p. 123; *Internationale Situationiste*, No. 7, April 1962, p. 36.
39 Vaneigem, *The Revolution of Everyday Life*, p. 46.
40 Charles Fourier, *Harmonian Man: Selected Writings*, edited by Mark Poster, Anchor Books, New York, 1971, p. 77.
41 Crevel, *My Body and I*, p. 124.
42 Leiris, *Manhood*, p. 120.
43 Vaneigem, *The Revolution of Everyday Life*, p. 22.
44 Rémila, "In Conversation with Raoul Vanegeim," p. 82.
45 Fourier, *The Utopian Vision*, p. 148.

7 *Détournement as Utopia*

1 Raoul Vaneigem, *The Book of Pleasures*, translated by John Fullerton, Pending Press, London, 1983, p. 28.
2 Fourier, *The Utopian Vision*, p. 145.
3 Fourier, *The Theory of the Four Movements*, p. 200.
4 Vaneigem, *The Revolution of Everyday Life*, p. 185. He borrows the idea from Brecht's Herr Keuner stories.
5 Vaneigem, *The Revolution of Everyday Life*, p. 264.
6 Eric Santner, "The New Idolatry," pressblog.uchicago.edu, September 6, 2011. See also Eric Santner, *The Royal Remains*. Santner sees this as part of a heretical extension of the properly religious into the secular domain. For Vaneigem, the heretical procedure of extending sacred poetics in every direction is not an excessive margin but the very center of sacred practice, for good and ill. For Vaneigem, as for Fourier,

it's not a question of pushing sacred sacrifice back into its proper box but of overturning its logic in all domains.

7   Imaginal, rather than an affect of the imaginary or the imagination, in that the imaginal is not the opposite of reason but the field within which reason is possible. The imaginal is social rather than merely individual. It constructs not just an imaginary bond between self and other, but the field of possible unities and connections. Détournement, which not only copies but corrects in the direction of hope, synthesizes aspects of both classical and romantic practices of imagination. See Chiara Bottici, *A Philosophy of Political Myth*, Cambridge University Press, Cambridge, 2010.

8   Herman Melville's story "Bartleby, the Scrivener" (1853) turns up as an exemplar of a certain kind of praxis in Gilles Deleuze, *Essays Critical and Clinical*, Minnesota University Press, Minneapolis, 1997, in Slavoj Žižek, *The Parallax View*, MIT Press, Cambridge MA, 2006, and in Michael Hardt and Antonio Negri, *Empire*, Harvard University Press, Cambridge MA, 2000, and also in Giorgio Agamben, *Potentialities*, Stanford University Press, Stanford CA, 1999. And this is to name just the most prominent examples. When it comes to the Bartelbization of theories of praxis, "I prefer not to."

9   Jonathan Beecher, *Charles Fourier: The Visionary and His World*, University of California Press, Berkeley, 1986, p. 490.

10 Vaneigem, *The Revolution of Everyday Life*, p. 187.

11 See J. D. Bernal, *Science in History*, Vol. 2, MIT Press, Cambridge MA, 1971. While Bernal is far more respectful of, and knowledgeable about, Newton's achievements, he is nevertheless alert to how implicated they were in the trade and industry of the time and the role they played in the rise of bourgeois thought. Fourier was not wrong to want to build on but diverge from Newton.

12 Fourier, *Harmonian Man*, p. 51.

13 Ibid., p. 49.

14 Jameson, *Archaeologies of the Future*, p. 248. I am indebted to Jameson's reading of Fourier throughout this chapter.

15 *Unlimited philanthropy*, Fourier, *Harmonian Man*, p. 83; *prodigal*, Fourier, *Harmonian Man*, p. 88.

16 Alice Becker-Ho, *The Essence of Jargon*, translated by John McHale, typescript, 2007, p. 28.

17 Fourier, *The Utopian Vision*, p. 200.

18 *Minimum of satisfaction*, Fourier, *The Utopian Vision*, p. 337; *the ravages it causes*, Fourier, *The Utopian Vision*, p. 339.

19 *Prohibition and contraband*, Fourier, *Harmonian Man*, p. 238; *poor in pleasure*, Fourier, *Harmonian Man*, p. 80.

20 A claim not actually the case with Fourier. T. J. Clark, "For a Left With No Future," *New Left Review*, No. 74, March–April 2012, p. 68. Here Clark turns from realist to tragic, but a form of tragedy that has not broadened—despite a nod toward Platonov—toward the popular. See Susan Watkins' reply in the same issue.

21 Fourier, *Harmonian Man*, p. 75.

22 Ibid., p. 83.

8 Charles Fourier's Queer Theory

1   Charles Fourier, *Des Harmonies Polygames en Amour*, Payot & Rivages, Paris, 2003, with a preface by Raoul Vaneigem.

2   On Fourier and Restif, see Mark Poster, *The Utopian Thought of Restif de la Bretonne*,

New York University Press, New York, 1971. On Fourier in the French utopian continuum, see Frank Manuel, *The Prophets of Paris*, Harper & Row, New York, 1962. For Rabelais' utopian order of the Themeites, see *Gargantua and Pantegruel*, translated by M. A. Screech, Penguin, London, 2006, p. 362ff. However, Fourier really stands alone in terms of sexual freedom and equality.

3   Vaneigem, *The Book of Pleasures*, p. 54.

4   Raoul Vaneigem, "Basic Banalities Part 2," in Knabb, *Anthology*, p. 167; *Internationale Situationiste*, No. 8, January 1963, p. 44.

5   For an account of aristocratic cultural forms of the kind Fourier détourns, see Johan Huizinga, *The Waning of the Middle Ages*, St. Martin's Press, New York, 1924.

6   Fourier, *Harmonian Man*, p. 262.

7   Ibid., p. 267.

8   Ibid., p. 263.

9   Ibid., p. 271.

10   For a fine — Rabelaisian — satire on civilized sex among the supposedly progressive middle classes, see Christina Stead, *Letty Fox: Her Luck*, New York Review Books, 2001. It hardly needs updating.

11   Fourier, *Harmonian Man*, p. 272.

12   See Raoul Vaneigem, *La Resistance au christianisme; les heresies, des origines au xviii siècle*, Fayard, Paris, 1993, ch. 7.

13   Fourier, *Harmonian Man*, p. 28.

14   Barthes, *Sade / Fourier / Loyola*, p. 78.

15   Rather like the coded color handkerchiefs worn at Mattachine square dances. See Stuart Timmons, *The Trouble with Harry Hay, Founder of the Modern Gay Movement*, Alyson Publications, Boston, 1990.

16   Stendhal, *De L'Amour*, Flammarion, Paris, 1992.

17   Beecher, *Charles Fourier*, p. 12.

18   Fourier, *Harmonian Man*, p. 40.

19   Vaneigem, *The Revolution of Everyday Life*, p. 26.

20   Nikolai Chernyshevsky, *What Is to Be Done?*, translated by Michael Katz, Cornell University Press, Ithaca NY, 1989.

21   See for example Jane McGonnigal, *Reality Is Broken: Why Games Make Us Better and How They Can Change the World*, Penguin, New York, 2011.

22   Francois Bott, "Raoul Vaneigem," *Le Monde*, September 12, 2003.

23   See Luc Boltanski and Eve Chiapello, *The New Spirit of Capitalism*, translated by Gregory Elliot, Verso, London, 2007.

24   Tiqqun, *Introduction to Civil War*, Semiotext(e), Los Angeles, 2010, p. 28, s. 8 (gloss), originally published in *Tiqqun*, No. 2, 2001, p. 5. The difference would lie in that itch *Tiqqun* can't help but scratch: critique of metaphysics. They spend more time worrying away at predicates than developing a mode of writing based on penchants.

25   "Premiers Matériaux pour une Théorie de la Jeunne-Fille," *Tiqqun*, No. 1, 1999.

26   Raoul Vaneigem, in *Charles Fourier, Des Harmonies Polygames en Amour*, edited by Raoul Vaneigem, Rivages, Paris, 2003, p. 7.

27   Raoul Vaneigem, "Aiming for Practical Truth," in Knabb, *Anthology*, p. 279.

28   Raoul Vaneigem, "Notice to the Civilized Concerning Generalized Self Management." The title, and some of the text, is a détournement of Fourier. Knabb, *Anthology*, p. 365.

29   See Paul Lafargue, *The Right to Be Lazy*, AK Press, Oakland CA, 2011.

30   Raoul Vaneigem, *Voyage à Oarystis*, illustrated by Giampiero Caiti, Éditions Estuaire, Brussels, 2005, p. 101.

9   The Ass Dreams of China Pop

1   Letter to Viénet, June 21, 1961, in Guy Debord, *Correspondance Volume 2*, 1960–1964, Fayard, Paris, 2001.

2   Meaghan Morris, "Transnational Imagination in Action Cinema: Hong Kong and the making of a global popular culture," *Inter-Asia Cultural Studies*, Vol. 5, No. 2, 2004.

3   My thanks to Julia P. Carrillo for pointing this out.

4   Jacques Rancière argues that Althusser's critique of ideology legitimated those within the French Communist Party who took the student revolt aspect of May '68 to be just a petit bourgeois tantrum. His own break with Althusserianism came at a time (1974) when it was being repurposed, against its will, as a prop for a return to intellectual order. He classifies it alongside the theory of spectacle as one of those doctrines based on "the idea that the dominated are dominated because they are ignorant of the laws of domination. This simplistic view assigns to those who adopt it the exalted task of bringing their science to the blind masses. Eventually, though, this task dissolves into a pure thought of resentment" (*Althusser's Lesson*, Continuum, London, 2010, p. xvi). Against this, Rancière insists on the equality of intelligences of the dominated with the dominators. While this break might have been welcome, Rancière makes it only by invoking a most fantastic version of the Chinese Cultural Revolution as its authenticating flag. The "penitentiary realities" of that movement he is still unable to quite acknowledge as late as 2010. Rancière almost always identifies the Situationist project with Debord's *Society of the Spectacle* (book and film), or his later texts: "The trajectory of Situationist discourse … is undoubtedly symptomatic of the contemporary ebb and flow of aesthetics and politics, and of the transformations of avant-garde thinking into nostalgia" (*The Politics of Aesthetics*, Continuum, London, 2004, p. 9). That this "Situationist project" was also, and already, seeding the very counter-practices he wanted to celebrate, and without recourse to the authority of the bloody flag of the Maoist violence, consistently eludes him. Not surprisingly, the originality of détournement as method also eludes him. The doctrine that "aesthetics has its own politics" (*The Politics of Aesthetics*, p. 60) is helpful if one wants to find an apparently legitimate reason to still be reading Flaubert, but it doesn't confront the Situationist proposition, at the heart of détournement, that aesthetics has its own *political economy*. Embarrassment at Maoism's "excesses" aside, there is still no retreat in Rancière from its fetishizing of the political.

5   http://sexdrugsandbottleservice.tumblr.com, February 14, 2009.

6   This and subsequent quotes are from René Viénet, *Can Dialectics Break Bricks?* (1973), most readily available at ubu.com.

7   Rey Chow, *Writing Diaspora*, Indiana University Press, Bloomington IL, 1993, p. 20. For a more affirmative account of specifically western Maoism, see Andrew Ross, *Nice Work if You Can Get It*, New York University Press, New York, 2010; Kristin Ross, *May '68 and Its Afterlives*, University of Chicago Press, Chicago, 2004. Smug liberal version: Richard Wolin, *The Wind from the East*, Princeton University Press, Princeton NJ, 2010.

8   On the genres and subgenres Viénet draws upon here, see Chris Desjardins, *Outlaw Masters of Japanese Film*, I. B. Taurus, London, 2005.

9   René Viénet, *The Girls of Kamare* (1974), most readily seen at ubu.com. Following Viénet quotes are also from this film.

10   "Address to Revolutionaries of Algeria and of All Countries," Knabb, *Anthology*, p. 189.

11   Mustapha Khayati, "Setting Straight Some Popular Misconceptions About Revolutions in the Underdeveloped Countries," Knabb, *Anthology*, p. 285.

12   ABC News, April 30, 2009; *New York Times*, August 11, 2009.

13   Other works by Poussin at the National Gallery were defaced in 2011.

14   Francis Deron et al., *Revo. Cul dans la Chine Pop: Anthologie de la presse des Gardes rouges*, Éditions 10/18, Paris, 1974. It was over censorship of Deron's writing about the "Maoist graveyard" that Viénet resigned as editor of *Monde Chinois* in 2008.

10   *Mao By Mao*

1   René Viénet, "Preface" to Simon Leys, *Les habits neufs du Président Mao*, Champ Libre, Paris, 1971. Viénet's other main source is Harold Isaacs, *The Tragedy of the Chinese Revolution*, Haymarket Editions, Chicago, 2009. For Leys, the Chinese Communists cease to be a revolutionary force when Mao tries to apply tactics from the guerrilla period to economic reconstructions, with disastrous results, during the Great Leap Forward. For Isaacs, the Communists had ceased being a revolutionary party in the 1920s, with the defeat of the Chinese labor movement. On this point, Viénet follows Isaacs.

2   See Elizabeth Perry and Li Xun, *Proletarian Power: Shanghai in the Cultural Revolution*, Westview Press, Boulder CO, 1997.

3   Francis Deron, René Viénet, Wu Zingming, *Mao by Mao*, 1977. The film represented France in the short film category at Cannes in 1977.

4   Avaliable on ubu.com as *Chinois, encore un effort pour être révolutionnaires, (a.k.a. Peking Duck Soup)*, English version by "Professor Stone," with narration by John G. Simmons, Archie Taylor and Jo Bouvier. Subsequent unattributed Viénet quotes in the text are from this film.

5   Debord, letter to Sanguinetti, April 25, 1972, in Debord, *Correspondance Volume 4: 1969–1972*.

6   The extent of the great famine in the wake of Mao's Great Leap Forward is only now coming to light. See Zhou Xun (ed.), *The Great Famine in China 1958–1962: A Documentary History*, Yale University Press, New Haven CT, 2012.

7   See Victor Serge, *Memoirs of a Revolutionary*, New York Review Books Classics, New York, 2011. Serge was also a perceptive critic of the Bolsheviks' China policy.

8   Li Yi Zhe, *Chinois, si vous saviez*, Christian Bourgeois, Paris, 1976. Published by Viénet and Deron in their Biblioteque Asiatique series, once it moved from Champ Libre. For an English translation, see Li Yi Zhe, "On Socialist Democracy and the Legal System," in Gregor Benton and Alan Hunter, *Wild Lily, Prairie Fire: China's Road to Democracy*, Princeton University Press, Princeton NJ, 1995.

9   Richard McGregor, *The Party: The Secret World of China's Communist Leaders*, Harper, New York, 2012.

10   *New York Times*, December 25, 2004.

11   Debord to Viénet, November 17, 1964, in Debord, *Correspondance Volume 2: 1960–1964*.

11   *The Occulted State*

1   *Now Public*, June 14, 2007.

2   Gianfranco Sanguinetti, *On Terrorism and the State*, translated by Lucy Forsyth and Michel Prigent, B. M. Chronos, London, 1982, p. 59; Gianfranco Sanguinetti, *Del Terrorismo e Dello Stato*, Sanguinetti CP, Milan, 1979, p. 33.

3 Retort, *Afflicted Powers*, p. 79. Retort is a San Francisco–based group including Iain Boal, Joseph Matthews, Michael Watts and T. J. Clark.

4 Retort, *Afflicted Powers*, p. 131.

5 Debord to Gallizio, July 17, 1958, Debord, *Correspondence*.

6 Debord, *Panegyric*, p. 51; *Oeuvres*, p. 1678.

7 Debord, *Considerations on the Assassination*, p. 60; *Oeuvres*, p. 1568.

8 Debord, *Panegyric*, p. 50; *Oeuvres*, p. 1677.

9 Guy Debord, *Preface to the Fourth Italian Edition of the Society of the Spectacle*, Chronos Publications, London, 1983, p. 12.

10 Debord to Sanguinetti, April 21, 1978, Guy Debord, *Correspondance Volume 5, 1973–1978*, Fayard, Paris, 2005.

11 Andrew Hussey, *The Game of War: The Life and Death of Guy Debord*, Jonathan Cape, London, 2001.

12 Sanguinetti, *On Terrorism*, p. 14; from the preface to the French edition: Gianfranco Sanguinetti, *Du Terrorisme et de l'Etat*, 2e edition, Groupment Graphique Gamma, Paris, 1980, p. 7.

13 Sanguinetti, *On Terrorism*, pp. 19–20; *Du Terrorisme*, p. 14. Sanguinetti is here a useful counterpoint to the range of views included in the seminal English-language document of the Autonomist movement: Sylvère Lotringer and Christian Marazzi (eds), *Autonomia: Post-Political Politics*, Semiotext(e), New York, 2007. See also Paolo Virno and Michael Hardt (eds), *Radical Thought in Italy: A Potential Politics*, University of Minnesota Press, Minneapolis, 2006. Given the Situationist interest in the critique of urban planning, a book of particular interest is Pier Vitorio Aureli, *The Project of Autonomy: Politics and Architecture Within and Against Capitalism*, Princeton Architectural, New York, 2008. But what is often lacking in the global celebration of autonomist writings is the immediate political context within which it was formed, something which this chapter seeks at least in part to remedy.

14 Particularly instructive here is Antonio Negri, *Books for Burning: Between Civil War and Democracy in 1970s Italy*, Verso, London, 2006, which reprints Negri's texts of the period. The break with Leninism is slow, painful, and perhaps somewhat incomplete.

15 Tiqqun, *This Is Not a Program*, Semiotext(e), Los Angeles, 2011, p. 21; "Ceci n'est pas un programme," *Tiqqun*, No. 2, p. 240.

16 *New York Times*, June 5, 2006. On conspiracy theories: Debord, *Comments*, p. 59; Jodi Dean, *Aliens in America: Conspiracy Cultures from Outer Space to Cyberspace*, Cornell University Press, Ithaca NY, 1998; Jack Bratich, *Conspiracy Panics: Political Rationality and Popular Culture*, SUNY Press, Albany NY, 2008.

17 Debord, *Comments*, p. 24; *Oeuvres*, p. 1607.

18 William Gibson, *Spook Country*, Putnam, New York, 2007, p. 74.

19 It sometimes appears as if more has been written about Wikileaks than the volume of documents they actually released. See Micah Sifry, *Wikileaks and the Age of Transparency*, O/R Books, New York, 2011. See also Suelette Dreyfus and Julian Assange, *Underground*, Random House Australia, Sydney, 2011, a reprint of an earlier study of the hacker culture from which Wikileaks sprang. Perhaps this could have been seen coming: McKenzie Wark, *A Hacker Manifesto*, Harvard University Press, Cambridge MA, 2004, the first version of which appeared in 2000.

20 *New York Times Magazine*, November 26, 2000.

21 *Highest ambition*, Debord, *Comments*, p. 11. On La Boétie, cf. *Comments*, p. 61. Now that journalists in Rupert Murdoch's employ have been caught tapping cellphone calls, and Scotland Yard caught sitting on what it knew of this, Debord's chiasmus

might thus be amended: Yet the lowest achievement of the disintegrating spectacle is to turn journalists into cops and cops into journalists.

22 Sanguinetti, *On Terrorism*, p. 58; *Del Terrorismo*, p. 32.

23 Debord, *Comments*, p. 82; *Oeuvres*, p. 1642.

24 Debord, *In Girum*, p. 65; *Oeuvres*, p. 1391. This statement is accompanied in the film by movie images of naval warfare. The image of war is itself the image of the war of images.

25 *Washington Post*, July 19, 2010.

26 Debord, *Comments*, p. 84.

12 The Last Chance to Save Capitalism

1 See Michel Foucault, *The Birth of Biopolitics*, Palgrave, London, 2008.

2 Censor (Gianfranco Sanguinetti), *Véridique Rapport sur les dernières chances de sauver le capitalisme en Italie. Traduit de l'italien par Guy Debord (suivi de Preuves de l'inexistence de Censor par son auteur)*, Ugo Mursia Editore, Milan, 1975 / Champ Libre, Paris, 1976, p. 147.

3 Censor, *Véridique Rapport*, p. 31.

4 Ibid., p. 128. After the war, the Italian Communist Party cached at least some of its weapons from the partisan struggle against fascism, but in 1948 renounced the option of armed insurrection.

5 Censor, *Véridique Rapport*, pp. 50–1, 48–9, 58.

6 Ibid., p. 68.

7 Ibid., p. 80; See Baltasar Gracián, *The Art of Worldly Wisdom*, Doubleday, New York, 1991, s. 40, s. 160. Gracián would put it more in terms of prudence, the measured use of the truth and the avoidance of outright lies.

8 Ibid., p. 91. This, for the Situationists, was the lesson of the Spanish Civil War.

9 Ibid., p. 94. See Gracián, *Art of Worldly Wisdom*, s. 214.

10 Ibid., pp. 106–10. See also Guy Debord, *A Sick Planet*, Seagull Books, Oxford, 2008.

11 Ibid., pp. 155–7. One could seek an explanation for the rise of contemporary art here.

12 Giuseppe di Lampedusa, *The Leopard*, translated by Archibald Colquhoun, Pantheon, New York, 1960, p. 40.

13 *Daily News*, August 11, 2010.

14 Debord, *Society of the Spectacle*, s. 2.

13 Anti-Cinema

1 The dissolution is documented in Debord and Sanguinetti, *The Real Split in the International*.

2 Champot, where he played *Game of War*, is lovingly described in *Panygeric*, p. 48.

3 Thomas Y. Levin, "Dismantling the Spectacle: The Cinema of Guy Debord," in Sussman, *On the Passage of a Few People*, p. 108. I am much indebted to this classic essay.

4 In this respect, Debord doesn't really belong in Martin Jay, *Downcast Eyes: The Denigration of Vision in Twentieth Century French Thought*, University of California Press, Berkeley, 1994. "The reigning deceptions of the time are on the point of making us forget that the truth may also be found in images. An image that has not been deliberately separated from its meaning adds great precision and certainty to knowledge." Debord, *Panegyric*, Vols 1 & 2, p. 73.

5   See McKenzie Wark, "Détournement: An Abuser's Guide," *Angelaki*, Vol. 14, No. 1, April 2009, *Special issue: Plagiarism! (from work to détournement)*, edited by John Kinsella and Niall Lucy.

6   *Philadelphia Inquirer*, December 26, 2008.

7   Isidore Isou, "Treatise on Slime and Eternity," in *Avant-garde 2: Experimental Cinema*, Kino Cinema, New York, 2007.

8   Interview with Martine Barraqué-Curie by Julia Carrillo and McKenzie Wark, April 27, 2009. Actually, the later film adds some material as well, not least on the Carnation Revolution in Portugal.

9   Lefebvre, *Critique de la vie quotidienne II*, p. 86. See the remarkable document by the Tiqqun group, "Premiers matériaux pour une théorie de la Jeune-Fille," *Tiqqun*, January 1999, reprinted as a separate text, VLCP, 2006.

10 See John Hartley, *Tele-ology: Studies in Television*, Routledge, London, 1992, p. 218ff, for a fine essay whose starting point on this is the birth of Kylie Minogue in 1968. Hartley detected early on the almost dialectical quality of what I will call The Girl, as both a controlling, patriarchal image for women, but also a surface on which a sense of the public coalesced. I followed in his footsteps in McKenzie Wark, *Celebrities, Culture and Cyberspace*, Pluto Press, Sydney, 1998. Hartley sheered the critical and francophone side of cultural theory away and relied on a nuanced and interpretive orientation to popular publics (derived in part from Terry Hawkes). His choice of Kylie over the Situationists in *Tele-ology* is something of a manifesto. My writings on the Situationists are among other things a belated dialogue with that strand of Anglophone cultural studies of which Hartley is a leading exemplar.

11 One should note that in Alain Badiou's *The Meaning of Sarkozy*, the Trotskyite remnants of the seventies come in for a brisk dismissal, but only some of the Maoist currents. Like his mentor Louis Althusser, Badiou remains relentlessly Maoist in not only political but also theoretical formation. Mao's injunction to "put politics in command" and reject Marxism as a critique of political *economy* has done lasting damage to critical thought.

12 Jaime Semprun, *La Guerre sociale au Portugal*, Champ Libre, Paris, 1975. See also Loren Goldner, *Ubu Saved from Drowning: Class Struggle and Statist Containment in Portugal and Spain, 1974–1977*, Queequeg Publications, New York, 2011.

13 Debord, *Complete Cinematic Works*, p. 223; *Oeuvres*, p. 1412.

14 *Correspondence* (to Frankin, July 15, 1959). See Gilles Deleuze, *Cinema 1: The Movement Image*, Continuum, London, 2005.

15 Debord, *Complete Cinematic Works*, p. 49; *Oeuvres*, p. 1203. See Julian Graffy, *Chapaev: Kinofile Filmmakers' Companion*, No. 11, I. B. Taurus, London, 2009.

16 Russian friends old enough to remember the Soviet era recall that *Chapayev* was détourned in everyday life via a series of jokes, often ribald or in dubious taste. See also Victor Prevelin, *Buddha's Little Finger*, Penguin, New York, 2001.

17 The parable does not quite appear in this classic form in Aesop. See Leslie Kurke, *Aesopic Conversations*, Princeton University Press, Princeton NJ, 2010, which finds the traces of a popular counter-knowledge in the fables of "classical" times.

18 On the suppression of the revolution by the Communists in Spain, the classic first-hand account is George Orwell, *Homage to Catalonia*, Penguin, London, 2000. It was published as *Hommage à la Catalogne 1936–1937*, Champ Libre, Paris, 1981.

14 The Devil's Party

1 Debord, *In Girum*, p. 50; *Oeuvres*, p. 1377. Actually the "name writ on water" is from Keats' epitaph for himself, détourned from Fletcher's "Philaster," but it is borrowed again by Shelley in "Adonais" and "Fragment on Keats," as well as by Christina Rossetti and Oscar Wilde. Shelley was indeed shipwrecked, and the shipwrecked above all perhaps have their names written on water. 'Shipwreckers' both détourns and corrects the thought. See Richard Cronin, *Romantic Victorians*, Palgrave Macmillan, London, 2002.

2 Debord, *Panegyric*, p. 15; Oeuvres, p. 1633.

3 Terence, "Homo sum: humani nil a me alienum puto," *Heauton Timoroumenos*, line 77.

4 Will Baker, *Jacques Prévert*, Twayne Publishers, New York, 1967; Edward Baron Turk, *Marcel Carné and the Golden Age of French Cinema*, Harvard University Press, Cambridge MA, 1989. The female lead in both films is Arletty.

5 Debord, *In Girum*, p. 33; *Oeuvres*, p. 1362.

6 *The Memoirs of Lacenaire*, translated by Philip John Stead, Staple Press, London, 1952, pp. 157–9. Here sounding as if he is détourning the Gospel of Matthew: "I come not to bring peace but the sword." Lacenaire is also mentioned in *Panegyric*, p. 7. Foucault compares Lacenaire unfavorably to another criminal-writer of the time: "No, I think that one must compare Rivière with Lacenaire, who was his exact contemporary and who committed a whole heap of minor and shoddy crimes, mostly failures, hardly glorious at all, but who succeeded through his very intelligent discourse in making these crimes exist as real works of art, and in making the criminal, that is Lacenaire himself, the very artist of criminality. It's another tour de force if you like: he managed to give an intense reality, for dozens of years, for more than a century, to acts that were finally very shoddy and ignoble. As a criminal he was a rather petty type, but the splendor and intelligence of his writing gave a consistency to it all." Sylvère Lotringer (ed.), *Foucault Live: Collected Interviews, 1961–1984*, Semiotext(e), Los Angeles, 1996, pp. 203–6.

7 Adorno, *Minima Moralia*, p. 111; Vaneigem, *The Revolution of Everyday Life*, p. 31.

8 Karl Marx and Fredrick Engels, *Collected Works, Volume 4*, International Publishers, New York, 1976, p. 82. Or as Lefebvre says, "man moves 'wrong foot forward.'" *Introduction à la modernité. Préludes*, Les éditions de minuit, Paris, 1962, p. 146.

9 Olivier Assayas, *A Post-May Adolescence: Letter to Alice Debord*, translated by Adrian Martin and Rachel Zerner, Synema, Vienna, 2012, pp. 49–50, 77, 101. See also Debord, *Considerations on the Assassination*, pp. 5–6. Assayas produced the DVD edition of Debord's films, and not much else of value in this context, except perhaps *demonlover* (2007). Of course, there were in actuality many "authors" of the Champ Libre editorial direction. See Éditions Champ Libre, *Correspondance Tome 1*, editions Ivrea, Paris, 1996.

10 Debord, *Considerations on the Assassination*, p. 3; *Oeuvres*, p. 1540.

11 Debord, *Considerations on the Assassination*, p. 9; *Oeuvres*, p. 1543.

12 "He smelled as if he hadn't bathed in days." *New York Times Magazine*, January 26, 2011. For Assange in his own words: Hans Ulrich Obrist, "In Conversation with Julian Assange," *e-flux journal*, No. 25, May 2011, e-flux.com, and Julian Assange et al., *Cypherpunks*, O/R Books, New York, 2012.

13 Debord, *Considerations on the Assassination*, p. 23; *Oeuvres*, p. 1550.

14 Debord, *Considerations on the Assassination*, p. 44; *Oeuvres*, p. 1560.

15 Guy Debord, *Des Contrats*, Le temps qu'il fait, Cognac, 1995; *Oeuvres*, p. 1843ff.

16 See Jacques Derrida, *Given Time*, University of Chicago Press, Chicago, 1996.

Derrida's critique is of the Christian-bourgeois idea of the gift as an unmotivated, selfless charity. But for ethnographers, and Situationists, the gift is always a stake in a game among rivals. See Jean Baudrillard, *Fragments*, Verso, London, 1997, pp. 127–8.

17   Debord, *Panegyric*, p. 17; *Oeuvres*, 1664.

18   See the documents collected and translated at tarnac9.wordpress.com, including an interview with Coupat from *Le Monde*, June 4, 2009; Giorgio Agamben, "Terrorisme ou tragic-comédie," *Libération*, November 19, 2008; Alberto Toscano, "The War Against Preterrorism," *Radical Philosophy*, No. 154, March–April 2009.

19   The Invisible Committee, *The Coming Insurrection*, Semiotext(e), Los Angeles, 2009. See also Benjamin Noys (ed.), *Communization and Its Discontents*, minor compositions, London, 2011. Most of the contributors to the latter are highly critical of *Tiqqun* and its offspring, such as the Invisible Committee, and pursue more theoretically rigorous concepts of an immanent Communism. Both a certain quality of the prose, and certain practical commitments, make *The Coming Insurrection* more germane to our story here, but interested readers can pursue these more *rigorous*, not to say *dogmatic*, versions of a Post-Situationist practice according to taste.

15   Guy Debord, His Art and Times

1   Interview by McKenzie Wark with Brigitte Cornand, New York, April 17, 2009.

2   See for example Cornand's later work on Louise Bourgeois.

3   Lefebvre, *Critique de la vie quotidienne II*, p 81; *Critique of Everyday Life* Vol. 2, p. 77. See Debord, *Panegyric*, p. 74; *Comments*, p. 19.

4   Letter to Leonardi, October 6, 1994. The music is from Monique Morelli, *Musique de Leonardi, François Villon*, Chevance, 1974.

5   Guy Debord, *Oeuvres Cinematographiques Completes*, produced by Olivier Assayas, Gaumont, Paris, 2005. See Keith Sanborn, "Return of the Suppressed," *Artforum*, February 2006, on some quirks of this DVD edition. Quotes from the film are from the English-language edition produced by Cornand and not included in the Gaumont box set. My thanks to Cornand for my copy.

6   Besides several books on French men of state, Franz-Olivier Giesbert is the author of *The American: A Memoir*, Pantheon, New York, 2005.

7   It would be amusing to compare the readings of Mallarmé offered by Debord to Quentin Meillassoux, *The Number and the Siren*, Urbanomic and Sequence Press, New York, 2012. There is no cult of contingency in Debord, for whom the rattle of the dice has more to do with the exigencies of historical time than the contingencies of cosmic time. Debord is no nihilist. Historical time is always an open invitation to roll the dice and take a chance on another way of life, if only for the pleasure of watching the blocks fall. We begin again, from the beginning, with neither hope nor resignation, but with a keen calculation of the chances, and for a chance to act in and against our time, for the ages. See also Debord, *Considerations on the Assassination*, p. 32; *Panegyric*, p. 15.

8   See Gil Joseph Wolman, *Défense de mourir*, Éditions Allia, Paris, 2001.

9   Comte de Lautréamont, *Maldoror and the Complete Works*, Exact Change Press, Cambridge MA, 1994, p. 234.

10   *The Australian*, November 16, 2006.

11   See McKenzie Wark, *Virtual Geography: Living with Global Media Events*, Indiana University Press, Bloomington IN, 1995.

12   Debord, *Panegyric*, p. 12; *Oeuvres*, p. 1662; cf. *Comments*, p. 78; *Oeuvres*, p. 1639

and *In Girum*, p. 33; *Oeuvres*, p. 1662; *Considerations on the Assassination*, p. 26. See Arthur Cravan, *Oeuvres: articles, lettres*, Éditions Gérard Lebovici, Paris, 1987; Carolyn Burke, *Becoming Modern: The Life of Mina Loy*, University of California Press, Berkeley CA, 1997, is probably the best English-language source on Cravan, whom Loy married shortly before he died. A suitably unreliable source on Cravan is Mike Richardson and Rick Geary, *Cravan: Mystery Man of the Twentieth Century*, Dark Horse, Milwaukie OR, 2005, which includes the delicious speculation that Cravan became the novelist B. Traven.

13 Benjamin Buchloh, *Neo-Avantgarde and Culture Industry*, MIT Press, Cambridge MA, 2000, p. 137. Interestingly, this volume contains an essay on Jacques Villeglé (who would have rubbed shoulders with Debord in the Saint-Germain heyday) which includes a brief appreciation of François Dufrêne, who departs from the Letterist International directly into the neo-avant-garde. Cf. Debord, *Comments*, p. 77.

14 See the Bernadette Corporation video, *Get Rid of Yourself*, 2003.

15 *Vanity Fair*, February 2007.

16 *Vanity Fair*, April 2007.

16   A Romany Detour

1 Hussey, *The Game of War*, p. 283.

2 Debord, *Panegyric*, p. 9; *Oeuvres*, p. 1660.

3 Jan Yoors, *The Gypsies*, Simon & Schuster, New York, p. 51.

4 Yoors, *The Gypsies*, pp. 31, 82, 116.

5 Ibid., pp. 121, 23, 135.

6 Ibid., *The Gypsies*, p. 34.

7 Ibid., *The Gypsies*, pp. 122–3.

8 Ibid., *The Gypsies*, p. 53.

9 Ibid., *The Gypsies*, p. 123.

10 *New York Times*, November 13, 2006.

11 Debord, *Panegyric*, p. 40; *Oeuvres*, p. 1673.

12 Yoors, *The Gypsies*, p. 93.

13 A certain caution is called for in any deployment of the figure of the "gypsy," a caution Becker-Ho and Debord don't always observe. See Adrian Marsh et al., *Gypsies and the Problem of Identities*, Transactions, Istanbul, 2006.

14 Isabel Fonesa, *Bury Me Standing: The Gypsies and Their Journey*, Knopf, New York, 1995, pp. 106–7.

15 Becker-Ho, *The Princes of Jargon*, p. 67.

16 Yoors, *The Gypsies*, p. 159.

17   The Language of Discretion

1 *New York Times*, September 21, 2004.

2 Becker-Ho, *The Princes of Jargon*, p. 41; J. Huizinga, *The Waning of the Middle Ages*, St. Martin's Press, New York, 1984, p. 10.

3 See Jonathon Green, "Romany Rise," *Critical Quarterly*, Vol. 41, No. 3, 1999.

4 Becker-Ho, *The Princes of Jargon*, p. 153.

5 Christopher Hitchens, *Unacknowledged Legislators: Writers in the Public Sphere*, Verso, London, 2000, pp. 3–9.

6 Becker-Ho, *The Princes of Jargon*, p. 67.

7   Alice Becker-Ho, *The Essence of Jargon*, translated by John McHale, typescript, 2007, p. 23.

8   Becker-Ho, *The Princes of Jargon*, p. 37. On the modern extension of the con from the Coquillards to Benjamin Marks to spam, and their relation to the development of transport and communication, see Graham Parker, *Fair Use: Notes from Spam*, Bookworks, London, 2008.

9   François Villon, *Complete Poems*, edited by Barbara Sargent-Bauer, University of Toronto Press, Toronto, p. 299.

10 Ibid., p. 309.

11 Ibid., lines 1667–8.

12 On Ghislain de Marbaix, see Jean-Michel Mension, *The Tribe*, Verso, London, 2002, p. 75ff.

13 Becker-Ho, *The Princes of Jargon*, p. 61.

14 Becker-Ho, *The Essence of Jargon*, p. 16.

15 *The Memoirs of Lacenaire*, p. 144.

16 Becker-Ho, *The Princes of Jargon*, p. 161.

17 Giorgio Agamben, *Means Without End*, University of Minnesota Press, Minneapolis, 2000, pp. 63–72.

18 Becker-Ho, *The Essence of Jargon*, p. 33.

19 Ibid., p. 23.

20 Ibid., p. 18.

21 Ibid., p. 21.

22 Debord, *Society of the Spectacle*, s. 204, quoted in Becker-Ho, *The Essence of Jargon*, p. 23. Debord distinguishes this approach to language from Roland Barthes' writing degree zero, the avant-garde of the time.

23 Becker-Ho, *The Princes of Jargon*, p. 143. See also Michel de Certeau's review essay on Foucault in *Heterologies: Discourse on the Other*, University of Minnesota Press, Minneapolis, 1986, which raises a similar point but settles for a more generic and less "dangerous" field of everyday practices.

24 *New York Times*, February 5, 2003. See also Edwin Black, *IBM and the Holocaust*, Dialog Press, New York, 2008.

25 Becker-Ho, *The Essence of Jargon*, p. 6.

26 Becker-Ho, *The Princes of Jargon*, p. 159.

27 Becker-Ho, *The Essence of Jargon*, p. 33.

28 Becker-Ho, *The Princes of Jargon*, p. 159.

29 Ibid., p. 159.

30 Ibid., p. 145.

31 Julia Kristeva, *Revolution in Poetic Language*, Columbia University Press, New York, 1984.

32 See for example "All the King's Men," in Knabb, *Anthology*, p. 152.

33 Becker-Ho, *The Princes of Jargon*, p. 17.

34 Debord, *Panegyric*, p. 24; *Oeuvres*, p. 1667.

35 Becker-Ho, *The Princes of Jargon*, p. 19.

36 Ibid., p. 47.

37 Ibid., p. 143.

38 Debord, *Comments*, pp. 1–2; *Oeuvres*, p. 1593.

39 Becker-Ho, *The Princes of Jargon*, p. 137; François Villon, *Complete Poems*, p. 299.

18   Game of War

1   Thanks to Michael Pettinger for this translation. Vida was the Bishop of Alba, where the inaugural conference of the Situationist International took place.

2   See Guy Debord, *Cette mauvaise réputation*, Gallimard, Paris, 1993; *Oeuvres*, p. 1796ff.

3   Alice Becker-Ho, "Historical Note (2006)," in Alice Becker-Ho and Guy Debord, *A Game of War*, translated by Donald Nicholson-Smith, Atlas Press, London, 2007, p. 7. See also *Oeuvres*, p. 285.

4   Debord, *Panegyric*, pp. 55–6; *Oeuvres*, p. 1679.

5   Becker-Ho and Guy Debord, *A Game of War*, p. 9.

6   *Strategist*: Jacqueline de Jong, in Stefan Zweifel et al. (eds), *In Girum Imus Nocte et Consumimur Igni: The Situationist International 1957–1972*, JRP-Ringier, Zurich, 2006, p. 240; Giorgio Agamben, in ibid., p. 36.

7   Debord, *Panegyric*, p. 61; *Oeuvres*, p. 1682.

8   On Surrealist games, see Susan Laxton, *Paris as Gameboard: Ludic Strategies in Surrealism*, PhD dissertation, Columbia University, 2004. Duchamp's book on chess is Marcel Duchamp and Vitali Halberstadt, *Opposition und Schwesterfelder (Gebundene Ausgabe)* Tropen, Berlin, 2001. François Le Lionnais is quoted in Allan Woods, *The Map Is Not the Territory*, Manchester University Press, Manchester, 2000, p. 199. Le Lionnais (1901–84) was a mathematician, chemical engineer, and a founder of the Oulipo group.

9   Becker-Ho and Debord, *A Game of War*, pp. 25, 26.

10 See Ed Halter, *From Sun Tzu to Xbox*, Thunder Mouth Press, New York, 2006.

11 Alexander R. Galloway, "Debord's Nostalgic Algorithm," *Culture Machine*, Vol. 10, 2009. On the one occasion Galloway and I played *Game of War*, on Alice Becker-Ho's own set, no less, the game ended in a draw. My position was weak, and I don't doubt Alex would have won had there been more time.

12 Becker-Ho and Debord, *A Game of War*, p. 156.

13 Ibid., p. 19.

14 Ibid., p. 21.

15 Antonio Gramsci, *Selections from The Prison Notebooks*, translated by Quintin Hoare and Geoffrey Nowell Smith, International Publishers, New York, 1971, p. 238. Of course Gramsci could also be wrong just on the facts. On the depth of Russian civil society's institutions, see Wayne Dowler, *Russia in 1913*, Northern Illinois University Press, Dekalb IL, 2010.

16 Becker-Ho and Debord, *A Game of War*, p. 24.

17 Class Wargames, *Guy Debord's Game of War*, 2009; Richard Barbrook and Fabian Thompsett, *Class Wargames Presents: Guy Debord's Game of War*, Unpopular Books, London, 2009. See classwargames.net. See also Richard Barbrook, *Class Wargames: Ludic Subversions Against Spectacular Capitalism*, manuscript, 2012. I should point out that on the one occasion I played *Game of War* against Class Wargames, I was soundly thrashed.

18 Becker-Ho and Debord, *A Game of War*, p. 22.

19 Ibid., p. 24.

20 Guy Debord, "Preface to the First Edition," in Becker-Ho and Debord, *A Game of War*, p. 9.

19   The Strategist

1   Becker-Ho and Debord, *A Game of War*, p. 26.

2   See Janet Afary and Kevin Anderson, *Foucault and the Iranian Revolution*, University of Chicago Press, Chicago, 2005, p. 263.

3   See Alain Badiou, *The Communist Hypothesis*, Verso, London, 2011, p. 101, where he describes Maoism as "the only true political creation of the sixties and seventies." Compare to the Chinese "new left" sociologist Wang Hui, *China's New Order*, Harvard University Press, Cambridge MA, 2003, pp. 148–9, who describes how Mao "used the socialist system of public ownership to establish a prosperous and powerful modern nation-state while at the same time working towards his principal goal of equality." The latter may have some justification, having to operate as a loyal opposition within the Chinese academy, for using the government's own official history against it. Viénet is a useful counterweight to the persistence of Mao idolatry in the West. A more consistent critical account of this history would be a much vaster and more demanding project.

4   Slavoj Žižek, *In Defense of Lost Causes*, Verso, London, 2008, p. 111.

5   Boris Groys, *The Communist Postscript*, Verso, London, 2010, p. 99.

6   Carl von Clausewitz, *On Wellington: A Critique of Waterloo*, translated and edited by Peter Hofschröder, Oklahoma University Press, Norman OK, 2010, p. 171.

7   Becker-Ho and Debord, *A Game of War*, p. 24.

8   See Manuel DeLanda, *War in the Age of Intelligent Machines*, Zone Books, New York, 1991; Paul Edwards, *The Closed World*, MIT Press, Cambridge MA, 1997; Fred Kaplan, *The Wizards of Armageddon*, Stanford University Press, Stanford CA, 1991.

9   Antoine de Jomini, *Précis de l'Art de la Guerre*, Champ Libre, Paris, 1977. The influence of Jomini on cold war strategy is also noted in Paul Virilio and Sylvère Lotringer, *Pure War*, Semiotext(e), Los Angeles, 2008.

10 Clausewitz, *On Wellington*, p. 105.

11 Carl von Clausewitz, *On War*, Penguin Classics, London, 1982, p. 121. An edition with few merits, other than the introduction by Anatol Rapoport, which shows exactly how *On War* was taken up in limited fashion in the world of game theory.

12 Clausewitz, *On Wellington*, p. 59.

13 Debord, *Comments*, p. 86; *Oeuvres*, p. 1644.

14 Stendhal, *The Charterhouse of Parma*, translated by John Sturrock, Penguin Books, London, 2006, p. 47.

15 Becker-Ho and Debord, *A Game of War*, pp. 25–6.

16 Debord, *Society of the Spectacle*, s. 143.

17 Georg Lukács, *The Historical Novel*, translated by Hannah and Stanley Mitchell, Merlin Press, London, 1989, p. 24.

18 Guy Debord, *Panegyric*, p. 57; *Oeuvres*, p. 1680.

19 Keith Sanborn, "Postcard from Berezina," in Napoleon, *How to Make War*, edited by Yann Cloarec, translated by Keith Sanborn, Ediciones La Calavera, New York, 1998, pp. 103–4.

20 Napoléon, *Comment faire la guerre*, Textes rassemblés par Yann Cloarec, Champ Libre, Paris, 1973; Carl von Clausewitz, *Campagne de 1815 en France*, Champ Libre, Paris, 1973.

21 Vaneigem, *The Revolution of Everyday Life*, p. 165.

22 Alice Becker-Ho, *Du jargon héretier en Bastardie*, Gallimard, Paris, 2002, p. 161.

20 The Inhuman Comedy

1 Clark and Nicholson-Smith, "Why Art Can't Kill the Situationist International," in McDonough, *Guy Debord and the Situationist International*, p. 467.

2 To cite just one classic version of history from below: E. P. Thompson, *The Making of the English Working Class*, Penguin, London, 2002.

3 Debord, *Panegyric*, p. 39; *Oeuvres*, p. 1673.

4 Loretta Napoleoni, *Maonomics: Why Chinese Communists Make Better Capitalists Than We Do*, Seven Stories, New York, 2011, tries to make the case that China won the cold war, that Deng Xiaoping's development strategy was essentially Marxist, and that the Chinese Communist Party is playing the historical long game. The attention to Deng-era China is at least a relief from Maoist nostalgia. Mao-era China does not much resemble the overdeveloped world in the twenty-first century. On the other hand, China in these same times does look a bit like the France and Italy of the postwar period. Rapid industrialization, transfer of populations from country to city, growing boredom with factory life, attempt by the integrated spectacle to compensate by expanding consumption and at the same time with selective repression. Situationist theory of history might have a certain ongoing relevance.

5 *New Yorker*, November 12, 2007.

6 For the idea of the improper name, I am indebted to Marco Deseriis, and his work on, and with, improper names, from Luther Blissett to the Yes Men.

7 Tiqqun, *This Is Not a Program*, Semiotext(e), Los Angeles, 2011, p. 117; *Tiqqun*, No. 2, p. 266.

8 See for example Gianni Vattimo and Santiago Zabala, *Hermeneutic Communism: From Heidegger to Marx*, Columbia University Press, New York, 2011.

9 Mina Loy, *Stories and Essays*, Dalkey Archive, Champaign IL, 2011; Claude Cahun, *Écrits*, Jean-Michel Place Éditions, Paris, 2002. See also Penelope Rosemont, *Surrealist Women: An International Anthology*, University of Texas Press, Austin, 1998.

10 Tom Levin claims that Dušan Makavejev's film *Sweet Movie* (1974) is dedicated to Vaneigem. If one takes that to be so, then it can be appended to the (anti-)canon of Situationist film as a quite astute analysis of The Girl. Interestingly, rather than find the Big Brother of the concentrated spectacle hidden in the diffuse spectacle, his analysis proceeds in reverse: he finds little sister's eastern double.

11 See Michael Gross, *Model: The Ugly Business of Beautiful Women*, Harper, New York, 2003. Wendy Steiner, *The Real Real Thing: The Model in the Mirror of Art*, University of Chicago Press, Chicago, 2010, restores some agency to the figure of the model, if only in the context of the art world. Jon Stratton, *The Desirable Body: Cultural Fetishism and the Erotics of Consumption*, University of Illinois Press, Urbana IL, 1996, takes some steps beyond the standard conflation of Marxian and Freudian theories of fetishism to consider The Girl as produced out of spectacular social relations. Still, the best thing on this subject is Ann K. Clark, "The Girl: A Rhetoric of Desire," *Cultural Studies*, Vol. 1, No. 2, 1987.

12 "Premieres matériaux pour une théorie de la Jeune-Fille," *Tiqqun: Organe Conscient du Parti Imaginaire*, Paris, 1999, p. 101.

13 Debord, *Society of the Spectacle*, p. 12.

14 Jean Baudrillard, *Seduction*, Macmillan, London, 1991. Baudrillard gives an account of his—oblique—relation to the Situationists in *Utopia Deferred*, Semiotext(e), Los Angeles, 2006, pp. 13–30. See also Craig Buckley and Jean-Louis Violeau, *Utopie: Texts and Projects 1967–1978*, Semiotext(e), Los Angeles, 2011. The Utopie group, in which he was an elusive presence, picked up the critique of architecture, design and the everyday from the early Situationists and took it somewhere else than the return

to council communism advocated by the latter Situationists. Seduction is one of the keys via which Baudrillard extracts himself from rhetorics of production and desire to re-establish a low theory of the everyday outside of such well-policed languages.

15   "Premieres matériaux," p. 105; Alexandre Kojève, *Introduction to the Reading of Hegel*, Cornell University Press, Ithaca NY, 1969.

16   Compare Debord's film to DJ Rabbi, *Society of the Spectacle (A Digital Remix)*, 2004, Djrabbi.com

Index